How Real Estate Fortunes Are Made

George Bockl

Prentice-Hall, Inc.   Englewood Cliffs, N.J.

Prentice-Hall International, Inc., *London*
Prentice-Hall of Australia, Pty. Ltd., *Sydney*
Prentice-Hall of Canada, Ltd., *Toronto*
Prentice-Hall of India Private Ltd., *New Delhi*
Prentice-Hall of Japan, Inc., *Tokyo*

© 1972 by

Prentice-Hall, Inc.
Englewood Cliffs, N.J.

This publication is designed to provide accurate authoritative information with regard to the subject matter covered. It is sold with the understanding that the publisher is not engaged in rendering legal, accounting, or other professional advice. If legal advice or other expert assitance is required, the services of a competent professional person should be sought.

> *... From a Declaration of Principles jointly adopted by a Committee of the American Bar Association and a Committee of Publishers and Associations*

Library of Congress Cataloging in Publication Data

Bockl, George.
  How real estate fortunes are made.

  1. Real estate investment. I. Title.
HD1379.B63   333.3'3   72-2886
ISBN 0-13-431098-5

Printed in the United States of America

Dedicated

to the memory of

My son Bobbie

A Word from the Author

This book is not limited to real estate men. It's for anyone who is daring enough to try new ideas to make a real estate fortune.

The principles of making money in real estate are difficult to grasp only when they are explained in abstract terms and do not touch the lives of people. They become a lot easier to understand when they are dramatized as human interest stories.

That's why this book is uniquely instructive. It deals with basic theory, yes, but only indirectly. It is people like you who hold the center stage. People who actually make the deals by using innovative methods.

For instance, describing the financing procedure of a $200,000 nursing home can be a dull exercise, but showing how a nurse financed it with only $10,000 in cash, and then increased her equity by several hundred thousand dollars—that awakens your interest. That's when the entrepreneurial juices begin flowing. That's when you want to do something about it yourself. That's what this book is about.

Much real estate literature is slanted for experts. I've decided to write in a style which will enable any man with average intelligence to grasp the ideas experts use, and turn them into profitable real estate deals.

Here is how this book can benefit you. If you have a big idea but little money, you may find the answer to your problem in one of the stories of how people like you solved them. Or, if you don't have any ideas, you may find them in this book, and learn how to borrow the money to put them over.

If you're a "horse trader" at heart, but know nothing about trading real estate—you will when you get through reading Chapter 7. It's a gold mine.

If you're young, you can become a conduit for elderly people who own real estate. You take over their ownership and problems, and they get a trouble free stream of income. It's a good deal for them, and a lot of profit in the pipe line for you.

There is also a lot of money to be made buying wholesale and selling retail. It's a good old American tradition. But few are doing it. Chapter 9 tells you how to do it.

This book will also help you manage property innovatively; judge an investment property scientifically; borrow imaginatively; sell losses and depreciation at a profit, and most important of all, make you aware of the real estate wave of the future—the opportunities in the small towns of America.

While all the success stories in this book are real, the names of persons and properties have been changed or omitted to protect the privacy of the individuals involved. I wish to acknowledge my gratefulness to the unidentified men and women who played the important roles in these stories. What they did is the living evidence that common sense, good judgment and imagination are more important than a lot of rules and scholarly knowledge. These people believed in manufacturing their ideas into real estate products—not warehousing them. They are the flesh and blood of this book. Without them I could not have written it.

George Bockl

What This Book Will Do For You

Many people believe that men who make fortunes in real estate possess some rare gift that sets them apart from ordinary men. Let me tell you from my own experience that this is not so. Real estate fortunes are made by those who know where the *opportunities* lie. This book will show you where those opportunities are and how you can turn them into fortunes.

Opportunities abound in every city, and I will try to help you recognize them. To do this, I have drawn on some of my own experiences and the successful experiences of others.

These fortune building examples are not based on theories of what might happen, but on concrete stories of what actually did happen. You will learn how ordinary men were catapulted into extraordinary successes because they did the unusual.

This step-by-step fortune-building-know-how is described in detail. When the veils of complexity are removed and the opportunities are revealed in all their money-making splendor, you may perhaps be moved to act, and enter into a new world of ideas and into a new dimension of profit-making.

HERE ARE THE FORTUNE BUIDLING OPPORTUNITIES

Who among us, with little or no money, would not be interested in making big money, if all they had to do was to emulate those who had done it? Read how a nurse, an unemployed young man and an electrician made fortunes by using the innovative ideas described in Chapters 6 and 8.

You'll see, perhaps for the first time, how fortunes are made in trading real estate. Whether you trade up or down, you can make money in either direction. You may not know what trading up or down means, but you will, when you finish the chapter on trading.

One of the great assets in real estate is youth. Unfortunately, the young often don't know how to sell it. Fortunes are awaiting the young when they learn how to convert their youth into a conduit for annuities for the elderly. If this interests you, turn to Chapter 8.

Have you ever heard of buying real estate wholesale and selling it retail like goods in a department store? Well, it's not only possible, but also profitable. See Chapter 9.

If you want to build new buildings without money, there are many ways to do it, and they are all described in detail in Chapter 9—if you have the ideas and the courage to be innovative.

There is big money in property management. The art of putting a building to its highest use is worth a fortune, and you'll see why when you read about it in Chapter 10.

It will pay you immeasurably to see and understand what's underneath the iceberg of a real estate investment. The four-way benefit test of an investment will open your eyes to new possibilities. Read about it in Chapter 11.

If a tight money market stymies you, there are ways to get around it. Read how to make end runs when lenders try to block you in Chapter 12.

Borrowing money imaginatively is an art. Chapter 13 is an adventure in borrowing, full of suspense and insight. Asking for money innovatingly is a fortune-builder.

Did you know that there is gold and golden living in the small towns of America? This is but one of the opportunities of tomorrow. Re-zoning the suburbs; replacing the ghettos with new developments; building subsidized housing for moderate and low income families, and creating new villages, are a few of the new ideas you'll be dealing with in Chapters 14 and 15.

HOW TO GET INTO A BIG DEAL WITH LITTLE MONEY

People often ask me how to get into a big deal with little money. Read the dramatic story of a young man who started with nothing and in eighteen months earned $90,000 in cash and a

$25,000 annual tax-sheltered income for ten years—worth $250,000.

How did he do it? By remodeling vacant buildings owners did not know what to do with and leveraging them beyond infinity. It means borrowing more money than what he paid for the property, but with the lender still having a safe loan, because the stream of income he created was big enough to cover all costs.

A nurse was earning $8,000 a year when she was shown how to acquire a $200,000 nursing home with $10,000 down. In several years, she ran up her equity to $300,000!

One of my students bought a $230,000 apartment building with no money down when I showed him how to use his borrowing imagination. He is now enjoying a $15,000 a year tax-sheltered overage in addition to his regular salaried job.

YOUTH IS MONEY

Youth has collateral value. A 30-year-old has a far better chance to pay off a 25-year mortgage than a 60-year old. Thus, a younger man becomes a good conduit for an older man who wants to convert his troublesome property into a trouble free annuity.

For instance, a gasoline service station attendant, earning $8,000 a year, was enchanted with a certain restaurant. "All my life," he told me "I've dreamed of owning a restaurant. Now, I've found one that I like, but I've only got $10,000. The elderly widow who owns it wants $215,000 in cash. What do I do?"

He was a good conduit candidate. He had character, stability and youth. I told the widow and her lawyer that selling the restaurant to the young man with $10,000 down made good sense because looking for a cash buyer was like looking for a needle in a haystack. "His youth is your cash—stretched out over 20 years," I said.

They took my advice. In five years, the young man had blossomed into one of the city's fine restaurateurs. A simple idea radically changed a young man's life.

THERE ARE A DOZEN WAYS TO BUILD A REAL ESTATE FORTUNE

Who would believe that sometimes it is advantageous to pay $2,000,000 for an apartment building rather than $1,000,000? On the surface it doesn't make sense, but when you read Chapter 8, you'll see that it does. It's a unique twist in financing that only a few are aware of. It's a brand new fortune-building tool.

You'll be amazed at the story of a 30-year-old lawyer who bought a 140 acre farm for $44,000 with $10,000 down. Then, using innovative road-widening negotiations and selling his above grade land for topsoil instead of paying an excavator to remove it, he got enough money to clear the farm of all debt. Finally, he ingeniously subdivided it for commercial use, and over a period of 20 years, he parceled it off and sold it for $3,000,000!

Three young men; a builder, a financier and a property manager, had lots of ideas but little money. Using several of the approaches I describe in Chapter 9 on the art of persuading "angels" to back sound projects, they built $30,000,000 worth of apartments in ten years. It's an astounding success story which can be duplicated in your city as well.

And if you're not comfortable dealing in millions, and feel more at home dealing in the hundreds of thousands, you will be enthralled by the innovative cost-cutting methods of a small builder who out-professionaled the professionals.

Yes, there's hope for the small-fry builder, if he knows what to do.

THERE IS BIG MONEY IN INNOVATIVE PROPERTY MANAGEMENT

In Chapter 10, I describe how a unique management idea added $500,000 in value to an old residential apartment hotel. There are hundreds of such hotels in the country which are either losing money or just hanging on. They could be turned into money makers by using the same innovative ideas. You probably never heard about the "Juneau Club" for the elderly and the "Home-Away-From-Home" for business executives. I have tested these ideas and documented their results, and you'd be passing up a sure-fire opportunity if you didn't seriously explore them in your city.

The host-guest property management concept I discuss in Chapter 10 gives a new slant to the landlord-tenant relationship and raises the occupancy rate. And what's more, it lowers business frustration as well. That's because it builds idealism and diminishes commercialism.

LOOK AT WHAT'S UNDERNEATH THE ICEBERG
IN A REAL ESTATE INVESTMENT

Most people see only the visible iceberg of an investment, not what's underneath. The underlying fortune building opportunities become visible only when we analyze a real estate investment on the basis of these four money-making benefits: (1) The value of overage, (2) The value of amortization, (3) The value of tax shelter and tax loss, and (4) The value of inflation.

Did you know that if you add them all up, your rate of return could be as high as 35%? Wouldn't you be foolish to invest your money at 5% when there's a chance for 35%? True, it's riskier, but armed with this knowledge, the risk is worth taking.

BOLD LEVERAGING

If you're on the flamboyant side, you will be intrigued by the story of a 31-year-old real estate man who bulldozed his way into a $5,000,000 office building project by merely signing a $25,000 note. He invested his time in what looked like a hopeless deal, but when he got through, he relieved the original entrepreneur of his worries, put the project on its feet, saved several small contractors from bankruptcy, and earned $100,000 in cash for himself. It's a fantastic story and it could happen in your city too. Read about it in Chapter 11.

You'll be sobered into caution by the story of a real estate genius who put all his eggs in one basket and scrambled them into a colossal failure. By being smart, but not wise, he laid the biggest egg of his life. See Chapter 11.

And to reinforce this note of caution, I relate a story about myself in which a small-town broker took me for a ride when I bought a building without checking a few vital facts. And that building has been losing money for me ever since. The moral of the story is to keep your eyes open for opportunities, but look for the pitfalls too. See Chapter 6.

THERE'S A RIGHT AND A WRONG WAY
TO GET STARTED IN COMMERCIAL REAL ESTATE

It's so easy to get started on a hit and miss basis. But fortunately, it's just as easy to get started on a sound basis. It will only take you a few minutes to read about the right way, and perhaps save you years of floundering.

First, check yourself in Chapter 4 to see if you have the qualifications for commercial real estate selling, and if you do, then read Chapter 11 and find out how to implement your qualifications so that you increase your chances for success.

HOW TO USE LEVERAGE WHEN BUILDING COSTS, REAL ESTATE TAXES AND INTEREST RATES ARE RISING

In Chapter 12, you'll see how a small town makes a wise investment in its future when it takes a $60,000 loss on land to give the developer the needed leverage to make a project feasible. As a result, both prosper—the town gets its needed hotel and enlarges its tax base, and the developer is able to stay in the black. In contrast, I cite an example of a bank which refused to take a loss to aid a developer, and compounded its loss.

Lenders are practical people. They're hard when they don't see a profit, but they soften quickly when they see one. For instance, in the same chapter you will read how a lender locks up a mortgage refinancing deal. But when you show him how he can make 17% interest by recasting it, he quickly unlocks it. It's a bit of mathematical footwork worth learning because by releasing a lender from a locked-in, low interest mortgage to a higher current rate, he can gain enough to give you what you want. It sounds a bit complicated, but it's worth digging into.

BORROWING MONEY IMAGINATIVELY IS AN ART WORTH LEARNING

Many a project does not see daylight because the developer lacks borrowing vision. To help you ask for money more imaginatively, I quote chapter and verse from my personal experiences, to show you how I turned impossible dreams into realities.

Involving spirituality can be a more powerful borrowing tool than intellectual acumen—if it is used with delicacy and good judgment. I'll tell you how it helped me get a $500,000 loan off dead center.

You'll be interested to read how I got out of a financial bind by tapping the entrepreneurial juices of an 82-year-old man, and floating an impossible $2,800,000 mortgage on an office building project. It was pushing borrowing into high adventure, a bit dangerous, but a lesson with a happy ending.

Honesty has not only moral value, but commercial value as well. Read how it cut the red tape of $20,000,000 worth of borrowing, and saved thousands of hours for both the lender and borrower. Trust in a business relationship saves money because it cuts endless formal detail.

Most people have a basic desire to do good. If your project

makes a worthy contribution to society, money lenders will go out of their way to help you. They may demand the maximum collateral and highest ,interest rates for mortgaging a whiskey warehouse or a bubble gum factory, but they'll be generous if a project makes a worthy contribution to the lender's community.

NEW WAVES OF THE FUTURE

There's big money and fulfillment in breaking up the ghettos, thinning out their congestion and replacing slums with new developments.

Forty per cent of the American people qualify for some kind of moderate and low income housing subsidy. Untapped fortunes are locked up in that statement. Untold opportunities lie in opening up the suburbs to millions of families where hundreds of billions of dollars are going to be spent in the near future. Read how, through FHA Title 236 and HUD Program 23, you can make big money and help a lot of people with no risk and little money.

The final chapter ends with a grand concept. You can build a village of your own and experience the thrills of creation. It's a heady idea, but it can be realized if you follow the practical suggestions and launch yourself into history.

LAYING THE FOUNDATIONS FOR FORTUNE BUILDING

Chapters 1 through 5 do not deal specifically with money-making, but they will give you a general insight into fortune-building. You'll find out how a $200,000,000 real estate mortgage insurance business was hatched in the back rooms of my real estate office by one of my salesmen during a bull session.

You'll read about some innovative methods used in finding and keeping real estate salesmen.

If you don't choose the sales category that fits your talent and personality, you could ruin your career. That's why I dwell on the different requirements needed for residential and commercial real estate selling.

The price and the prize of real estate developing are carefully analyzed—the pitfalls and the fulfillment.

And perhaps, when you sort out your options, you'll decide that managerial rather than entrepreneurial action is your cup of tea. It's a lot easier on the nerves.

And finally see if you do not agree with me that you should be proud, not sorry, when salesmen leave you to go into business for themselves.

DON'T FESTER UNDER THE PLASTER

It's very likely that you'll find several new ideas here. If you're plastered down by old thinking, you can now remove the plaster .with a new idea, and let some fresh air in. Or you can remain comfortable and fester under the plaster. My advice is to remove it, even if it hurts.

Fortune-building requires courage and action which strips off the old and makes you vulnerable to the new.

I acknowledge with gratitude the assistance of Wade Mosby, whose professional editorial touch was most helpful.

CONTENTS

PART I

THESE IDEAS BUILD ORGANIZATIONS

How a pupil used his teacher as a stepping stone to a fortune. A simple suggestion struck gold. A bull session gives birth to a $200,000,000 real estate insurance company. The tremendous selling power of sincerity. Is it practical to care for your customers the way a clergyman cares for his parishioners? Can idealism be converted into fortune making?

From garbage inspector to owner of 200 rental units. From a $3,500-a-year teaching job to a net worth of half a million. From a vacuum cleaner salesman to a builder of homes. From biology to real estate. He gives up dentistry for real estate. From boredom to happy selling. His education didn't help him. There is more money in saying it than writing it. A good manager is hard to find.

Ethical standards produce stability. Instilling a sense of purpose. How to manage friction between salesmen. Concrete ways of caring and sharing. Should a broker allow his salesmen

PART II

THESE IDEAS PRODUCE ASTUTE INVESTORS

PART III

THESE IDEAS BUILD FORTUNES

PART I

THESE IDEAS
BUILD ORGANIZATIONS

Chapter 1

The Role a Real Estate Organization
Can Play in Building a Fortune

How do real estate fortune makers get their start? How do financial nobodies become financial somebodies? By either discovering their own potentials, or having their talents discovered by others.

One of the most fertile grounds for discovering ability, either through self awareness or recognition by others, is the real estate organizations of America. Whether it's a one man or a hundred man sales office—that's where talent meets opportunity, and real estate fortunes are conceived.

It is said that the rubber industry got its start when a chemist accidentally dropped some substance on a stove. It changed its consistency and caused it to bounce. Great real estate ideas are conceived just as accidentally, but they're more likely to occur in the workshop of a real estate office than in a scholarly ivory tower.

Textbook real estate information is necessary, but the gutsy ideas are forged on the firing line of action. That's where plans burst in the open and men are put to their highest and best use.

Innovation—remember that word—is born in the stress and strain of making projects work. Like a golden thread, you will find innovation running through the pages of this book. That's because it's the basic stuff out of which real estate fortunes are made.

HOW A PUPIL USED HIS TEACHER
AS A STEPPING STONE TO A FORTUNE

A real estate broker ought to feel a sense of accomplishment if one of his salesmen leaves and surpasses him. And that's not sour grapes. Doesn't a wise professor feel that way when his pupil becomes more famous than he? Well, that's what happened to me.

Burt didn't know the difference between a cottage and a bungalow when he started selling real estate for me. He was fresh out of college, stuffed with legal and accounting knowledge. He was an introvert—hardly a promising background for a salesman. I hired him because he was my friend.

While my more flamboyant salesmen did more talking than thinking, my shy young salesman did more thinking than talking. He was eagerly absorbing the practical lessons of a busy real estate office.

For three years Burt was selling and learning; but learning more than selling. In between sales, he was blue-printing his own career.

When he left he said, "Thanks for a crash course in real estate You've taught me a lot—now I know there's little money in brokerage. My intuition tells me the big money is in building, and that's where I'm going."

I was but a few years older than Burt and too inexperienced at the time to have recognized that under his shy exterior was a hurricane drive to succeed with plenty of ability to match. Hidden under the surface of his introverted personality were the guts of a successful builder, the stamina of a bull, and the financial shrewdness of a Wall Street wizard.

Within a few years he was building and selling a thousand homes a year. As he gained momentum he began building apartment complexes, office buildings and university dormitories.

"You see, George," he told me ten years later, when he had become a multimillionaire, "you taught me that there's no money in brokerage. Now let me teach you something. The big money is in building—if you learn these three bedrock principles: One, how to build at rock-bottom costs; two, how to keep rental occupancy near 100%, and three, financing your projects at 100% or beyond. The third becomes easy if you learn the first two."

He awakened me to the fact that there was little money in brokerage compared to the big money in building. My building efforts were in the tens of millions while his were in the hundreds of millions. The student had surpassed his teacher.

He hatched his building dream in my organization, just as many have done in other organizations.

A SIMPLE SUGGESTION STRUCK GOLD

Often an ordinary idea, clearly articulated at the right time, can aim an ordinary man into an extraordinarily high earning career.

One of the first real estate salesmen I hired was a department store shirt salesman. He was personable, intelligent and impatient.

After four months, he said, "When I was selling shirts, people were saying yes to me 20 to 30 times a day. I made sales and commissions every day. Here, so far, no one has said yes in 120 days. I don't think real estate is for me."

"Listen and listen carefully," I said, "because what I'm going to say could make or break your real estate career. You're an impatient guy with a lot of bottled-up potential. But it won't come out unless you adopt a new selling tempo. This is what I mean. Instead of selling 20 shirts a day and earning $10, you've got to get used to selling one property a month and earning $500. That's like selling a thousand shirts at one crack. Trust me. I know what I'm talking about. Relax and see what happens."

I could see my wilting salesman perk up. Within 30 days he made his first sale. During the next 25 years, he and my organization split one and a half million dollars in commissions.

This is not meant to be an example of a fortune builder. He didn't have the entrepreneurial savvy that goes into fortune making. But building an earning record of $30,000 a year for 25 years is not bad—much better than earning $75 a week.

My salesman could not have achieved this enviable earning record without the motivation and psychological support of a real estate organization.

A BULL SESSION GIVES BIRTH TO A
$300,000,000 REAL ESTATE INSURANCE COMPANY

Bull sessions in real estate offices often waste a lot of time. But they can also lay the foundations for real estate fortunes. One of my restless salesmen brain-stormed an idea in one of my backroom offices which mushroomed into a $300,000,000 company. It's earning $15,000,000 a year and still growing.

My imaginative salesman introduced the proposition to our sales meeting that there was as much logic in insuring mortgages against default as there was in insuring homes against fire. A few of my salesmen raised eyebrows. The rest, including myself, let the idea glance off without giving it another thought.

But my salesman persisted. He went to one of the lawyers who closed real estate deals for me and described his plan.

"Did you know that insuring mortgages failed in the 1920's?" my attorney asked.

"But is that a good enough reason for it not to succeed in the 1950's?" my salesman retorted.

"All right," the lawyer said, "I'll talk to my partner."

Now and then an idea meets a man, and their affinity for each other bursts into a success story. My attorney's partner was that man, and my salesman had that idea. They matched perfectly.

The first attorney liked business, but he loved the practice of law more. He wasn't the man. His partner liked law, but he loved business more. He was the man. He was a born innovator. But that was only the beginning. He had much more. He had a quick, mathematical mind. He knew how to spot administrative talent. He was a rock of emotional and physical stability. And a perennial optimist. Oh, was he an optimist!

Life insurance, fire insurance—these people understand. But insuring mortgages—that required a promotional campaign that needed a million dollars. Now, if your friends and relatives are millionaires, that's no problem. But if they're mill-run wage earners and small fry entrepreneurs, raising a million dollars is like moving a mountain—with hand and shovel.

But he did it! Many of his friends, relatives and acquaintances bought stock in his company, not on its merits, but to do him a favor. His barber, his haberdasher, his grocer, his struggling lawyer friends—all came to his aid. Most of them are millionaires now because anyone who bought $5,000 worth of stock and kept it, is worth over a million dollars today.

It's a great fortune building story, and it all began in the back room of my office.

THE TREMENDOUS SELLING POWER OF SINCERITY

My first year as a salesman in a small real estate office taught me the practical and crucial importance of sincerity. I soon realized what a powerful fortune building tool it was. This early discovery laid the foundation for my real estate success.

One of human nature's innate drives is to find someone to trust. If one is blessed with sincerity—the kind with no reservations—he has a bankable asset. It's an invaluable business tool—one which converts prospects into loyal customers.

Sincerity is not something you put on or take off like a suit of clothes. You have to feel it and live it out of conviction and with commitment. When this is blended with innovation, problems become manageable, solutions fall into place.

For instance, during my first year in real estate selling, I told my prospects, "Let me do your home buying research. Make it my job, not yours. When I find the home that answers your needs, I'll call you."

It was a new twist. Nothing exceptional, but it worked. My prospects were willing to let me do their looking, as long as I gave them a progress report and showed them what I had found. That was the key—letting them know that I looked and cared. Three months after I began my real estate career, I had 25 families waiting for me to find them homes. My prospects became my clients.

I began making sales—one a month, sometimes two a month. At that time, sincerity was my only selling tool because I had very little knowledge.

I happen to have a terrible sense of direction, and several times when I took my prospects out to look at homes, I became lost. I noticed that when I confessed my ignorance, my prospects eagerly and courteously offered to help me find the way. Had I been defensive and allowed my pride to cover my weakness, I couldn't have developed a sense of trust and camaraderie which drew us together. Each sort of leaned on the other. It personalized our relationship—and what a powerful selling tool that is!

This may sound naive and simple, but it's not. I don't care how sophisticated one is if he relies on contrivance rather than on sincerity, he's bound to fail one way or another.

If someone had lectured me on the efficacy of sincerity, I could never have grasped it as completely as when my prospects taught it to me on the firing line of action.

When I opened my own real estate office, I made sincerity the cornerstone of my business philosophy. All my masthead signs carried these words: "A Dependable Real Estate Institution." And I meant it.

IS IT PRACTICAL TO CARE FOR YOUR CUSTOMERS THE WAY A CLERGYMAN CARES FOR HIS PARISHIONERS?

Real estate conventions can be a gold mine for new ideas, or they can be a waste of time—depending on how you use them.

I once heard an industrial salesman give a talk which revolutionized my concept of property management. True, I improvised on it somewhat, but the germ of the idea was his.

"You know," he said, "my minister has his flock, and I have my flock too. He ministers to their spiritual needs, and I minister to my 300 customers. I give them the same care my minister gives his parishioners. Whatever they need or whenever they want it, it is theirs at a fair price and with the most courteous service. I cater to their minutest needs. The commercial aspect is only a backdrop for the friendships I have developed with each of my customers. It's a caring relationship both ways—and as meaningful a one as my minister has with his parishioners. Or at least, that's the way I look at it."

As I was listening to him, a thought came to me which went something like this:

Why not turn property management into a host-guest relationship? Isn't the tenant our guest, whether he rents a hotel room, an apartment, an office or industrial space? Why should the commercial relationship dominate instead of a friendly host-guest friendliness?

When I got back to my office, I made a few moves to put the host-guest concept into practice. You'll read more about it in Chapter 10. It not only improved my relationship with my tenants, but the profitability as well.

Wouldn't you say that 98% occupancy for apartments, office buildings and industrial space is a pretty good record? That's the occupancy rate I've enjoyed for years, and a great deal of the credit is due to the industrial salesman's inspirational talk. I only take credit for being alert to his advice.

CAN IDEALISM BE CONVERTED INTO FORTUNE MAKING?

As far as I know, there is no other business that offers a more fertile field for innovation than real estate. Shelter is a basic industry, and there's no limit to the ways we can find to improve it.

The best place to start is in a busy real estate office. That's where the sparks fly, and some of them can be ignited to light the way to fortune making.

Artists have no monopoly on exhilaration that comes from creative work. In my opinion, real estate men who create new shelter to elevate the lot of people, can experience as much inspirational exhilaration as those who write poems, compose concertos or paint masterpieces.

If the real estate man's motives are altruistic and not exploitive, his contribution to society can be as meaningful as that of an artist. In fact, by using idealistic innovation in renewing the central cities, dispersing the poor, thinning out the megalopolises and beefing up our small towns, the real estate man can raise the quality of life more practically and pervasively than our philosophers or artists.

Chapter 2

How to Find Salesmen

Before we can train salesmen, we have to find them. But where? A little originality helps.

Some brokers recruit salesmen through advertising, others hire them through agencies. There's nothing wrong with these methods, but they're not as effective as prospecting for a salesman—like prospecting for gold—looking for finds in the most unusual places.

That's how I handpicked about sixty salesmen. About a third stayed with me for more than fifteen years; about half went out on their own to become huge successes; and a few, very few, didn't work out.

That my method of selecting salesmen paid off is attested by the fact that from 1940 to 1970 my organization sold close to $300,000,000 worth of real estate—the equivalent of selling every house, office, factory and apartment building in a typical city of about 75,000.

FROM GARBAGE INSPECTOR
TO OWNER OF 200 RENTAL UNITS

I happened to see an amateur play one evening. One of the actors radiated an unusual charm. At the end of the play, I introduced myself and asked him what he did for a living.

I'm a city garbage inspector," he replied.

"Do you like your job?" I asked.

"Yeh," he said pleasantly. "It's not very exciting, but with all the fringe benefits, it offers a dependable living. You might say it's a smelly job, but secure." He ended with a laugh.

My next remark changed the young man's future.

"Don't you know," I said, "that uncertainty is what makes life interesting? Just think how boring life would be if you knew exactly what was going to happen to you for the rest of your life."

"I never thought of it that way. What would you suggest I do to make my life more uncertain and exciting?"

"Join my organization and sell real estate," I said breezily. "I promise you lots of uncertainty, and lots of excitement."

"I may just do that."

Several weeks later he came to my office. I hired him. He was with me for fifteen years. When he left to form his own company, he had earned upwards of $250,000. He now owns 200 rental units and lives in a $75,000 home.

FROM A $3,500 A YEAR TEACHING JOB
TO A NET WORTH OF HALF A MILLION

Jim and I played a lot of tennis together during our college days. We were good friends. While I was languishing in idleness during the depression, he was building a career teaching high school geography.

"Jim," I said to him one day after I had formed my real estate company, "I'm going to jar you out or your complacency. I want you to join my organization."

"You must be nuts, George. You want me to give up teaching and security for pie in the sky?"

"I'm offering you more than pie in the sky," I said. "You happen to be one of the most stable guys I know, and a delightful schmoozer. You're like an old shoe—people are comfortable with you. If you'll let me aim you right, you can't miss becoming an extraordinarily successful real estate salesman."

The fact that I had three successful years behind me, and an organization of six, high-earning salesmen, gave me the confidence to ask him to come with me. He yielded to my judgment and joined my company.

"Jim," I said, "here is the way I want you to get started. Each day, call fifty home owners listed in the city directory, and ask them to list their properties. It's a tedious job, but don't give up until I do. And I don't give up easily."

A week and 250 calls later he came into my office and said:

"George, I am getting discouraged. People like to talk to me all right, but all I hear is 'no.' "

"Next Monday," I said, "is the beginning of another week. Let's not draw any conclusions until you've been at it a month."

The next week he listed his first property. Three weeks later, he sold it. His informal schmoozing was paying off. Within several months, prospects were inviting him to their homes, weddings and social affairs. In return, he was visiting them periodically with small but thoughtful gifts.

In his first year, he earned three times what he was making as a teacher, and during the thirty years he's been with my organization, he has lived well, and accumulated a net worth of about $500,000. We're still buddies, except instead of playing tennis, we've now slowed down to golf.

FROM A VACUUM CLEANER SALESMAN
TO A BUILDER OF HOMES

One evening a young man came to our home to sell us a vacuum cleaner. He spoke with a strong foreign accent.

In spite of his accent, he set up a trade deal for my old vacuum cleaner in language so persuasive that I said yes in a few minutes. But I did more than that. I saw an opportunity for both of us.

"Would you mind if I asked how much you make a week?"

"About $75," he replied directly.

"How would you like to make $20,000 a year?" I asked.

"Doing what?"

"Trading homes instead of trading vacuum cleaners."

"What makes you think I'd be able to trade homes?" he asked.

"You exude trust, and that's a rarity. Also you know how to handle numbers. It's especially effective in selling real estate. I have a hunch you'd make a dandy home trader.

"I'm sure of making $75 a week selling vacuum cleaners, but real estate—I'm not so sure. You see, I have a family to feed."

"Trust me. I think I can make a big change in your life. To make it easier for you to decide, I'm willing to guarantee you $75 a week for half a year."

A month later he started to work for me. He learned the trading technique with ease, and more important, he communicated it so clearly and persuasively, that before long he became involved in two–, three–and four-way trades that tested the financial wizardry of the attorneys who closed our deals.

He averaged $20,000 a year for the five years he was with my organization. He then struck out on his own and became one of the quality home builders in our state.

FROM BIOLOGY TO REAL ESTATE

I heard of a young man whose grades were not high enough to get him into medical school, and he was now floundering in a fog of uncertainty.

"John," I said after I talked to him for about an hour, "I know you must think that healing is a nobler calling than selling, but what if I told you that selling is but another form of healing? If you dedicate yourself to helping people find the homes they've been dreaming about, in the price ranges they can afford, in locations they like—you can affect their lives as intimately and as healingly as many doctors do. You can give them peace of mind by meeting their basic need—shelter—a home in which they can be happy. And that's a contribution to health—it's practicing preventive medicine."

His face broke out into a smile. He was responding. There was an innocence about him that assured me I was on the right track.

"If you practice real estate the way I described it, you'll not only make a lot of money, but you'll be happy too."

I knew I struck gold! John was with me twenty years. During that time we split close to a million dollars in commissions. I made a notable contribution to his life, and of course, he made a valuable addition to my organization also.

HE GIVES UP DENTISTRY FOR REAL ESTATE

This rarely happens—a successful dentist leaving his profession to go into selling real estate.

One day a fifty-five-year-old dentist friend of mine said:

"George, would you think I'm crazy if I gave up dentistry at my age to go into real estate with you?"

"Doc," I answered, "knowing how frustrated you are being cooped up in an office all day, and watching your wheeling and dealing mind in action for some time, I'd say you're not only not crazy, but probably very wise."

"Here's the way I look at it," he said, "if you were able to make successes out of teachers and vacuum cleaning salesmen, you ought to be able to make a super salesman out of me. It sounds like bragging, and it is, but I think you and I could do great things together."

"If you decided to come with me," I said, "I wouldn't start you with selling homes, I'd put you directly in commercial real estate. That's where you belong."

A month later he closed his office and joined mine.

In a matter of weeks he found a vacant loft building, and he insisted we buy it. Several months later he found a businessman who wanted it. With a little help from me, we master-minded a buy and a sale and a profit of $25,000. Three months later he sold an A & P Store building to an investor. Our commission—$7,500. Soon he began crowding me with development deals, and for a piece of the action. He was no longer satisfied with commission deals. He wanted development and entreprenurial action.

After two extremely successful years together, he came upon a piece of raw land which he wanted to develop with me. I said: "Doc, I know it's a good deal, but I just can't let you monopolize my time. It wouldn't be fair to the rest of my salesmen. And you know something? Isn't it about time for you to go out on your own."?

"I'm glad you said it first, George," he said with a smile. "I'm so grateful for the start you've given me, I just couldn't get up enough nerve to leave you. But now that you've said it, you make it easier for me to say thank you for a happy and most profitable two years."

He went on to make over a million dollars in the next ten years.

FROM BOREDOM TO HAPPY SELLING

A sixty-year-old retired, small corner-store groceryman came into my office one day and said;

"I'm bored. I have enough money to live on, but I don't know what to do with myself. Perhaps you can find something I can do."

I looked at his baggy pants, ill-fitting jacket and dishevelled hair. Yet, there was something pleasant about the little man— gentle and grandfatherly.

I surveyed him quietly for about a minute. Then a thought flashed across my mind.

"How would you like to spend four hours a day talking to housewives in their back yards as they're hanging their wash to dry? Leisurely, go from yard to yard, asking them whether they would like to sell their homes. And if they don't care to sell, ask them whether they know anyone who does."

"I think I would be good at it," he said eagerly. "I've been dealing with housewives all my life."

After several months of study, he barely passed his real estate examination.

On a warm May afternoon, he went out on his first day of work. He was as excited as a youngster in his first job. He talked to twelve housewives. He reported to me the next day that two of them said they were thinking about selling their homes. Within a month, he listed four properties. Within six months, he became the leading lister in our office. His boredom vanished. He was bubbling with happy activity.

He earned $8,000 his first year, more than he had ever earned in his corner grocery store.

"Why didn't I meet someone like you twenty-five years ago? I would have turned this town upside down."

There are tens of thousands who are not discovered and aimed to reach a higher percentage of their potential. Rene Dubois, famed micro-biologist, claims that most of us use only 10 per cent of our talents and abilities. That's why salesmen prospecting can be so profitable.

HIS EDUCATION DIDN'T HELP HIM

One of my friends graduated from a university with high honors, but he couldn't get a job. After a year of floundering, he came to me and said,

"George, I'm desperate. I've got to do something. Will you let me try selling real estate? I know some of the fellows in your office have little education, yet they're earning big money. Why can't I?"

"All right," I said, "let's find out."

I accompanied him on several calls to show him how to interview blue-collar families—lathe operators, tool and die makers, janitors, etc. On one of these occasions, I let him do all the talking. I squirmed in my chair as he made his explanations. They were learned, stiff and formal. He was talking down to his prospects, and I could see they were reacting negatively. There was no give-and-take communication.

The ability to absorb facts is important, but the art of communicating them is more important. My college friend was learning it fast—with humility.

After six months, I said,

"Ernie, selling is not for you. You're brilliant at sopping up information, but digesting it, and spoon-feeding it to the average man so he can understand it, is a talent you obviously don't have. But don't worry, fellows like you will soon be in great demand." It was in the late 1930's, just when our economic depression was beginning to lift.

Eventually, Ernie got a job with the federal government, where he did an excellent job. He became a reservoir of knowledge for his superiors, whose more important job was to communicate it.

THERE IS MORE MONEY IN SAYING IT THAN WRITING IT

Back in the mid-fifties, I was managing twenty salesmen. I needed an advertising man to streamline my public relations. I hired a young publicity writer for the job. After several months, I became convinced he was a better salesman than a writer.

"Steve," I said to him one day, "I think I know you better than you know yourself. You see, I'm very much like you. I've tried to be a writer and found I was a much better salesman. We're made of the same stuff. I think you could earn more money selling real estate than doing publicity. Want me to prove it to you?"

His eyes lit up. "Prove it to me."

"Okay," I said. "What do you think of the slogan, 'You can trade your home just like you've been trading your car'?"

"Sounds good to me. But what are you driving at?"

"Well," I said, "there are only a few people in this town who really know how to trade property. The car people are way ahead of us in this field. I think with your background you could become a hell of a successful real estate trader."

He joined my company and became an instant success. He perfected home trading into a science. After staying with me for fifteen years, we formed the Bockl Development Corporation, with the aim of pioneering the revitalization of the small American town, with him in control. But more about this exciting idea in a later chapter.

A GOOD MANAGER IS HARD TO FIND

Side by side with finding salesmen, we must also discover and develop managerial talent to manage the salesmen. Managers are a different breed of men. In a salesman, the motivational quotient is high on the list of assets. In a prospective manager, it's the stability quotient that counts. Is he fatherly, patient and ethical? Like the head of a family, the manager is charged with the responsibility of setting the tone of activity in an organization and of holding it together.

An ideal manager is a middle-of-the-road man who has the resiliency to absorb the shocks of volatile and high-strung salesmen. Unlike them, he must know how to live in the living room, that is, not like many of his salesmen who emotionally often run up to the attic or down into the basement. A competent manager is basically a competent teacher—compassionate, organized, understanding and firm.

"Joe," I said to one of my leading salesmen one day, "I would like you to manage my men, but I can't pay you a salary equal to your commission earnings. To make up the difference, I'll sell you part of my stock, and you can pay me for it out of stock dividends."

He listened attentively. I had a hunch he would like my offer because basically his forte was management, but I had to figure out a formula which would appeal to him. He turned out to be a good choice, and the formula made sense for both of us because he remained with me for thirty years.

I found out that one manager cannot give personal attention to more than fifteen men. When my organization increased to thirty, I divided my real estate activity into north side and south side office. I needed another manager.

When it came to choosing between men who were as brisk as rabbits or plodding as turtles, I always chose the latter. I shied away from the type who shines like fireworks in the night for one moment, and disappers in the darkness the next. I prefer the plodder who burns slowly, the rock type of a man around whom less stable men can rally when the going gets rough.

When I chose Lee to become assistant-manager, many of my successful salesmen thought I made a mistake.

"I earn twice as much as he does," several complained. "How can he lead us?"

But I stuck to my guns. Lee surprised many of my hot-shot salesmen. He became a top-notch manager. What they didn't realize was that stability in a manager is of a greater value than brilliance. Razzle-dazzle doesn't build an organization—dependability does.

That's why I chose "A Dependable Real Estate Institution" as the slogan for my company.

Chapter 3

How to Keep Salesmen

What thinking man would not prefer democracy over dictatorship? If democracy is good for a large organization, should it not be equally good for a smaller one—like a real estate organization, for instance?

Those who worship efficiency and results are apt to rebel against giving salesmen too much voice in policy making. And that's why we have many one-man business dictatorships. Efficiency may be good, but perfectionist authoritarians take all the fun out of work. Ask anyone who's lived under Communism and he'll tell you.

As for me, I prefer democracy in all levels of relationships. Salesmen can give us a lot of trouble, if we let them in on policy making, but it's worth it. Inefficient democracy is superior to efficient dictatorship.

When my organization consisted of six men, they balked when I kept looking for more salesmen. They felt that prospect leads would be diluted among too many men. I had to spend several days explaining to my men that by hiring more go-getting salesmen their earnings could actually be increased by the new listings the new men would bring in. They gave in grudgingly. Fortunately, I turned out to be right. I would have lost them if I hadn't.

On one occasion a top-notch salesman wanted to join our organization. His reputation was questionable, but being a reformist at heart, I felt I could straighten him out. I put hiring him to a vote, and my men voted him down. I lost a good man because he subsequently formed his own company and did a bang-up job.

If we want the fruits of democracy, we must be willing to take our chances of winning or losing. Only in a dictatorial situation does one have it one way—his way.

ETHICAL STANDARDS PRODUCE STABILITY

To keep salesmen, it is imperative that a set of ethical standards be formulated, agreed upon and adhered to. Unless management fights for integrity, it cannot expect its salesmen to have it. By setting an example of dependability and reliability, an employer can help wavering and weaker men toward higher ethical behavior.

Just as law and order stabilize a society so do sound ethical standards stabilize a business. Without an undergirding of integrity, an organization disintegrates from top to bottom.

I have often told my salesmen that in dealing with people who know less than they, such as elderly widows, or any uninformed buyers or sellers, they insist these people be represented by lawyers or knowledgeable members of their families.

"Remember," I warned them, "the little old lady could be your mother or your grandmother. Would you want anyone to exploit them? Then don't do it yourself."

It's easy to misrepresent in real estate. It's a complicated transaction. Those who know can easily take advantage of those who don't. A broker has the responsibility to instruct his salesmen to do the right thing not only when the law is breathing down their necks, but even when the law is not looking. That's when clients begin to trust real estate men—an asset which redounds to the benefit of broker, salesmen and public.

A company which does not hold the line on ethical standards will not be able to hold the line on its salesmen. They'll over-run it with a dog eat dog philosophy.

Our company sold $300,000,000 worth of real estate from 1940 to 1970. It's an impressive record. But what I believe is more impressive is that we closed approximately 20,000 deals under the watchful eye of the incorruptible and competent Wisconsin Real

Estate Brokers Board, our regulatory agency, and, except for a few minor disagreements between buyers and sellers, and on very rare occasions between either of them and our company, these very personal transactions, involving perhaps 75,000 people were handled in an orderly professional manner.

This is a tribute to our salesmen and the reward of management which tried to do what was right. Practicing integrity plays a vital role not only in keeping salesmen, but helping them earn more money in a happy environment.

INSTILLING A SENSE OF PURPOSE

Making money must be linked to something bigger or it degenerates into spiritless and aimless activity. Unless it is subordinated to a search for raising the quality of living, work lacks spontaneity and purpose, it becomes a bore and a chore. Is it possible to sell real estate with a sense of dedication? It certainly is. Seen in its proper light, it is as significant as practicing medicine, law, or social work.

I often told my salesmen that if they thoughtfully and caringly matched 30 families with 30 comfortable homes a year, they not only could make a good living, but could make as much of a contribution to the families' mental and physical well-being as psychiatrists and physicians do. If a salesman finds the ideal type of home his prospect is looking for, the location he wants, monthly payments he can afford, near the church and school he prefers—that salesman is meeting a basic family need. He is indirectly practicing preventive medicine.

Salesmen must be made to feel that they are not involved in an ordinary humdrum job. They should be made to feel that they are playing a vital role in the lives of people.

I believe that real estate selling makes a more vital contribution to society than many other careers I can name. "When you sell a home to a family," I have said at meetings, "and see their glow of satisfaction, you can put your head on the pillow at night and rightfully feel a sense of contentment."

Selling real estate can be a work of dedication, and those who are thus motivated become better and happier salesmen.

HOW TO MANAGE FRICTION BETWEEN SALESMEN

It is healthy to have differences of opinion, and they should be expressed, but it's much more fun to disagree agreeably, than let it deteriorate into hostile confrontations.

Democracy grinds slowly and frustratingly because we so often become unreasonable and disagreeable, but we should be grateful to solve our differences in a spirit of give and take, rather than in an atmosphere of arrogant authoritarianism.

I could have solved many disagreements between salesmen by simply making a unilateral ruling, but that would not have proved as effective as my decision to have a grievance committee, composed of salesmen, make such rulings. The grievance committee, elected by the salesmen, made final decisions involving tens of thousands of dollars. It ruled on who misappropriated calls from whom, and what the penalties ought to be. Generally, however, its main work involved commission divisions between salesmen.

Now and then there were differences between salesmen and the company. Under those circumstances I would add a management member to the grievance committee, and take my chances on winning or losing. I remember losing one thousand dollars to a salesman in a decision I considered outrageous, but when I thought it over, I realized it was better to lose in a business democracy than win under the rules of an autocracy.

Isn't business democracy at its finest when salesmen and their employer can present their cases, as they do in court, and be willing to abide by whatever the outcome? Solving frictions on the grass root level eliminates the lingering recriminations when there are no rules, or when the employer has the sole authority to make the final unilateral decision.

CONCRETE WAYS OF CARING AND SHARING

To keep salesmen happy and producing we must, or course, give them something more concrete than democracy, ethical standards, and a grievance committee. This is why very early in our company history, we provided many types of bonuses, accident and health insurance, and a profit-sharing plan. These are practical ways of sharing and caring. Many large forward looking companies throughout the country have been providing these fringe benefits to their employees for years, and there is no reason why small companies shouldn't do the same. It's good economics and good sociology because this type of help gives men a sense of security, and raises their productive capacity.

"In sickness and in health" is not only a compassionate marriage vow, it can be a thoughtful business vow, as well. During times of illness when accident and health insurance is not enough to see a family through a trying period, it's not only a decent act but good business for the employer to volunteer a loan. This is not a time to play hard to get, but to give graciously.

Selling on a commission basis is a feast-and-famine business, and an alert employer will level out the peaks and valleys with timely loans on a selective and deserving basis.

A salesman may need several thousand dollars to help him buy a home. No thoughtful employer ought to allow him to pay exorbitant interest rates to some loan shark companies. He should furnish such loans either interest free or, if the company is short of cash, at least co-sign with the salesman at its—or his—bank.

Over the years, we have made dozens of loans to salesmen, and while we lost about $40,000 in the process, the good we've done makes this loss an excellent investment.

Running a small business is like extending familial responsibility to a greater number of people. Wayward men have to be helped back into the fold. Sometimes we have to play the role of psychiatrist and father confessor. My managers and I have listened to many of our salesmen's troubles, tried to lift them up when they were down, and when they lived high off the hog, we tried to make suggestions on how to get down to earth.

Though we stressed sales, we also challenged them to find something bigger to live for than mere success. Occasionally, during sales meetings, and more often in private discussions, we raised the question of the indispensability of the spiritual life.

It's true that most of them would turn off when we discussed the quest for quality living—for finding something big to live for, but enough of them listened to make the time spent worthwhile. Of course, we stayed away from preaching—we merely raised the spiritual question in the hope it would influence their decision-making on the business battle front, where the bullets are live, where the problem of making a living was on the line, and where the question of morality was more practical than theoretical.

SHOULD A BROKER ALLOW HIS SALESMEN
TO INVEST IN REAL ESTATE?

At first blush the answer is no. And many fine brokers do not allow it. Their rationale is that they don't want their salesmen competing against their clients. This can be justified by brokers who like to run their salesmen with an iron hand, giving consideration to their firm, their clients, and their salesmen, in that order.

I believe it is easier to attract and keep salesmen if we reverse that order, and give priority to salesmen, but without jeopardizing the interests of clients or the firm. I think it can be done if management lays down a policy of disclosing all the facts to sellers, letting them know that in certain instances, the firm's salesmen are ready to pay as much for a property as any buyer.

Why should a salesman be deprived from investing his hard-earned money in real estate? It's true, there may be a conflict of interest, and it may be abused, but if all the facts are brought out in the open, the hardship on clients is less than it would be on salesmen if they were deprived of the right to secure their future in real estate.

Dozens of my salesmen invested in real estate with varying results. Several of them lost all their savings. Others accumulated small portfolios of investment property which stabilized their fluctuating commission incomes, and gave their families a feeling of security. In analyzing their investments across the board, I'd say they did no better or worse than the hundreds of buyers who invested their millions through our organization.

The number of parcels our salesmen bought for themselves was probably less than 1/10 of 1% of the properties they handled for our clients. Giving our salesmen the opportunity to use their judgment and risk their earnings like anyone else, brought no harm to our clients or our firm and, in my estimation, helped us to keep them satisfied.

TEACHING SALESMEN—IMAGINATIVELY

A forward-looking company should develop imaginative ideas to stimulate its salesmen. For instance, a playlet depicting a buyer and seller encounter with all the human interest nuances can be both entertaining and informative. On the other hand, setting forth, point by point, in syllabus form, how to qualify a buyer and seller is good, but it does not have the impact of a skit in which the telling selling points are easily remembered.

Knowing why a prospect wants to buy or sell is the first golden step in selling. The how to sell then becomes secondary. In selling, as in living, the why is always more important than the how.

Another way of putting it is that to be wise is more important than to be smart. We can be loaded with facts, but if we communicate them with contrivance and insincerity, we may get a few results but never a wholesome feeling of accomplishment.

Surface knowledge or psychological tricks may entice some people into buying, but if we want to make selling a profession, there is no firmer rock to build on than a foundation of spiritual wisdom. Is this some naive pie in the sky? Not at all. In my estimation, that's where genuine sincerity comes from. And sincerity is selling power. It's more powerful than any learned technique. It's putting why ahead of how—the secret of successful selling.

LOOK FOR PROSPECTS IN THE RIGHT PLACES

Living in a democracy is a privilege, and to keep earning that privilege an enlightened company should encourage its salesmen to participate in the various democratic institutions. Salesmen should be urged, for their benefit, for the firm's good, as well as for the community's welfare, to join civic, political and social service groups.

Salesmen should circulate to encourage encounters with people. But they should be selective. Talking endlessly at bars and running to race tracks trying to get something for nothing is not the way to search for promising prospects. Such activity wastes time, empties pocketbooks and dulls minds. The best prospects are found at service clubs, school meetings, political gatherings, etc.—wherever responsible people meet.

Salesmen should try to convert prospects into friends. It's more fun that way. This can be done by inviting them to social, civic, or athletic affairs. That's where formal relationships are thawed into informal ones.

Above all, a salesman should be free of all traces of either ostentation or obsequiousness. It poisons the salesman-prospect relationship.

SHOULD SALESMEN BE OFFERED STOCK IN THE COMPANY THEY WORK FOR?

If you're the type who likes to run things your own way, if you work best when you're not sidetracked by others, then don't sell any of your stock to salesmen. The chances are nine out of ten that your minority stockholders are going to give you trouble.

I've had a salesman, who owned 10% of my stock, tell me he didn't see why I should draw a salary, and not he. Another 3% stockholder felt peeved when I didn't inform him in advance about the moves I planned for my company.

A small business does not have the committees, formal meetings and agendas big companies do. The typical broker is usually an individualist, who does not like formalities or have minority stockholders tell him what to do.

Should you decide to sell some of your stock to your salesmen, and I think you should in spite of the looming difficulties, be sure you retain majority ownership, and don't sell it to stubborn, argumentative men.

I sold as much as 45% of my stock to my salesmen. When we developed differences, I had to repurchase some of it at 50% profit to them. Yet, I do not regret it. I believe in experimentation. When an idea does not work out, correct it. Nothing ventured—nothing learned.

It was a challenging experience battling eyeball to eyeball with my stockholders. Sometimes they sharpened my plans and sometimes they shattered them. Often they clipped my wings when I wanted to soar. But what they contributed far outweighed the few headaches they caused me. We became wiser after every battle because one or the other won or lost, and we had to accommodate ourselves to new situations. That kept us on our toes.

HOW A COMPANY SHOULD SELL ITSELF TO SALESMEN

To say that a broker is an employer and his salesmen are his employees is not an imaginative way of describing a broker-salesman relationship. The better way, and perhaps the more accurate way, is to point out to real estate salesmen that they are in fact in business for themselves. They purchase services from the broker at a price of half their commissions. It could even be said they are employing brokers to furnish them real estate services at a price

That's selling point number one. There are others, and they should be dramatized.

For instance, a broker should emphasize that a dependable real estate institution opens doors to unknown salesmen. Its image of integrity and respectability gives him trust and acceptability in the minds of prospects. Salesmen usually are not fully aware of the value of these selling assets.

When an imaginative broker livens up a weak listing with effective advertising that brings the inquiries and the sale—it is management's know-how which plays a partnership role in converting a mediocre man into a star salesman.

Many deals live or die depending on the broker's ingenuity in financing them. A broker who knows how to leverage deals for financially weak buyers—and they're the majority—becomes a tremendous selling aid to the average salesman. Salesmen should be made aware that it takes unusual skill to steer deals through demanding buyers, troublesome sellers and overly-cautious lending institutions.

Half of our sales would not have closed had it not been for the financial expertise of my manager. Our salesmen bought his genius at bargain prices, because he blew life into dead deals which literally put millions of dollars of added commissions into my salesmen's pockets. Of course, our organization profited too.

A broker who attracts unusual salesmen can make this a selling point to attract other salesmen, because rubbing shoulders with men of different selling styles is a valuable selling experience. The spirit of competition, if it is not allowed to degenerate into "dog eat dog," is a mind-sharpener. It raises a man's potential. When teaching is tactfully blended with motivation, lead is turned into gold, ordinary men become extraordinary.

Among the less visible services the broker offers to the salesmen is his responsibility to the state licensing agency, to the federal government for tax withholding procedures, to seeing that deals are closed properly, that buyers and sellers are given full legal protection, and the myriads of unsung details which go into managing a smoothly functioning office. And the record-keeping the broker provides, the office space, stenographic service, telephone, accounting, advertizing and public relations should somehow be made visible, and not be taken for granted.

It is the broker who takes the entrepreneurial risks—the salesmen can't lose—only their time. It is not inconceivable for a top-notch real estate salesman, freed from all detail, to make more than a successful broker. Over a period of 30 years, our firm averaged a gross commission of about $500,000 a year. $250,000 or 50% went to the salesmen for commissions. Our costs to run our office averaged $225,000 a year, or 45% of our 50%. Thus, our firm averaged about $25,000 a year profit, after an average salary for myself of about $20,000 a year.

Many of my salesmen earned more than $30,000 a year, year after year. They were buying my firm's many-faceted services for much less than if they had to furnish it themselves. Brokers often don't do a good selling job in impressing their salesmen with the bargains they're getting.

There is no big money to be made in residential brokerage. When I delegated my sales managment responsibilities to my managers, and turned to real estate development, on several occasions I made more money in one deal than I did in 10 years of brokerage. But that's another story, another dimension in real estate with which I deal elsewhere in the book.

Chapter 4

Choose Your Sales Category
Carefully--It's Crucial

Real estate selling is many-faceted. Obviously, selling a home involves less imagination than promoting a shopping center. It is important for one contemplating a real estate career to know the various categories of selling, how they differ, and the type of men who best fit the various selling classifications.

Salesmen often are unaware of their potentialities, and frequently lack the curiosity to investigate the nature of the sales options available to them. Thousands of careers are sidetracked because the salesmen's abilities are either underdeveloped or overmatched.

A training program should be tailored to match a man's capacity, maybe a size larger for growth. But not too much larger or he'll give up in frustration. The proper training goals put a man to his highest and best use.

The following are the main real estate selling categories and, as will be noted, they attract men as radically different as the categories themselves.

PROFILE OF A DEVELOPER

Men who promote shopping centers, office buildings, multi-family apartment complexes, industrial parks and land development take the greatest risks, make the most money when they are successful, and take the greatest physical punishment. To say that developers work hard is an understatement—they are driven. And only the few with bulldog tenacity, emotional stability and rare judgment prevail. The great majority fail, and many of them end up with serious coronary flirtation.

Developers have to be able to sell superbly on many fronts. They must convince the city fathers of the worth of their projects. They have to sell the money-lending institutions their projects' feasibility. They must hold the reins on their architects so they don't design them out of their budgets, and most important, they must find tenants to fill the projects. The competition is fierce among these real estate giants, sometimes ruthless.

There are areas where fatal mistakes can be made—building costs underestimated and the availability of tenants overestimated. When a project takes a turn for the worse, anyone without emotional stability could freeze into inaction, throw in the sponge prematurely, or go to pieces. Even those with courage and emotional stamina fail, if they lack a sense of timing, a little bit of luck, and above all, good judgment.

The typical developer gambles his talents for high stakes. He can become ferocious. If someone tries to block him, he'll first try to run around him, but if cornered, he may try to run over him. When a competitor accuses him of being ruthless, he salves his conscience by calling it efficiency.

He's a driver and drives others. There is no sweeter music than the applause which comes to him when his strenuous efforts meet with success. Because a developer is highly result-oriented, he is more likely to rationalize questionable means to attain his ends. A success-driven man is less likely to take the time to choose between right and wrong than one who lives at a leisurely pace.

There are gradations of developer entrepreneuers. There are those who are so hell-bent for success that they lose touch with what is decent, and will breach the law, if they have to, to get what they want. They lose touch with reality. Results and rewards become their ultimate concerns. The quality of their lives doesn't concern them.

There are others who strenuously fight for success, but moderate it with self-discipline. They do not seek to bend people or laws. They take pride in being fair and honorable, but they don't slacken their desire to keep moving forward and upward. These are not the sluggers, the killers who operate with no holds barred. They are usually the more imaginative and stable.

But even the more honorable ones pay a high price for going through the wringer of pursuing success. Without finding something bigger to live for than results and rewards, their bodies become coiled and rigid, and their personalities warped with eager intensity.

I have seen dozens of such men in action. Men in their fifties, worth millions, who could not possibly consume their net worth in five lifetimes, roar out into the business world to block and punch and go in for the kill, when all that's involved is adding another several hundred thousand dollars to a fortune that already is more abstract than functional—more shadow than reality.

These are the psychological pitfalls real estate developers can get sucked into, if they do not learn to decompress, to lower the fervor of their desires.

Success is meaningful only when it is not made ultimate. Only when one is armed with this wisdom is it safe to plunge into real estate development.

PROFILE OF A SUCCESSFUL BROKER

Organizing and running a brokerage firm is worrisome but not hazardous. It can make money but not a lot of money. The type most likely to succeed as a broker is a good family man, because running a brokerage firm is an extension of family responsibility. A successful broker is usually a fatherly, caring type, likely to be more wise than astute, more dependable than colorful.

Anyone who does not have a feel for detail better think twice before becoming involved in running a brokerage company. Unless he can shore up salesmen who are notorious for their lack of detail, they will all flounder together.

A broker should not only like people, he should enjoy molding and guiding their destinies. He should become involved in their hopes and aspirations—that's when he is most likely to meet their financial needs as well. The ideal broker has compassion, understanding and leadership. They are qualities salesmen appreciate most.

A slugging developer usually makes a poor broker because he is too wrapped up in his own projects, and does not have the empathy to lose himself in the problems of his men. He can only lose himself in himself. If a developer wants to remain in the brokerage business while developing projects at the same time, he would be wise to delegate responsibility to a manager who has the fatherly qualities of a broker.

Why do some brokers continue to be successful year after year, while others last a year or two and fall by the wayside? Invariably, the answer is that the successful ones build men, who in turn build an organization. The unsuccessful ones have money on their minds, not the welfare of men. They look for the quick buck, and find out just as quickly that it isn't there.

I know two of the leading residential real estate brokers in the midwest. Here are the reasons why they are successful.

The first is a religious man who looks after his salesmen as a clergyman does after his parishioners. He believes and lives the strenuous life, prodded more by biblical ethic than his desire to make a lot of money. Mixing hard work with sincerity and originality, he became the largest residential broker in the state.

He didn't learn his real estate in any college, he learned it on the firing line where the bullets are live and decisions have to be wise and practical. His integrity had a spiritual fervor, and it spread among his men, giving his organization stability and dependability.

He imbued his salesmen with dedication to service, and they grew with him. Home buyers responded to this commitment with their trust, and he built on it—successfully.

The second successful broker is a laywer, a conservative laissez-fair individualist, the kind who is looking for new Wests to tame. He is a law-and-order idealist who will dispute his government's interference with his rights as readily as he fights those who interfere with the laws of his government.

Laissez-faire, as a way of life, is as deeply embedded in him, as he embedded it into his business. He surrounded himself with men who believed the way he did, and together they built an organization using 19th century ideals, but modernized with 20th century business insights.

There is something eloquent about a man who says to government, "Leave me alone and I'll show you what I can do with the old-fashioned virtues of hard work and self-reliance." There is something dependable about a man who lives what he believes, who is as proud about the service he renders as he is of his country's Establishment.

His conservative ethic did for him what the religious ethic did for the first broker. His ideal tapped a well of energy which he drew on and used to charge up his men. It built a strong-willed, stable organization.

It is no wonder then that successful real estate brokers are by nature conservative, reluctant to change things in a hurry.

And to categorize the successful real estate brokers still further, as they relate to developers and salesmen, I'd say that the developers usually own a city, the brokers usually run it, and the salesmen usually enjoy it.

PROFILE OF AN UNSUCCESSFUL BROKER

Two competent men with "big-money—making" propensities, but without the fatherly wisdom of running men, decided to organize a real estate brokerage firm—in a hurry. They made the following mistakes . . .

Within several months, they hired ten men. They weren't creative in their hiring practice. Instead of discovering unusual men, they hired the first ones who answered their ads.

Their second mistake was getting involved in a real estate development, and not hiring a manager to look after their salesmen. The partners were more interested in their project than in their men—and their men knew it. There was no caring at the top and no cooperation below.

Within a year the partners began to quarrel and their poison spread to the men. There was dissension among salesmen, and eventually between salesmen and the brokers. The company folded as quickly as it was put up.

Another broker who didn't make the grade was a brilliant real estate man who tarnished his brilliance with whiskey. He knew all the hows but none of the whys. He was smart but not wise. He could have directed men to earn a lot of money, if he could only have learned to direct himself.

He had the competence to lead a thirty man organization to the heights of success, but instead he and a few cronies settled for mediocrity. They earned only enough to sustain themselves—squandering their talents because they found nothing bigger to live for than the next drink. A far cry from the ideals that bound the men together in my description of the two successful brokers.

Another broker I knew had many favorable qualities. He was attractive, articulate, full of energy and knowledgeable. People liked him. He was well-known in his community and his ten man sales organization did a creditable job.

But he lacked stability. His emotional volatility ignited relationships between him and his men so often that he had little time left to direct them.

One day he came to my office and said:

"George, I'm a free man. I've just fired all my salesmen. Every damn one of them! They were driving me batty, I tell you. I'm on my own now—at last!"

My broker friend didn't have the fatherly stability to sooth the bickering between his salesmen, nor the wisdom to compose the differences between himself and his men.

He was jolly and full of humor one day and ready to punch someone in the nose the next. When he was emotionally high, he figuratively ran up to the attic, and when he was low, his spirits plummeted him into the basement. He did not have the stability to enjoy the living-room.

PROFILE OF A "LONE WOLF" BROKER

The broker who fired his ten salesmen is a good candidate for the lone-wolf category. In fact, that's what he became, and made a success of it. Thousands of lone wolf brokers make a quiet living. They feel more relaxed without the responsibilities of running an organization.

As a group, they are self-starting individualists, but satisfied with limited horizons. They are not interested in molding and directing men, they are more interested in putting their own abilities to their highest and best use. It's a good life. Several examples will illustrate this.

B. J. was a city-wide personality. Almost everybody in the real estate business knew him. He made millions of dollars for brokers and developers in his forty years of bird dogging and brokering deals.

"I want to sleep nights," he used to tell me. "You wheelers and dealers can make the money and have the headaches that go with it. I just want peace of mind. It's more valuable than money."

He called on developers and brokers, offering them propositions, and making his commissions. He was well-informed on land values, and in improved real estate of all categories. He rarely sold to the public direct. He would "smell out" the deals and let others do the risking and the selling.

Working three to four hours a day, he was able in his quiet way to make enough money to send his boys through college, live in comfortable middle-class style, and subsidize his two university degreed sons after they were married and had families of their own.

He was a walking encyclopedia of deals. It was his stock in trade. By visiting four or five brokers a day, he absorbed and exchanged enough information to make him a valuable man to know. Brokers, and especially developers, lionized him.

B. J. made hundreds of thousands of dollars for our organization. He was always welcome because he always had information I could not obtain from anyone else. He sold his knowledge honestly, imaginatively and, I might add, with a great deal of humor. He looked upon himself as a harbinger of good news. And he was because he made many men wealthy.

John was a pro. He knew every phase of the real estate business. He was a master appraiser and broker. Methodical and scholarly, he could have run any good-sized real estate organization. But he had no desire nor disposition to do it. He was a real estate scholar more than a merchandizer. Testifying in court on complicated real estate matters was his forte. He made appraisals for banks and other responsible financial institutions. Now and then he sold a good-sized piece of property.

He practiced real estate like a lawyer practices law or a doctor medicine. Though he made several feeble starts to build an organization, they fell short of success because his heart wasn't in it. He was more at ease with facts and theories than in molding and motivating men.

Scholars seldom become millionaires because one seldom makes millions on fees or salaries. Developers, on the other hand, seldom are scholars. They live by their wits rather than their knowledge. They are forced to risk and innovate to make what little knowledge they have work for them.

John didn't have to risk or innovate. His specialized knowledge was in such high demand that he was able to employ himself for as many hours as he wanted to work. John, the scholar, explained things, others who knew less, made them happen.

PROFILE OF A MANAGER

A manager is a chip off a broker's block. He assumes the broker's administrative responsibilities but not his financial risks. He prefers teaching to selling, a steady salary to fluctuating earnings. He is at his best leveling the lives of those who by the nature of their rising and falling fortunes need a steadying influence.

Managers do not have the high motivational quotient of brokers. They are gentler and prefer to play for lower stakes. Feast or famine earnings are anathema to them. They don't mind hard work as long as they can enjoy emotional tranquility.

Managers are the cement of organizations. They can make heroes or bums out of brokers and salesmen. They can build or tear down organizations. Among the most vital decisions brokers have to make is choosing qualified managers and to learn how to manage them.

Good managers are primarily teachers. They motivate salesmen to organize their selling talents for maximum production. Managers are usually long on techniques and short on selling performance. Like the unheralded music teachers who do their best to draw the talents out of their pupils, managers are content to bask in the performances of their salesmen.

Managers are seldom as cunning as brokers or selfish as developers. They are not as success-driven, and consequently are not pressured by eager-beaver pulsations. They are more calm and relaxed. They are creative in small matters, not in the sweeping concepts. They fill in the details after the brokers or developers paint the general picture.

When uptight developers, bulldozing brokers and fatherlike managers use good judgment in creating feasible and saleable deals, they set in motion the opportunities for our next subject—the salesmen.

PORTRAIT OF A SALESMAN

The career real estate salesman, the real professional, becomes the sparkplug of his company. He is the one who makes those at the top look good or bad. He colors the bottom line of a business operation red or black.

What are the behavioral patterns which differentiate the superior, mediocre and poor salesman? Here is an attempt at an answer.

THE SUPERIOR SALESMAN

The top-notch salesman possesses a blend of originality and sincerity. He knows how to mix interest with energy to produce enthusiasm.

That's why even an introvert with a bland, low-profile personality can become a star salesman when he sincerely superimposes new ideas on old problems. The yeast he injects into a stalemated problem gives rise to solutions which personality selling and technique cannot match.

The superior salesman has a knack of getting on target, of taking the confusing details out of a deal. He knows how to get to the heart of a proposition. Just as a good writer gets to the point quickly without redundancy, so does a good salesman know how to get to the area of decision quickly and diplomatically.

The superior salesman genuinely feels that his work is important. He does not make the mistake of comparing himself to others, and although this might goad him to greater effort, comparison brings on more anxieties than improvements. Only the wise know that, and that's why they have more productive energy then those who jealously ape others.

The key to selling success is to convince ourselves of our uniqueness, our importance, and the importance of our work. No matter how menial our work may appear in comparison with greater works, we dare not feel inferior. That's what saps our motivational energy. Comparing and competing is not wise. It hurts and demeans.

The superior salesman must have empathy—a liking for people. The more he can genuinely enjoy relating himself to others, and meeting their needs, the smoother will be his flow of selling energy. It is impossible to be a good salesman and dislike people.

Empathy grows out of wisdom—in which is rooted a generosity to deal with the good and the bad in people. The superior salesman enjoys dealing with the good guys, but he gives a lot of room to the bad guys too. He knows how to take abuse with equilibrium, and accusations with equanimity. Sometimes he is even wise enough to turn the other cheek. Those are marks of great salesmanship because they have the power to change clients.

The superior salesman has a great deal of ego power—a sustained flow of motivational energy. He doesn't lapse into moods of discouragement—signs of energy blockages. He prefers common sense to technique in overcoming sales resistance.

The superior salesman doesn't make a great to-do about orderliness. He falls into it naturally. It's simpler to be orderly than confused, and since simplicity is one of his strong points, he automatically prefers order to disorder.

There are no perfect salesmen because there are no perfect men. However, there are salesmen who come closer to perfection than others. I have had the good fortune of discovering and training several salesmen who became near perfect and I admit, in exchanging experiences with them, they taught me more than I taught them.

Take Joe. He was a natural. He had a constant flow of new ideas, and seldom wasted time on old ones. He was loaded with ego power, but of a quiet kind—one with little bravado and a lot of depth.

He was with my organization less than six months when he came into my office one Monday morning and laid five sales contracts on my desk.

"How did you manage to sell five properties when you held only one open house Sunday?" I asked him.

"Well," he said with his introvertive smile, "I called all my prospects during the week to go through all of our open houses on Sunday, and come to my open house if they liked any of them. After I sold my open house, four others came back and said they liked the house I sent them to see."

"But how did you know the details of the other listings—the selling prices, the mortgage balance, and the terms of sale?" I asked in amazement.

"I memorized them," he said matter-of-factly.

He did more than that. He not only knew more about the properties than the listers, he developed sales plans which went beyond what the ordinary salesmen mapped out. He was an improviser, and his ideas quickened both buyers and sellers. And I might add, his broker too.

Then there was Jack—a battering ram of a salesman. He had so much empathy that people didn't mind and hardly felt his sledge-hammer blows. With the stamina of a bull and the patience of a saint, he bore in on a twenty-deal front, unobtrusively nudging and pushing his buyers into areas of decision.

His typical day called for a half-dozen cold-turkey calls, ten warm-up calls, and two or three showings. The typical week consisted of signing up two purchase and sales agreements, and closing one or two deals.

He could charm the gold out of people's teeth, if he wanted to—that's how much they loved him. But, of course, he never did. He made his prospects feel that their needs were all that mattered. He gave each and everyone his complete and total attention.

But what made his pouring out of energy so electric was that he was sincere—completely sincere. Service to him was not some motto one reads on a letterhead. It was a duty—almost a compulsion. He turned a promise into a vow. And it was easy for him to live up to it, because the desire for performance came out of the depths of his feelings, and it molded him into a master salesman.

THE MEDIOCRE SALESMAN

Some men do not know how to innovate. They think and live in ruts made by others. And when they do occasionally get a new idea, they lack the confidence to uproot themselves from the old.

The mediocre salesman doesn't see the airplane view of a proposition. He doesn't see the forest because he squanders too much of his energy on the trees. Like a mediocre writer who loses his reader in unrelated detail, the mediocre salesman loses his buyer with too much explanation.

The moment a salesman loses his sense of dedication, he sags into mediocracy. If he doesn't feel he's doing important work, he will not have the wisdom to make his work important. If he is satisfied to be average, he becomes average.

The mediocre salesman may have empathy, but tends to lose it too quickly and on too many occasions. He loses it when people act spitefully or vengefully. He resents unjustified accusations, and too often will get into hassles with those who make them. The mediocre salesman does not have the wisdom to turn the other cheek, nor does he have the patience and generosity to turn a nasty guy into a good one.

He has lapses of discouragement, because when the going gets rough, his ego drive sags, and his empathy loses its zest. Only a superior salesman has the resources to sustain his ego power and empathy, even though the odds are against him. The mediocre salesman cracks under the strain.

The mediocre salesman is short on wisdom, and is more susceptible to addictions and emotional instabilities than his superior colleague. An unstable home life due to promiscuity and drinking are pitfalls more likely to trap him than the superior salesman, because the latter is cognizant of their debilitating effects and avoids them.

I have trained more mediocre men than superior ones. The latter are rare. The challenge in training men is to lift the poor ones into the mediocre category, and to raise the mediocre ones into superior class.

Take Jim. He was triggered for mediocracy. Though he showed streaks of superiority, like fireworks that flash for a moment, they would die just as quickly.

At times his awkward contriving would drag him below mediocrity, but somehow he would always raise himself by his boot straps and get back into his mediocre groove. He would always take too long to tell a story, and take just as long to get on target in making a sale. But what he lacked in clarity, he made up in persistence, and it was the latter that kept him from sliding into the poor category.

Jim was not dedicated to his work. He had average energy, average interest, and average enthusiasm. He was wise enough to know it was safer to row the boat than rock it. He kept his home life stable.

Because he had no emotional hangups, he was able to channel his sales efforts at a steady pace. His median earnings were $15,000 a year. He never burst into brilliance, but neither did he break below mediocrity. Because he was in the midst of a highly motivated group of men, he kept his ego power up, faltering now and then when his empathy fell below normal, but getting back on his feet again because of his perserverance. What he lacked in airplane view, he made up by keeping his feet on the ground, but it was not enough to make him extraordinary.

THE POOR SALESMAN

The poor salesman has neither wisdom nor stability. He is not innovative, nor does he grasp the sales value of sincerity. His ego power sputters, and whatever empathy he possesses comes out in spurts. He is long on promises and short on performance.

Deep inside in many a poor salesman there is a desire to make a go of things, but unless he is shored up by a wiser and more dependable man, he flounders all his life. He has a weak sense of uniqueness and self-importance.

When a poor salesman is neglected by his superiors, when he's used rather than helped, his emotional weaknesses can flare into addictions, and he becomes a candidate for skid row. Many unthinking managers and brokers have kicked men down there, because they put sales ahead of a man's welfare.

What such managers and brokers don't realize is that salesmen who flounder in their weakenesses can be healed and helped if they're caringly and patiently shown how to hold their jobs. A fatherly broker or manager can often do more good than a psychiatrist in helping a "failure" get up after he's been kicked from job to job on his way down to a physical or moral breakdown.

Fred is a case in point. When he got into a minor altercation with the law, his broker fired him. The adverse publicity ostracized him from his community and none of the respectable brokers would hire him. When he came into my office looking for work, I could see the tell-tale marks of a rejected and dejected man. He was listless and disheveled. I hired him.

Fred had the marks of a poor salesman, but he was a good guy. He was filled with good intentions, but he didn't know how to channel them. He liked people but he conveyed it uninterestingly. He stretched stories with such dull and unnecessary detail that he lost his listeners in a maze of inconsequentials. And to top it all off, he had a drinking problem.

At first blush, I suppose, the businesslike thing to do was not to hire him, not to waste any time. But that would have been the easy way. I was charmed by this slow-talking middle-aged man because, though he was no ball of fire, he was guileless. He was devoid of cunning and contrivance. He stood there with all his weaknesses flashing, but mixed with it was a shining innocence that was intriguing.

I spread the umbrella of our company's image over him and put him to work. I was more interested in seeing what I could do for him than what he could do for me.

I challenged him to match my faith in him with his faith in himself. I suggested that he try to lose his drinking problem by losing himself in helping families find the homes of their dreams, in locations they always wanted, with mortgage payments they could afford.

"Fred," I said, "I want you to look upon your work as an opportunity to help other people. But don't just say yes—believe it—and then prove it to me."

If Fred were a sophisticated intellectual, or an ambition-driven materialist, he might have raised a supercilious eyebrow at my emphasis on helping people rather than making money. But Fred, fortunately, was not that kind. He accepted my suggestion wholeheartedly because he was so innocently honest. He actually began to feel a sense of dedication. That made him feel important. He was finding his identity. In fact, his passion to help people became so absorbing, it was subduing his lesser passion for drink.

Fred didn't set the world on fire. Where others worked with twenty prospects at a time, he could only follow up three or four. But the few he worked with responded to his caring service. Being devoid of greed, he wasn't jealous when he was averaging one deal a month while many of my salesmen were closing more than one a week.

But he had what many of my salesmen didn't have—imperturbability—a sort of slow serenity. He took his role of healer so seriously that he healed himself.

His infrequent sales were big events in his life. I sought him out to let him know that I was as proud of them as he was. While some of my salesmen probably snickered behind my back when I equated selling with healing, Fred I know, was not one of them. He appreciated the opportunity for stabilizing his life in my organization, and he conveyed this gratitude to his clients. All of us gained.

Fred was a $6,000 a year man who held his head high because he was a functioning member of his community. And I felt good because I shored up a man who otherwise might have stumbled and become a community problem.

Isn't such help a form of healing?

RESIDENTIAL SELLING

Residential real estate selling is becoming a woman's job. Several years ago when I addressed a combined meeting of several Real Estate Boards in the Detroit area, of the some 900 salesmen present, about half were women. This is the trend thoughout the country. And it is logical that it be so. Isn't it logical that a woman should know more about the amenities of a home than a man? Isn't her response to a home buyer bound to be more comprehending?

Of course, many men make good residential salesmen because they usually have more expertise in the financial arrangements, a very important factor in selling residential real estate. Another reason why men are still in demand as residential salesmen is that women who usually make the buying decisions prefer to deal with men. They seem to have more confidence in them. However, this is changing because women are becoming as well informed as men.

Empathy, patience, personal charm and a knowledge of home amenities are more important in selling residential real estate than a knowledge of leverage, financing, tax shelter and depreciation. What sways sales in residential selling are architectural niceties, an unusual kitchen, a quiet street, proximity to church or school, the kind of neighbors, location, the beauty of a back yard, and sometimes even such a small item as a beautiful tree. Selling a home is selling a way of life, as contrasted to selling commercial real estate which has a money making dimension.

Patience is one of the great attributes of a good residential salesman. This was dramatically illustrated to me on one occasion when I saw one of my salesmen flounder as he tried to explain to a home buyer how he was going to finance the deal. I was pressed for time, so I hurriedly walked over to them and asked if I could help. Without waiting for an answer, I hurriedly explained the salient financial points of the deal, and ended with, "That should clear it up."

As I walked back to my desk, I knew I had not hit the mark, because I could still see the puzzled expressions on my salesman and the buyer. A day later when I had a chance to talk to my salesman, he told me that the buyer was very unhappy with my intrusion.

"The buyer apparently preferred to stumble patiently with me," my salesman told me, "to having someone rush through something that's very important to him."

I learned my lesson. How much one knows is not as important as how caringly and clearly he tries to communicate it. My salesman in his halting manner was more effective than I was with my greater knowledge and hurried attitude.

In dealing with commercial real estate buyers, quick and precise explanations are excusable, but we should be slow in using them with residential buyers. They grasp less quickly and want more time to make up their minds. And I can't blame them. In making decisions involving a way of life, all the factors should be weighed carefully. It's that important!

COMMERCIAL SELLING

Selling investment or commercial real estate requires a wide background of tax laws, depreciation, income shelter, trading up or down, cash flow, etc., and the ability to communicate that knowledge with clarity, but above all with innovation and improvisation. Residential selling is to commercial selling what high school work is to post-graduate work.

A commercial or investment real estate salesman should be able to handle himself with ease among top-flight executives who usually have sophisticated backgrounds in finance. He should be well-grounded in theory as well as in the practical aspects of the advantages of owning real estate as against investing in stocks, bonds or other types of competitive investments. He should have a grasp of the economic history of our country and some basic explanations for projecting its economic future. This gives him the background and rationale for projecting a future stream of income of a commercial or investment project.

But above all, he must understand financing and, especially the principles of leverage, so he can advise a prospect how to buy a lot of real estate with little money, or when to use a lot of cash to leverage price in his favor.

There are many variables playing upon a typical investment project, and the ability to improvise on any of them can often solve a knotty problem. Sometimes changing the major premise of a deal solves the problem. Changing an H-shaped building to a U-shaped building saved me $100,000 without altering the basic concept or square footage of an office building.

The typical commercial or investment real estate deal has the following elements: Depreciation, tax shelter, location, management, leverage, short-range return, long-range return, continuity of the stream of income, residual value, inflation, deflation, effects of changing neighborhood, interest rate fluctuation, the competition of stocks and bonds as investment alternatives, and dozens of other lesser variables. An astute commercial real estate salesman must be able to steer his deal through all these variables and show his buyer how it measures up as a prudent investment.

Few mental disciplines test the imagination more than commercial real estate selling. It is problem solving at its finest, involving big stakes and rare judgment. Enchanting, fascinating and intriguing—all these adjectives describe it.

In later chapters I shall show how unyielding real estate problems yield to unorthodox approaches. Deals that reached an impasse were successfully concluded when new selling ideas were innovatingly superimposed on hard facts, softening them up for solution.

Chapter 5

Be Proud--Not Sorry--
When Salesmen Leave You
To Go Into Business for Themselves

Without my knowledge, one of my top salesmen was preparing to go into business for himself. While he ostensibly worked for me, he rented an office and induced another of my salesmen to become his partner.

When I discovered this, I was furious. Without thinking, I called him into my office and said:

"Pack up and leave! You can't serve two masters—working here and planning your own business."

He looked at me and then, without raising his voice, said:

"Who says you're my master, and what's wrong with going into business for myself? Didn't you do it?"

"But I did it in the open."

"But I didn't take anything away from you," he said quietly. "Your only complaint is that I should have told you. Well, I'm sorry."

His imperturbability emptied me of arguments. I was upset for the rest of the afternoon, and lost a few hours of sleep that night.

In the morning, I was a new man. My thoughts had twirled in my mind and then found a new insight: It should be a matter of pride to me when salesmen use my organization to learn, make money, and then go out into business for themselves!

As soon as I got into my office, I called my departing salesman to share my new attitude.

"I've had a sort of an awakening," I said. "While we may have had some honest differences about the way you were leaving, my problem was that I clutched too tightly at my welfare without thinking about yours. As you said, you haven't taken anything from me. You're right. Stay here until you're ready to move, and you have my best wishes."

"Thanks for your new attitude. It'll help me get rid of my guilt. Leaving you the way I did, bothered me, I must confess. I've learned something, too. Were I to do it over again, I would put my cards on the table, instead of under it."

We shook hands, and though he carved out a successful brokerage business in competition to mine, we have remained friends to this day.

Brokers and developers are individualists. They're usually go-getters. They prefer entrepreneurial action to becoming involved in reforming society. And being more interested in creating wealth than distributing it, they tend to hold onto salesmen for as long as they can, because they're an important business asset.

But the typical real estate salesman will work for them only as long as he knows he cannot do better on his own. And the better a salesman becomes, the closer brokers get to losing him.

Knowing this, what should a broker or developer do? My advice is to create as financially rewarding an environment as possible, in the hope of keeping as many salesmen as possible, for as long as possible, and then relax. The ambitious, success-driven salesman will leave you no matter what you do.

Should you hire a prospective salesman even though you know he will leave you as soon as he learns the ropes? My advice is yes. If he stays with you a year, you'll enjoy a year of his productivity, perhaps longer. What if he learns a few of your secrets while you're training him? Why not look upon it in the same manner as a professor regards his students? The more they learn, the happier he is, and the more famous he becomes.

Why not look upon salesmen as students, not as potential competitors? This empties you of anxieties, helps the salesman, and in the long run you will get a bigger bite of the action, as you will see when you read on.

This enlightened attitude has paid off financially, but more important, when I tested it in the heat of battle, it soothed my nerves, and gave me that relaxed feeling which professors are reputed to experience in their ivory towers. Why not have the best of two worlds—the excitement of business, and the calm of teaching?

I KNEW HE WOULD LEAVE ME

Even as I was interviewing Bill, I knew he was not the type to work for another—for long. His eager face, his quick grasp of my explanations regarding commercial real estate, his nervous stirring in his chair—these were telltale signs that here was a man champing at the bit to make money.

When he told me that he closed down his successful ready-to-wear business because it was too confining, and that he wanted work that engaged his imagination more extensively, I was sure that he had the stuff for success, and just as sure that he would leave me as soon as he was ready.

For the first three months, he appeared to be lost, floundering from one unsuccessful deal to another. But he was absorbing what I had to say, what my training team was telling him, and what he could learn from my salesmen. During the next three months, he began making small deals—but nothing that really excited him. I knew he was waiting to pounce on a big one.

He risked his time on hundred-to-one shots, fifty-to-one shots, deals that were big, but the odds of making them small. Then he struck. A triple A tenant bit on one of his propositions, and although he was a bit short on knowledge and finesse, he hauled in a $20,000 commission. That was the beginning of the end of our broker-salesman relationship.

Did I make a mistake in hiring Bill? I should say not. He represented me and himself with integrity. My gain was of a short duration, but it was a gain.

When he left to go into business for himself, he said;

"George, I will be forever grateful to you for taking me on. I knew, you knew, that I wouldn't stay very long, yet you hired me. You gave me a short but thorough course in commercial real estate. I hope that when I become as successful as you, that I will be big enough to do for other salesmen what you've done for me."

We shook hands and he left. He is now a successful real estate entrepreneur on the West Coast.

I TANGLE WITH A FOX

Randolph was a lawyer, and smart as a whip. Due to conditions beyond his control, his business career careened out of control when he was in his mid-forties and he was out of a job, and with very little money. But he was loaded with ability and he knew it. I came to know it, too.

"George," he said after we had several long visits together, "I would like to work with you, but I don't want to join your large organization. I would like to start a new division for you specializing in high-level commercial real estate, and I would like this division to bear your name and mine, and I would like fifty per cent of the ownership."

This was quite an unusual demand for one who had never earned a dollar in real estate, but I also recognized that here was an unusual man. We formed the partnership along the lines he suggested.

After about six months, and after we had a dozen learned discussions about the theory of selling commercial real estate, he was ready for the firing line.

I dinned into him that the art of using leverage, that is, controlling the maximum amount of property with the minimum amount of money, is one of the key financial tools in building a real estate fortune. Knowing how to communicate this creates buyers. And the equally important corollary, I pointed out, was that one doesn't leverage unless an investment project is feasible, and the yearly stream of income ascertainable.

What Randolph needed now was to have several doors opened for him leading to important people. I introduced him to the president of a large Milwaukee utility, and within one year, he obtained three excellent locations for it. Commission $12,000. I blueprinted a trade deal for him involving an exchange of land between the second largest bank in the state and the second largest savings and loan association. The bank got the additional land it needed to build its future office building, and the savings and loan association got the land it desperately needed for parking. Both profited, and so did we—$15,000 in commissions

I learned that a certain piece of downtown property was for sale and suggested a possible prospect. That's all I did. It took about ten minutes of my time. Randolph did all the rest. We earned another $10,000 commission.

After several years, Randolph needed none of my guidance. The new division became all Randolph. I was involved in many other projects and was no longer making any significant contribution to the partnership.

I began to get the feeling he didn't need me anymore but was too polite to tell me. But I also knew that Randolph was too ambitious to continue passing on income to another who he thought did not deserve it.

I made my move before the awkwardness of our commercial relationship infected our friendship.

"Randolph," I said one day, "although I started you in business, lent you my name, and made some contribution toward your success, now that you're running the show, I imagine you're not too keen about paying me a percentage of the profit. Isn't that so?"

Randolph smiled and said, "You're reading my mind, George. I don't mind saying that I'd like to buy you out."

Within three months, we consummated our deal and he became the sole owner. He is now one of the nationally prominent real estate men of our country. Using his own name now, he not only conducts a nationally recognized commercial brokerage business, but teaches real estate in many states of the Union.

Certainly, I would have liked Randolph to stay with me longer. But if I had tried to hang on to my ambitious friend, I would have been foolhardy. Besides, it's always wiser to get off before you're thrown off. It's just common sense.

I earned about $100,000 during my association with Randolph. I have nothing to complain about. I was well compensated for my contribution. I consider this a mutually successful association. I was a teacher who was well compensated for his work.

I GIVE MY COLLEGE CHUM A LIFT

My college chum was a robust fellow who met obstacles with gusto. After twenty-five years, he had hammered his way in and out of several businesses in several cities.

When we renewed our friendship after a quarter of a century, he was in between enterprises—down but not out.

"Need a little help, Butch?" I asked him after we went over old times.

Though my old-time buddy was aggressive, he was also proud "Do you think I can do you any good?" he asked.

I knew he could do me some good, and I also knew that he was the kind who couldn't be happy unless he worked for himself. But I felt this was not the time to worry about it.

"Let's start it out this way," I said. "I will guarantee you $15,000 a year against commissions while you're learning the ropes in my organization, and then we'll play it by ear."

He earned $20,000 his first year, $30,000 the next year. Within three years, he found another "ball of fire" like himself, and together they formed a partnership in direct competition to my organization.

Did I lose, losing Butch so quickly? I should say not! If I don't mind teaching real estate to students at the university for nothing, why should I mind helping an old pal get started? Besides my encounter with him was a profitable one. Wasn't he making money for me, while he was making it for himself?

This is not a case of sour grapes. The fact that I helped him more than he helped me is no reason to feel that I was a loser. The way I look at it, whatever Butch poured into my organization was a positive gain—for me and for him. And what's more, this enlightened attitude kept our friendship intact. Isn't this a gain also?

I DISCOVER AND LOSE ONE OF TODAY'S LEADING TYCOONS

Little did I know that the unimpressive looking young man who came to my office and asked me for a $50 a week draw, so he could propose to his girl friend, would become one of the top real estate developers in our country. But it didn't take me long to find out. A year later I knew his days with my organization were numbered.

Armand was packed with compressed mental acumen. During his first year, the future empire builder not only was soaking up all the knowledge I and my salesmen were making available to him, but some of his was already beginning to spill over onto us.

There were moments when I thought he would take all my salesmen, and leave me, so that I would have to start all over again, and I think he could have done it. Fortunately, he was brilliant, but not mean.

Then it happened. One day he came into my office and said:

"George, I'm leaving and taking Herman along. Thank you for a wonderful education."

We shook hands, and he left to build one of the largest real estate firms in America. Soon he left Herman behind. Herman was used to taking little steps, Armand took only giant leaps.

Armand remained a friend of mine, close enough for me to chide him that though he became a real estate giant, he was paying too high a price for it.

"Armand," I said, "you're exhausting yourself running on a money-making treadmill, and you don't know how to get off. I can no longer teach you anything about real estate, but as an old friend, I'd like to see you put your mind to some new concern. Something more ultimate."

"Like what?"

"Like finding something bigger to live for than making money."

"I don't know what it is."

"Then look for it, and perhaps you'll find it. Why don't you launch on an odyssey to find an ultimate concern?"

While his money making addiction was not as bad as getting hooked on alcohol or drugs, it did prevent him from venturing into new thinking, leading into more peaceful and graceful living. Armand had intelligence to burn, and he burned it—on the alter of success worship.

THE BOCKL COLLEGE OF REAL ESTATE KNOWLEDGE

The "Bockl College of Real Estate Knowledge", as some in our community dubbed my organization, launched several dozen successful real estate organizations. It's where the heads of the new firms trained, and made enough money to go out on their own.

It's true that as each of these men left me I experienced a diminishment, but the way I look at it, as long as I was innovative enough to plug it up with a replenishment—I lost nothing. In fact, I gained—a great deal.

In each case, while these men were building themselves, they were also building my organization. It was through their personal efforts that new clients were brought to my firm, and made it grow. True, when the salesmen left they took some clients along, but enough remained from each, so that the cumulative increment was impressive. So impressive, in fact, that my firm sold $300,000,000 of real estate in 30 years.

As long as I kept replenishing what I was losing, I was gaining rather than falling behind. I was running a school, graduating salesmen into brokers and developers, selling more and more real estate, and making money too. What more could I ask?

But this point of view, mind you, can only be maintained with a teaching attitude. It helps create an atmosphere of fun and freedom within an organization which minimizes conflicts and maximizes camaraderie. It removes some of the strain from work, making it a more light-hearted and selfless experience. It's especially rewarding when we can teach and earn money too.

This less competitive and combative attitude makes more practical sense than hoarding knowledge and driving ourselves to coronary brinkmanship, trying to get the most dollars out of our salesmen and ourselves.

This more mellow, and I think wiser point of view, is the opposite of the conglomerate point of view, where men, not content with the profits in their own businesses, try to cannibalize smaller ones to satisfy their hunger for more profits. The sharing and caring point of view is lost here, and those who swallow are swallowed—all dehumanized and sacrificed at the altar of BIGNESS.

America would be more democratic, and a stronger nation, if we had more small businesses and fewer big ones. That's why I feel I have made a contribution to our community by giving birth to about thirty new businesses. Those who swallow others cannot make that statement.

It's true this concept defies the advantages of mass production, but a famed psychiatrist put it this way when he was discussing the advantages of small businesses versus huge conglomerates at a seminar at Aspen, Colorado:

"What do you want, independent, happy people, or mass-manipulated unhappy ones?"

Those who make a game out of becoming big are playing with social dynamite. They are as irresponsible as those of the far Left who want revolution just for the hell of it. Neither is truly interested in improving the quality of life. One is only interested in quantifying it and the other in ripping it apart.

I was fortunate enough to have an organization big enough to be interesting, and small enough to be kept on a personal basis This is the way we can win disenchanted youth back into business. One of their main complaints is that big business is too impersonal.

Not feeling sorry for myself when salesmen left me reduced hostility in me, and in my men. Holding on to the teaching concept encouraged me to be more sharing and caring. Mixing idealism with commercialism is blending know-how with know-why, and giving meaning and purpose to work

PART II

THESE IDEAS PRODUCE ASTUTE INVESTORS

Chapter 6

Innovative Ideas that Change Ordinary
Men into Astute Investors

Simple language is the shortest line of communication between buyer and seller. Not long ago, I was involved in converting an old warehouse, located near a hospital, into a medical center. I prepared an office layout for the chief of staff of the hospital and invited him to become my tenant.

He was familiar with the dust-laden warehouse, and in looking over the colored rendering I presented to him, he asked,

"How do I know it will be as beautiful as I see it here?"

"Doctor," I said, "how do I know if you operate on me that the result will be beautiful? But I'd risk it with you. I'm asking you to risk it with me."

The doctor looked at me, smiled, and said,

"Okay, I'll take a chance."

He signed a five-year lease.

While there were many favorable factors which induced the doctor to sign, I know that my answer clinched it. Honest, home-spun language has triggered many, many a deal.

More important than using direct language to explain old ideas is to concoct new ideas. Here are several which have changed ordinary men into astute investors.

HOW TO GET INTO A BIG DEAL WITH LITTLE MONEY

It was Wednesday. Everything seemed to be falling into place that day. My creative juices were flowing. Late in the afternoon, I took a few hours to prepare my lecture for the evening on how to get into big real estate deals with little money.

I studied the faces of some forty men and women who had come from a radius of 30 miles to learn how to make money in real estate. Among them were teachers, electricians, accountants, a lawyer, one or two social workers and a goodly number of real estate salesmen and brokers.

"I'm going to stress only one single idea tonight," I began. "How to substitute time for money in buying real estate. I'm assuming most of you have more time than money." There was a ripple of laughter, then I could hear a pin drop. I had everyone's total attention.

"I'm not exaggerating when I say that there are today, in our city, from 500 to 1,000 vacant buildings whose owners are not imaginative enough to find the right tenants. These buildings are gathering dust and losing money. What has that got to do with you? Everything! These vacant buildings are your opportunities to make money. But you say, 'How?' Listen carefully.

"Keep in mind that one of the most important real estate axioms is that a property increases in value when it is put to its highest and best use. Millions have been made by those who implemented this real estate truth.

"Let's get to specifics. You have lots of time but no money. Take off a few afternoons or evenings, and study several vacant buildings. Go through them. Now go to some quiet place and try to think of some logical users. Take several hours. Jot down your ideas. Now go through the Yellow Pages. They will stimulate a few more ideas. Now comes the hard part that separates the men from the boys.

"How many of you are ready to make twenty, thirty or fifty cold turkey calls to try to rent buildings you don't own. Most of you will back off. I can see a few of you already relaxing, and probably saying to yourselves, 'what's so new about that?'

"You're already out of the game. For you, this will only be an intellectual discussion. A few others may look at one or two vacant buildings. And fewer still will get on the telephone to make calls. The chances are they'll make two, three, or five calls and quit. It's not pleasant to be refused. And I agree. But perhaps one or two of you will go all the way—make the fifty calls and perhaps one of you will get a *bite*. If any of you are fishermen, you'll know what I mean. Now the excitement begins to mount. What do you do next?

"What follows is easier than what has already been done—but it requires timing and some knowledge. Go to the owner of the vacant building and try to get an option for 60 or 90 days. Tell him you have a potentially interested tenant and that you need the time to sign him up and arrange the financing.

"If you strike a jealous owner, he'll stall you, or he may angle to take the tenant away from you, and all your work will have been done for nothing. At this point, you might wish you had never listened to me, and I wouldn't blame you.

"But the chances are the owner is sick and tired of his vacant building, and will gladly give you an option. Hotfoot it to the tenant and get a letter of intent, stating the terms of the lease, then get over to the bank to arrange for interim financing, and then to the savings and loan association for a permanent mortgage. With all the ends neatly tied together, you call in your attorney and ask him to draw the formal lease and arrange for the closing."

The lecture continued in this vein with many interruptions and explanations.

There was one young broker of about 29 who seemed more interested than the rest. He asked penetrating questions. He seemed excited, like he was going out the next day to try out my idea.

He did, with fantastic results. Without a dime of his own money, and following the instructions of my lecture almost to the letter, he leveraged himself into a combination cash and equity position worth $350,000—in 18 months.

He found a 5,000 square foot building that had been vacant for several years. It was on a business corner, but it didn't do any business. A grocery store failed there, and so did an appliance shop. It was now a $10,000 a year drain on the owner's pocketbook He tried to sell it for $100,000, then $80,000, finally $70,000. No takers.

While the owner was languishing with his vacant property, our young broker, who took my lecture seriously, began making his 50 cold turkey calls. The answers up to about number 37 were cold and brusque. But on the next call he heard an answer which sent a warm glow through him.

"Yes," the voice said, "we're looking for about 5,000 feet in that location. Can we take a look at it?"

It was a triple A tenant who was looking for office space. Would he spend about $20,000 to remodel it for their needs their representative asked after he looked it over. If so, they would be willing to pay $18,000 a year rent.

The young man came to my office, breathless with excitement, and asked, "What do I do now?" I suggested he get a letter of intent from his tenant, and on the strength of it, go to a bank and obtain an interim loan to close the deal. I advised him to skip the option period for fear the owner might stall the deal during which time he could lose the tenant. After he obtained the letter and interim financing, he went to the owner of the building and offered him $60,000 for the property, with $1,000 down, and $59,000 in cash upon date of closing.

The owner grabbed the offer. It is interesting to note that our young hero had to borrow the $1,000 from the bank to make the down payment. The deal closed in 30 days.

How did he finance the $20,000 remodeling money? Good question. On the strength of the lease from the triple A tenant, he went to a savings and loan association and arranged for an $80,000 permanent mortgage, but with a payout only after the building was remodeled. With the permanent $80,000 mortgage commitment, he had no trouble getting another $20,000 from the bank to make the tenant improvements.

When the tenant moved in, and our neophyte broker had signed the $80,000 mortgage and paid off the bank's $80,000 interim financing, the deal stacked up as follows;

The new owner had fixed expenses of $14,000 a year, including the debt service, and a rental of $18,000 a year, leaving him a $4,000 a year overage, which was tax sheltered because of depreciation. He had no money in the deal.

What is the $4,000 a year stream of income worth? $40,000? At least! Perhaps more.

Not bad for a young man who knew nothing about real estate but pounced on a new idea and made it work.

But this was only the beginning.

One of the largest commercial brokers in the area had a vacant building of 12,000 sq. ft. for sale. It was appraised for $135,000. But there were no buyers, and the owner was very anxious to sell. Our young real estate hero looked it over and went to work. Instead of spraying his shots, he used a bit of savvy. He called the triple A tenant who leased his 5,000 sq. ft. building on the far north side and asked him if he needed office space on the far south side.

He did! Our neophyte had struck gold on his first call. It had taken a month of calling on the first deal before he hit pay dirt.

But this deal had a new wrinkle. His triple A tenant needed only 7,000 sq. ft. But he remembered that a shoe store chain turned him down on his first deal because they wanted space on the south side. He quickly called them. It was exactly what they wanted.

Armed with two letters of intent, he took the same intricate financial route I mapped out for him on his first deal, and it worked like a charm.

The second deal shaped up about as follows;

My young protege paid $95,000 for the vacant building. He spent $65,000 in improvements to meet the needs of the two tenants. The total rent was $38,000 a year. He obtained a $200,000 mortgage, which was $40,000 more than his total cost, and which he retained without having to pay any income tax. His total yearly expenses, including his debt service on his $200,000 mortgage was $32,000 so that he had a $6,000 yearly overage. All this without a dime of his own money.

It sounds fantastic, doesn't it? It is. And what is equally un-believable is that all profited by these deals.

Here is how. Certainly our young hero did well, so well, it opened a new business dimension for him. The tenants didn't overpay. In fact, their rentals were about 15% below market. The mortgage companies made safe loans because the income from the tenants assured their amortization with plenty of cushion to spare.

Two facts made all this possible. One was that the unimagin-ative owners of the vacant buildings sold them for about 60% of their potential value. The other was the imaginative maneuverings of our young broker. The juxtaposition of these facts made it possible for the tenants to get good deals and for the mortgage companies to make safe loans.

These two deals certainly illustrate that it's possible to get into big deals with little money—in fact, with no money.

As dramatic a story as this is, it is not the end. The triple A tenant was so pleased with their two tenancies that they asked their young landlord to build them a 24,000 sq. ft. office building in another town.

Elated, he came to my office to tell me all about it. Here is how he handled it—without my help. He bought a lot for $75,000. By this time he had built up enough credit with the bank so that it advanced him the money. And since he had a construction background, he cut enough corners off the bidders that he was able to "sub" out the building for $375,000. He obtained a loan of $500,000.

The figures for this deal lined up about as follows:

Yearly rent $105,000. All expenses, including debt service—$90,000. Cash flow $15,000. Cash from overfinancing, or for smart entreprenurial effort—$50,000.

Within 18 months after hearing my lecture, our innovative young man had earned $90,000 in cash (tax free), and was enjoying a (tax free) cash flow of $4,000, plus $6,000, plus $15,000, for a total of $25,000 a year.

Would all this have happened if the young man had not attended my lecture? I would like to think not, and that's where I get my motivation for teaching and writing this book. And that's how sharing becomes a glowing experience.

A SMALL CONTRACTOR IS AMAZED WHEN HE IS SHOWN HOW TO BUY A $230,000 APARTMENT BUILDING WITHOUT ANY OF HIS OWN MONEY

Here is a variation on the theme of getting into profitable deals without any money.

One evening, I described the following real estate deal to my commercial real estate class at the University of Wisconsin-Milwaukee. I put the following figures on the blackboard:

1. Price: $230,000
2. 28 Efficiency Apartments and 3 Stores:
3. Gross income . . . . . : . . . .$ 38,000
4. Expenses:
   a. Fixed expenses—taxes, heat, janitor,
                    insurance, etc. $16,000
   b. Debt service—Interest and principal
                on $115,000 mortgage . .16,000
5. Yearly fixed expenses and debt service . . . . .$ 32,000
6. OVERAGE . . . .$ 6,000

"Now, how can we buy this property without any money?" I asked my students. "How can we raise the difference between the $230,000 selling price and the $115,000 first mortgage, or $115,000?"

There were these other conditions, I told them.

    1. The seller was willing to take back a second mortgage of $65,000 with payments of approximately $500 a month, including interest and principal. I said this was available because the owner wanted an annuity as part of the down payment. The balance of $50,000 had to be in cash.

    2. The buyer had to be someone who did not have to live off the overage of the property. He had to have other income. The buyer also had to have enough credit with his bank to borrow about $50,000.

    3. The property had a potential for a rent raise of about $10,000 a year, enough to amortize the $50,000 bank loan in about 6 years. The apartments and stores were poorly managed.

After I delineated the deal's anatomy, I turned to the class and asked, "Are there any questions?"

A small contractor, still in his working clothes because he came directly from work to my class, sitting at the back of the room, called out, "I like that. Is there such a building available?"

"Yes," I replied. "I have the listing."

At the end of the lecture, he came to my desk and said, "I could meet all the conditions you've outlined because, as you see,

I'm a handy man, and I also know how to raise rents, but I've never had any need to borrow more than $5,000 from my bank. Borrowing $50,000 scares me, and I'm afraid it might scare my banker, too."

"Do you keep $15,000 to $20,000 on deposit with your bank?" I asked him.

"Yes," he said, "and often a lot more."

"Well, why don't you look the building over thoroughly tomorrow, and satisfy yourself that it is poorly managed, and that the rents can be raised, as I indicated. Your only hurdle, as I see it, is to convince your banker that you have the know-how to raise the rents from $38,000 to close to $50,000 a year."

Several days later, my student called and said,

"I got the bank to loan me $40,000. I'm $10,000 short."

I took a note from him for $10,000 of my $11,500 commission, payable at the rate of $140 a month, including interest and principal, until paid.

Two months later, my student became the owner of an apartment building which he had never dreamed was within his means to own. Within a year, he fulfilled the promise he made to the bank—that he would clean up the building and get the rent up to $50,000 a year. The bank's $40,000 advance, which was risky at the start, became a prudent loan.

As is so often the case, someone's inadequacy becomes somebody's opportunity. By shoring up a sagging project with hard work and good practical sense, the contractor created more than $10,000 a year of additional income. What is it worth? Perhaps $75,000. Was this done at the previous owner's expense? No! Because he was satisfied to run his building with a minimum of effort, he had to be satisfied with a lesser price. Good managers are unwilling to pass on their potential gains, in the form of a higher price, to poor managers.

There are hundreds of such cases in every city. And there are many reasons why properties run down—indifference, poor health, lack of ability. There are also many ways to build them up—astute financing, wise management and hard work.

I wish there were ways for owners of problem properties to fare better at the hands of those who buy them at bargain prices. But there aren't any. The ideal solution, of course, is for the owners to become as imaginative as the buyers, but if they lack imagination, what can they do?

There will always be winners and losers. All we can hope for, since capacities and talents are not evenly distributed, is to learn to win with humility and lose with equanimity.

WE CAN'T WIN ALL THE TIME
SOMETIMES ROSES TURN INTO DAISIES

Several years ago I was invited to give a talk to a Board of Realtors in a small town.

After I cited several examples in my speech how challenging problems were solved by ingenious approaches, a real estate broker during the question-and-answer period confronted me as follows:

"I've got one that defies all solution. I have a listing on a 35,000 square foot, 3-story building that has been vacant for ten years. It's on our Main Street, a block away from our largest department store and a half a block from our leading bank. It's in a 100% location. I don't know what to do with it, and I challenge you to give me the answer."

After the meeting, the broker drove me to the building. It was a stately structure occupied earlier by a large retail chain, but it had been gathering dust since they moved out 10 years ago. The owner wanted $175,000 for it when he lost his tenant, but as the years rolled by, the price dropped to $150,000 then to $100,000, and now he was ready to take $75,000.

I suggested several uses for it to the broker, but in each case he said, "We tried it, and it didn't work." Finally, he turned to me, and said, "Why don't you buy it and see what you can do with it?"

Flushed with confidence after having made what I thought was a good speech, I said,

"Okay, I'll take it if you can get it for $50,000."

A week later, the broker called me.

"You're a lucky man, you've just bought the 'Glenmark' building for $50,000."

What looked on the surface like a bargain turned into a financial fiasco. As of this writing, three years after I bought the building, and after having shaken up every conceivable tenant in the sleepy town, I still have a vacant building on my hands. Taxes and interest have now brought my costs up to $80,000.

What went wrong? The big-gun lecturer turned into a pop gun because he didn't know what was going on in the small town. Soon after I bought the property, a promoter began building an end-of-town shopping center. The AAA tenants left the main street and moved into the shopping center. A dozen smaller stores followed the big department stores. My sweet 100% location turned sour. I had a white elephant on my hands. It was eating $10,000 worth a year in interest and taxes, and producing nothing.

I used my wits in entertaining and informing my small town audience with stories about solving real estate problems. But a small town broker did me one better. He used his wits to sell me a building, and thus solved his own problem.

All of which points up the fascinating uncertainities of commercial real estate. The reader will recall how a young neophyte broker bought a vacant store, one-third the size of the 'Glenmark' building, and in a fourth rate location, for $95,000, and came out smelling like a rose. But my 'Glenmark' deal doesn't smell so good.

This is what makes commercial real estate so excitingly interesting. Nothing is ever certain until something new is super-imposed on something old—changing lead into gold. The 'Glenmark' building problem will be solved, if not by me, then by someone else. And if he does it, he's entitled to all the money he can make, and I, to all the losses I deserve.

HOW TO FIND AND LEVERAGE A DEAL 100% WITHOUT ANY RISK WHATSOEVER

There are thousands of owners of buildings whose mortgages are more than ten or fifteen years old, and whose straight line or accelerated depreciation is not enough to shelter the accelerated principal payments. There are gold mines in those situations. Let me explain.

Twenty years ago, a friend of mine bought a building for a million dollars and simultaneously found a triple A tenant. This enabled him to obtain a million dollar loan on the basis that all of the rental (after deducting fixed expenses) would be used to pay off the mortgage at 4½% interest.

After ten years of mortgage amortization, my friend found himself in this position. His depreciation was averaging about $20,000 a year, but since he was paying principal at about $60,000 a year, he had to pay income tax on $40,000. And what made this difficult for him was that he had no overage with which to pay it. And since he was in a better than 50% tax bracket, he had to take more than $20,000 from "home," out of his pocket, for taxes. And the tax bite was getting bigger every year.

I knew my friend well. He was a wheeler and dealer who always needed money for new projects. He didn't relish the idea of being trapped into paying Uncle Sam *now,* for a windfall 10 years *later* when the property would be free and clear.

I got my friend on the phone one day and said:

"How would you like to get $300,000 in cash, and as a sweetener, stop paying income tax on a profit you're not getting?"

"I'd like that. How do I do it?"

"Sell me your building on Main Street for a million dollars," I said. "I'll pay you $300,000 in cash and assume your $700,000 mortgage. That's how you can do it."

"You're talking about the best and most trouble-free investment I've got," he said.

"But it's not doing you any good, and you know it. Just think what you could do with $300,000 in cash. What excitement you could have, compared to sitting on your safe investment."

"You know," he said, "you've got something there. How about having lunch?"

He couldn't resist my twin arguments of getting $300,000 in cash and saving about $20,000 a year in taxes. We made the deal.

And here is the interesting kicker which makes this deal, and all others like it, so financiable and so appealing. I borrowed all of the $300,000 equity money from my bank by simply assigning my interest in the triple A tenant's lease.

I pointed out to the bank's loan officer that in 10 years the building would be free and clear. That he would then have a prime lien or first mortgage on a million dollar building. His only risk, I suggested, was whether the lessee would continue to pay the rent. And that was no risk at all because my tenant was worth fifty times the net worth of the bank. I got my $300,000 loan.

By upping my depreciation base from $700,000 to a million dollars, and taking the interest deduction on the $300,000 loan, I showed a profit of less than $10,000 the first year. As the profits increased, I was able to shelter them because I put the building in a corporation that had enough depreciation from other properties to shelter the increasing profits in this one.

One of the conditions of the lease was that at its termination the lessee had the option to purchase the building for $750,000. As it turned out, the lessee did exercise his option, and when the deal was closed, I received the $750,000 in cash and paid the bank its $300,000 loan, netting a profit of $450,000. Since I had two partners in the deal, each received $150,000. All this without a dollar of my own money.

This was a prudent deal for all. Every financial move was conservative and practical. My friend got into other lucrative deals with his $300,000, which earned him far more than he would have earned if he had kept his investment. My bank received its interest regularly for ten years, and enjoyed one of the safest loans it had· on its books. The government didn't do badly either. First, it got a chunk of taxes from· my friend when he received the $300,000 from me. Then when the lessee exercised its option, the government received a tax on the $450,000 profit.

And, of course, I and my partners came out the best of all.

On the face of it, it seems like the owner of the building gave up too much. If he were an ordinary investor, I might say yes. But not in the case of a creative wheeler and dealer who is more interested in money *now* than what will happen ten years from now. To a man like that time is money.

There are many deals like this in every city. It doesn't take any intricate knowledge of higher mathematics to figure them out. Any ordinary salesman or investor who understands the simple principle explained here, can make such deals, if he can nose out the situations I described, and communicate their advantages to the various parties.

This is a tremendous selling and fortune building idea. Super-imposing ideas like these over a set of ordinary facts is what creates new situations and new capital formations. It's a dramatic illustration, in my opinion, how innovative ideas create super salesmen.

An innovative idea, more than any other factor, is what separates the ordinary from the extra-ordinary salesman or investor.

MAMA-PAPA MOTEL IDEA MAKES AN ASTUTE INVESTMENT OUT OF AN UNEDUCATED MAN

Tony couldn't pass a sixth grade geography test. He couldn't understand what was going on in a high school algebra class. He couldn't hold a $7,000 a year job in any white-collar business office.

Yet, Tony was worth a couple of hundred thousand dollars. Why? Because he was forced to live by his wits, and he did better with them than others do with their scholarship.

One day he came into my office and said;

"George, you're always looking for new ideas. Well, I've got one that tops them all."

"Go ahead, Tony," I said, "I'm all ears."

"About two years ago, I heard 'Continental Inns' was going to put up a big motel on the outskirts of our city. I bought a piece of land close to the motel and put up 20 rooms. I put in a mamma-papa management team, and I'm now 80% occupied with the overflow from the 'Continental Inn'. Believe it or not, those 20 rooms are netting me $20,000 a year."

"That's a great idea," I said. "Did you stop just with this one?"

"Hell no!" he said. "I got another 20 rooms going in Florida. I did that when I was on vacation there. And that's earning about $20,000 a year too, I now have four others in the works, and if I weren't getting older so fast, I'd go national with the idea. I tell you, George, it's a sleeper."

"What's the arithmetic of the deal?"

"Well," he said, "I buy the land for a song, and get myself a small contractor, and put up the rooms at half the cost of a 'Continental Inn'. Would you believe it, I can put up 20 rooms, plus the land and all the furniture and equipment for less than $100,000. And the beauty of it is that I can mortgage it for about the same amount. My debt service and taxes are only about $15,000 a year. I pay the mama-papa couple $5,000 a year and living quarters, and with another $10,000 of miscellaneous expense, I have a total operating expense of about $30,000. I average about $2,500 a room per year on the basis of about 70% occupancy, and that gives me a gross of about $50,000, and a profit of about $20,000. Not bad, hey?"

Tony was a little man who enjoyed wheeling and dealing, and enjoyed bragging about it even more. I was a good listener and that's why he often chose me as an object of his exultation.

Tony was an innovator, and probably would not know the meaning of the word. But he overcame his deficiencies by pushing himself to think creatively. He used his wits in the absence of knowledge. It turned an ordinary man like Tony into a super salesman.

Chapter 7

How Trading Real Estate
Makes Sales and Builds Fortunes

TRADING IS PRACTICAL AND PROFITABLE

Exchanging real estate is practical because it meets people's changing needs. It's profitable because it is a sophisticated way of selling real estate, as well as building real estate fortunes.

Trading property is a merchandizing art which trains salesmen to be innovative. It is the science of matchmaking. It solves real estate problems. It is at once simple and profound, simple because no great knowledge is needed, profound because it works best with those who seem to have an intuitional wisdom, a sort of knack for it.

There are thousands of excellent real estate brokers, but there are only a handful of good traders.

My friend Charlie became a millionaire trading real estate. He didn't seem to know a great deal, yet when it came to trading, his acumen was uncanny. Matching real estate seemed to make his thinking juices flow. Although my friend Charlie was never required to use more than simple arithmetic, he earned about $50,000 a year for some 25 years, while scholars and scientists dealing with higher mathematics earned only $15,000 to $20,000 a year.

You don't have to be a full time trader like Charlie to make money in leveraging and trading properties. You can do it on a part time basis while holding down another job. You can be a writer, a lawyer, an accountant, or a lathe operator, and still moonlight in the art of trading real estate.

HOW AN ENGINEER COMBINED LEVERAGE AND TRADING

One winter afternoon while I was perspiring in the 175° sauna room of a health club, I overheard a man saying to his companion:

"You know, I've read Bockl's real estate book on leverage, and it makes a lot of sense. I bought three properties which I can trace. . . ."

"Hold on Hal," his buddy, who knew me, said laughingly. "See that guy there? That's George Bockl."

"So you're George Bockl," Hal exclaimed. "Well I'll be damned– the author in the flesh."

His buddy introduced us more formally and we became good friends.

I learned that Hal bought an 8-family, a 12-family and a 20-family apartment building in the last four years in which he had invested about $25,000. Because he had a good job, a good credit rating and a good knowledge of leverage, he was able to maximize his holdings with a minimum of cash. And using good managerial skill, he developed a $10,000 overage so that when I asked him what he thought his equities were worth, he very casually announced;

"Oh, about $100,000."

"How would you like to trade them," I asked, "for a million dollar apartment building?"

"If your trading advice is as good as your leverage advice, I'd say yes. Where's your million dollar building?"

It just happened that I knew of a 72-family apartment which the owner had allowed to run down and which he was very anxious to sell. And he was ready to sell it on a land contract with $100,000 down and a $900,000 balance to be amortized over 25 years. But he did not want Hal's properties. He was fed up with management. He wanted the down payment in cash. Here is how I worked out the deal which satisfied everybody.

I drew an exchange contract between Hal and the owner of the 72-family apartment building (let's call him B), in which each agreed to assume the other's mortgages. That is, Hal assumed the $900,000 land contract balance, and B assumed $400,000 in mortgages on Hal's three properties.

However, since B was not interested in Hal's properties, we had a contingent clause in the trade agreement that I the broker, had to purchase Hal's properties subject to his mortgages for $100,000 and turn over the proceeds to B. I took six weeks to close the deal. This gave me time to find buyers for Hal's properties because I had to have $100,000 ready at the time of the closing.

For arranging this trade deal, B agreed to pay me a $50,000 commission, but not in cash, since he considered the $100,000 down payment too low out of which to pay commission. I agreed to take it at the rate of $5,000 a year, for 10 years, without interest.

Before the six weeks were up, I sold all three of Hal's properties for $95,000, subject to their mortgages. That meant I had a $5,000 cash investment in my $50,000 commission note. I also was careful to state in selling Hal's properties, that the sales were subject to the consummation of the trade deal between Hal and B.

Note how logical and constructive this trade deal was for all concerned. B was grossly mismanaging his 72-family building, and its value was eroding. Hal with his superior management was B's insurance for the continuation of his stream of income. And Hal, who was giving up about $10,000 a year overage in his $500,000 worth of real estate, was positioning himself to get about $30,000 a year overage in a million dollar project. Since the rate of amortization of the smaller and the larger projects was about the same, the advantage to Hal, in addition to the larger overage, was that when the mortgages were paid off, he would own free and clear a million dollars worth of real estate, instead of half of it. The buyers who made down payments on Hal's properties, subject to the trade deal being consummated between Hal and B, were satisfied, because in order to make quick sales, I sold Hal's apartment buildings somewhat below the market price. And I, of course, was satisfied because though it took dozens of hours of hard work shoring up the various props which were holding up this intricately balanced trade, I had a fairly safe $5,000 annuity for 10 years in which I had only $5,000 invested.

Our office has made dozens of similar trade deals. But we didn't make this one. Though contracts were signed, it fell apart.

Fortunately, I unraveled it before it reached the courts. I relate it only to illustrate two important points. One was to describe the anatomy of a typical trade deal. The other was to point out that one has to risk weeks and months of time, and be ready to get nothing for it but valuable experience.

Why did Hal, my sauna friend, back out of the deal? He felt comfortable using my leverage theory on his 8, 12 and 20-family apartments, but getting into a million dollar deal awed him. He was losing his nerve. Leveraging and trading combined was a little too much for him.

As it turned out, the 72-apartment project was sold several months later, and the new owner is getting the $30,000 a year overage I predicted Hal could have gotten with good management. The present owner can now get $150,000 more for it than Hal could have traded it for. Well, such are the risks, the stakes and the could-have-beens of trading.

THE PHILOSOPHY OF TRADING UP

It's easy to get started in the business of trading real estate, especially trading up. When we've refined it, we don't call it a business anymore, we like to call it an art. And it is an art.

Let's get started by buying a four-family apartment for $50,000, subject to a $40,000 mortgage. Let's say the cash flow, what's left over after all fixed expenses and debt service, is $1,000.

Put an ad in your local newspaper, saying that you are willing to trade your equity in a four-family for an equity in a larger apartment building. You will get many responses because there are more people who want to trade down than up, that is, they want to cash out. One of the respondents could be the owner of a sixteen-family apartment building who is having trouble with it, and would like to either get a smaller property so he could eventually sell it and cash out, or move into one of the flats himself, if it's in a location he likes, and use it as a trouble free smaller investment.

Let's say your ad finds the owner of the sixteen-family apartment building, and you exchange properties with him. He assumes the $40,000 mortgage on your 4 family, and you assume the $140,000 mortgage on his sixteen family. And what makes the deal logical and attractive for you is that you see a possibility of increasing the cash flow on the sixteen-family from $1,500 to $3,000 a year.

Six months later, after you've increased the cash flow to $3,000, by making improvements, cutting expenses and raising rents, you're ready to trade up again. Your former $10,000 equity in your four-family is now worth about $30,000, because your cash flow has increased from $1,000 to $3,000. You now have a lot more to trade.

Again, put an ad in your local newspaper, advertising that you're willing to trade your sixteen-family for a thirty-family and up. Let's say an owner who is sick and tired of his forty family tenants' complaints (and there are many such owners) reads your ad and decides he wants something smaller with fewer headaches. Let's also assume that the owner of the forty apartments has a $350,000 mortgage on it, and is realizing only about $3,000 cash flow, out of a potential $8,000 cash flow, because of poor management.

You have a natural trade here. Your cash flow of $3,000 on your sixteen-family, subject to a $140,000 mortgage, will look good to the disgruntled owner of the larger building with the larger mortgage. He'll get the same cash flow with fewer problems. All right, you make the trade.

Now your managerial skill, which is the right arm of your trading skill, comes into play. By upgrading the building physically, that is, painting hallways, remodeling the lobby, modernizing the light fixtures, and perhaps a few other eye catching improvements, the building gradually improves its image. And equally important, the public relations with the tenants has to be improved, too. Now you're ready to make your move to increase the rent so you can realize the $8,000 cash flow potential which the previous owner missed. When you've done that, you're ready to trade up again. You now have a potential equity of $80,000.

There is nothing to stop you from going on, like trading your forty family for a mismanaged seventy family. Am I exaggerating? Not at all. It has been done, and you can do it. Remember, there are more poor managers than good ones. In time, as you continue to trade up and increase your cash flow and equity position, you may want to stop, let's say, at a point where the cash flow is about $25,000 a year and the mortgage about $1,000,000.

You're now worth about $250,000, starting with an initial investment of $10,000, and you don't have to pay any income tax on the increased equity until you sell the building. And what's more, the chances are that by taking accelerated depreciation your $25,000 cash flow will be tax free also.

And now comes the greatest bonanza of all. At the end of, let's say, 20 years, if you had kept the original four family and paid off the $40,000 mortgage, you would own a building worth about $50,000, while now, after the series of trades, after paying off the $1,000,000 mortgage, you would have an estate worth about $1,250,000. That's what trading can do for you, and as it is doing for thousands of others across the nation.

The basic prerequisite for trading up, profitably, is managerial skill. Without it, you're only half a trader. Another is the ability to find owners of properties whose managerial problems are too much for them and who are eager to trade for something that's trouble free, blue ribboned and smaller.

THE PHILOSOPHY OF TRADING DOWN

Suppose you inherited, or bought an investment property which had a single triple A tenant on a 20-year lease, and the mortgage was $275,000, and the cash flow about $8,000 a year. It's true that if you keep it you will have a trouble free $8,000 a year overage for 20 years, but that's all. There's a definite ceiling to your income.

Now come along with me and see what you can do by trading down, that is, exchanging your safe, but limited income property, for smaller properties. After just finishing explaining in glowing terms how one makes money trading up, you perhaps are beginning to wonder how it is possible to make money trading down. Take my word for it, it is possible, and here is how it can be done.

Put an ad in your local newspaper which should read about as follows:

ARE YOU TIRED
of your old properties
which are giving you trouble
and whose incomes are uncertain?
Then trade them all in
for a net lease, trouble-free
Investment.

```
Gross rent ............................... $48,000
    All fixed expenses ................ $12,500
    Debt service on $275,000 mortgage ... 27,500
    Total yearly outlay .............. $40,000
Net Cash Flow ........................... $ 8,000
```

CALL JOHN DOE

You'll be deluged with calls. Your problem will be to check out the "cats and dogs" from those which make real estate sense.

There are many owners of small equities who would like to consolidate them into one investment property, but don't know how to do it. Such an ad will get their immediate attention.

Let's suppose now, that after checking out 15 or 20 replies, the one that looks the most promising has the following properties to trade for your trouble free investment:

1. A summer home, free and clear, worth
   about . . . .$ 10,000
2. A residence worth about . . . .$ 20,000
3. A 30-year-old four-family apartment
   building . . . .$ 30,000
4. A free-and-clear apartment site for 25 families,
   worth about . . . .$ 35,000
5. A 20,000 sq. ft. loft building (½ vacant
   because owner doesn't care to bother at
   his age to fill it) having a net of $5,000 but
   could be $10,000. Value . . . .$ 30,000

   TOTAL VALUE $125,000

It would not be difficult to convince the elderly owner of all these properties that he would be making a good deal if he could trade all of his odds and ends for a sure $8,000 a year net cash flow, over and above what he would be paying off on the $275,000 mortgage. To clinch the trade deal, it should be pointed out to him that by exchanging he saves paying a commission on each of his properties, and equally important, he is selling and buying in one operation, saving himself the trying chores of closing six transactions. Also, at the time of selling, he knows what he's buying. Let's assume the trade is consummated.

Now, instead of standing still with an $8,000 a year net, you can start moving. You now have five properties with which to start trading up in five different directions. First of all, you now own property worth about $125,000 which you exchanged for your equity of about $80,000. But that differential is just the beginning. Now, if you're a "horse trader" at heart, and you don't have to be in the real estate business to be one—some of the best traders are in different businesses—you start trading up in the following manner. Put these ads in your local newspaper;

Ad No. 1

Will trade summer home, free & clear for a 4-family, an oil station site, or what have you?

Ad No. 2

Will trade beautiful 3 bedroom home for any income property you may have.

Ad No. 3

Will trade four-family for small office building, or what have you?

Ad No. 4

Will trade excellent corner apartment site for raw acreage or any income property.

Ad No. 5

Will trade my 20,000 square foot loft building suitable for light manufacturing, or as a wholesale distribution point, for an apartment site, raw acreage, or any income property.

I have shown earlier in this chapter how an owner starting with a four-family kept on trading up until he became the owner of a million dollar apartment building. There is no reason why you cannot do the same, starting with each of these five properties, and trading them up. After a lot of hard work and master matchmaking, you too can become involved in the ownership of millions of dollars worth of real estate. I have outlined the skeleton how it can be done, all you have to do now is to flesh it out.

I can visualize a situation where a master trader could hire several men, either on a salary or give them a part of the action, or a combination of the two, and keep 30 or 40 trade deals moving simultaneously. It then becomes a masterful game. And if it is played with integrity, it is possible that all the participants involved could benefit.

One inclined toward cynicism might object to this statement, contending that someone has to lose if the trader keeps making money as he trades up or down. The answer to that objection is that the needs of the various participants vary as, for instance, the variables of age, income status, how hard one wants to work, and if you can fill them, no one gets hurt.

Let's remember that most people are neither able nor interested in wheeling, dealing and horse-trading, and if you are willing to immerse yourself in this type of problem solving you are entitled to all the fruits of your labor.

Just as the horse trader of yesteryear was usually the most alert and aggressive man of his group, so the property trader of today is usually the most alert and aggressive among the brokers. Though he may be a bit more sophisticated, he and the horse trader live more by wit than knowledge.

Here are a few additional trading hints:

1. Apartment building owners who are unhappy with fluctuating incomes and problems of management, and yearn for a safe and stable return, should not sell them and then buy trouble-free buildings with triple A tenants. They should trade for them. There are many apartment owners who would like to give up their uncertain 12% return for a certain 9% return. To them I say, find a good trader and let him do it for you.

2. Those who bought land for speculation, and find that instead of the quick profit they hoped for, the cost of holding on is a drain on their cash, should trade it for income property. Uneasiness can develop into anxiety,

and so to have peace of mind, the would-be speculator would do well to exchange his yearly loss in vacant land for a yearly gain in income property. For many, peace of mind is worth more than a potential profit.

3. If you're in a high income bracket, and you own income property upon which you have to pay additional high income taxes, it might be wise for you to trade it for vacant land which has an appreciation potential. There are two advantages in doing this:

a. You eliminate the additional taxable income from your improved property and,

b. The real estate taxes on the land and the interest on the mortgage, which you should be sure to place on it, are deductible against your ordinary income.

A high income friend of mine who made such a deal, trading his income property for land on the basis of $50 a front foot, sold it 15 years later at $500 a foot. Here is how he gained three ways. During the 15 years that he was losing on the land, he was making a lot of money, and used his loss as a deduction. When he sold the land at $500 a front foot, he was at an age when he began to decompress his activity, and his earnings were much lower. Also, when he sold the land, his profit was taxed on the basis of capital gain income. It was a cagey trade deal all the way around.

Trading is to brokerage what a doctor's degree is to a bachelor's degree. And I suppose there are fewer doctorate than bachelor degrees for the same reason that there are fewer traders than brokers.

HOW A SIMPLE TRADE SUGGESTION
SAVED A MAN $12,000

Several years ago, a small unsophisticated real estate broker came to my office and said:

"I have taken a down payment on a 12-family apartment building I have owned for ten years. Someone told me I was making a mistake, because there is a way of trading it, instead of selling it, which avoids income taxes. First, tell me how I can get out of my deal, and second, would you explain in simple language how this non-taxable trade works?"

I was not surprised at this broker's naivete. There are many brokers who don't take advantage of trading real estate, and, of course, thousands of laymen lose millions of dollars every year because they don't understand the advantages involved in exchanging properties.

Was our unsophisticated broker making a mistake? Could it be corrected? He was about to sell his apartment building for $100,000. His cost after depreciating it for ten years would be $50,000. Therefore, if he sold his building outright, he would have a profit of $50,000, and he would have to pay to the government a long-term tax of $12,500.

I asked the broker what he would do with his $100,000.

"I want to buy a bigger building," he said, "and I already have a twenty-family in mind which I think I can get for about $200,000. But now I'm stuck, because I have signed a purchase and sales agreement on my building, and I don't know how to get out of it."

I told him to get a lawyer to write up a trade deal between the owner of the $200,000 building and himself on the following basis:

"You assume a $100,000 mortgage on the 20-family," I told him, "and convey your building free and clear to the owner of the larger building. And since the owner of the $200,000 building wanted to cash out, the trade deal should be subject to him being able to sell your $100,000 building to your present buyer. This will get you off the hook, and make everybody happy."

Of course, that presented no problem because it didn't make any difference to the buyer of the $100,000 building who the seller was, as long as he didn't have to pay any more for it.

By thus trading his 12-family building for the higher priced building, our broker saved $12,500 in taxes, or, more accurately, he delayed paying it until he resold the 20-family building. Had he not taken my advice and sold his 12-family direct, and then bought the 20-family with the proceeds, he would have had $12,500 less with which to buy the bigger building.

It's simple, yet so many keep on making these mistakes.

Just as there are excellent reasons for trading up, as the foregoing example illustrates, so are there excellent reasons for trading down. That is, trading a higher-priced property for a lower one.

Let's take an example. You own a twenty-family apartment building, subject to a $150,000 mortgage and the property is a headache to you. You're getting old and the problems of management are becoming a burden. You've tried to sell the property for $200,000 subject to the mortgage, but unsuccessfully. That's the time to try to sell it via the trade route.

Here is how to do it. Advertise that you're willing to take a four-family in trade for your 20-family apartment building. You should get plenty of calls from young owners of properties who are on their way up, and should be trading up. Perhaps you may be fortunate to get a call from someone who has a four-family with a depreciated cost of $25,000, but worth $50,000. This would be a natural for both of you.

It's easier to sell a four-family than a twenty-family. There are many more buyers in the lower price category. Someone with $10,000 down can get a $40,000 mortgage on it, and presto, you have your $50,000 in cash. Take my word for it, it's a lot easier selling a twenty-family this way than taking the straight cash sale route.

A FOUR-WAY TRADE DEAL
THAT MADE EVERYBODY HAPPY

Some years ago, Andrew came to my office and said;

"Mr. Bockl, I'm in trouble. I own a restaurant, a grocery store and cold-storage locker plant, all on one large lot, and they're all driving me batty. My nerves are on edge. I don't seem to be able to please my customers, and what's worse, I'm not pleasing my creditors either. In short, I can't make ends meet. Could you please trade me out of my headaches?"

I felt sorry for him. It was all too apparent that his problems were pumping up his blood pressure.

Within half an hour, I established the following facts:

He had a modern 140 seat restaurant in a good location, but he didn't have the temperament or ability to run it. And his relatives who were in charge of the grocery store and cold-storage locker plant knew less than he did. And on top of it, he loaded himself up with $30,000 of short term equipment loans which taxed him beyond his ability to pay. This was in addition to a $50,000 mortgage in favor of his bank.

"What would you like to trade your 'troubles' for?" I asked with a smile.

"A place in the country with a few cabins for about 20 or 30 tourists, where I can breath fresh air and enjoy peace of mind."

This was more than a real estate problem. I now became a healing adjunct to his doctor who told him that his business pressures were endangering his life.

. After I looked over his properties, and decided they were worth between $90,000 and $100,000, I called Andrew, and told him to put his family in his car, and look over a list of about a dozen small resorts in Northern Wisconsin which I knew were for sale.

Ten days later, refreshed and calmer than when I first met him, he came to my office and said he liked several of them.

"But," he said, "if you could get the 'Blue Haven Resort' for me, I'd be the happiest man in the world."

I called his first choice. The broker who handled the 'Blue Haven Resort' wanted $50,000. I told him over the phone that I might be able to sell it for him for $40,000 with $10,000 down, and the balance to be paid off at the rate of $350 a month, including interest and principal. The broker must have fallen off his chair when he heard my offer because, as I learned later, the owner of the resort was as desperate to sell as my buyer was desperate to buy. I heard the broker say, "It's a deal" altogether too quickly.

Several weeks later, we closed the deal. The transactions were handled the following way. I bought Andrew's properties for $10,000 in cash and assumed his debts of about $80,000. With this $10,000 as a down payment Andrew bought the 'Blue Haven Resort'.

A year later, Andrew came to town to visit his relatives and he made it a point to visit me. He was a picture of health. He pumped my hand with gusto, and if I hadn't pulled away, I think he would have kissed me. He was not only doing fairly well in his 'Blue Haven Resort', but he became a big man in his small community. They ran him for sheriff. He was now a resort owner and law officer, and he loved it.

"If someone guaranteed me $100,000 a year to come back and run my businesses, so help me, I'd turn it down," he told me happily.

I satisfied Andrew, but now let's continue with the story. I sold the grocery store to one of his relatives, and the locker plant to a food purveyor. But the restaurant was a problem. No one seemed to want it, and I certainly didn't want to run it. I didn't know how, nor did I care to learn.

Then I struck on a bright idea. About two blocks away was a small hamburger stand. Would it be so far fetched to inquire whether the hamburger stand owner might be interested in the restaurant? This was reaching for a straw, but why not? There were no better alternatives.

"Yes," said the hamburger stand proprietor. "I've always dreamed of owning this restaurant, but I have no money. I've got lots of help—my wife, my sisters, and my brothers, but I have no money."

"Don't give up too easily," I said. "Do you own the building you're in?"

"Yes," he answered. "I live upstairs. But I've got an $8,000 mortgage against it."

"Well," I said, "let's say your building is worth $13,000. Now you have $5,000. How would you like to buy the restaurant with $5,000 down, and take over a first and second mortgage, totaling $60,000? In other words, you'd be buying my restaurant for $65,000."

"If you can arrange it so my payments aren't too high, I'd be willing."

We arranged a trade on the following basis: I assumed the $8,000 mortgage on his building, and he signed a $35,000 first mortgage with a savings and loan association, and a $25,000 second mortgage to me. Since I needed the cash to pay off all the debts against Andrew's properties, I immediately sold the $25,000 second mortgage at a discount for $15,000 in cash, so that I ended up getting $50,000 in cash for the restaurant, plus a $5,000 equity in the little hamburger stand building a few blocks away.

There wasn't a happier family in the country on the day they opened their new restaurant. It turned out that this family knew how to cook and was willing to give extraordinary service. The customers responded, and the restaurant became an outstanding success.

Now I owned the· hamburger stand building. I remembered a certain gracious middle-aged lady who served wonderful hamburgers in a coffee shop at one of the department stores where I'd stop for a quick snack now and then.

"How would you like to own a hamburger stand of your own?" I asked her one day.

"I've always wanted a little restaurant of my own," she said, "but I have no money."

"Don't you own anything?"

"I own a little cottage that's worth perhaps $8,000."

"Is it mortgaged?"

"Yes. We owe $4,000."

"Lady," I said, "you've just realized your dream. You can now own a restaurant of your own."

I described it to her, and a day later I took her through the building. I arranged the deal as follows:

I had her convey her cottage to me, subject to her $4,000 mortgage, and I conveyed the restaurant building and equipment to her, subject to the $8,000 mortgage.

Her husband quit his job, and together they became the proud owners of their own business. The living quarters upstairs suited them fine. They did so well that in a few years they paid off the $8,000 mortgage out of earnings. They owned their business and living quarters free and clear. They were solvent, depression-proof and happy.

I was now left with their cottage, subject to a $4,000 mortgage. I decided not to carry on this trading any further. I sold it for $7,000, and ended one of the most interesting series of trades I have ever participated in.

Let's see how all the people fared. Andrew, of course, came out the best. He regained his health. The original hamburger stand owner made such an outstanding success of his new restaurant that he sold it five years later at a huge profit, and got into a quarter of a million dollar restaurant, cocktail lounge and bowling complex. All this from a little $5,000 equity in a hamburger stand.

My elderly department store waitress did well too. She and her husband got what they had always wanted.

As for myself, after selling the grocery store and locker plant, and then guiding the restaurant through the series of trades, I recouped the $10,000 I advanced to Andrew, plus a profit of $15,000 for all my pleasant and interesting work.

But the greater profit came in the glowing feeling of healing and helping the people involved in all these deals.

Chapter 8

The Conduit Idea--a New Leverage Tool

We have often heard the expression, "time is money." But few have been able to turn this phrase into cash. Equating time with money can be a powerful selling tool, especially effective in real estate.

If time is money, then youth is a valuable commodity, and a young man should learn to sell his youth in a way that will bring him the highest return.

In real estate, he can do it by offering himself as a conduit for money to flow through from real estate projects. As it flows, some of it is diverted for fixed expenses, some to the money lenders, and a little of it remains with him. What I'm suggesting is that a young man who has managerial skill but no money, should find ways to convince elderly property owners to sell him their real estate with nominal down payments. This, as I will explain, has advantages for the elderly who have made it, and for the young who want to make it.

Let's say you know a 65-year-old man who owns a $100,000 apartment building. At his age, the chances are he owns it free and clear, and that he has used up most of his depreciation. And if he should happen to be in a 70 per cent income bracket, then you have a sure-shot opportunity to try out your conduit idea—selling your youth in a way that converts his real estate equity into an annuity.

Here's how. Tell him you are an ambitious young man who would like to make it the way he did, and that you're willing to work hard for it. For this information, he will give you a benign smile. But don't be discouraged. Tell him that if he sells his apartment building to you with $5,000 down and carries the balance on a 4 per cent mortgage, you can show him that he will have more spendable money left than from owning his property. This will perk up his 65-year-old ears.

He will probably say:

"Young man, you must be talking out of your hat. How will I be better off selling you my property with $5,000 down at an unheard of low 4 per cent interest rate?"

What you're going to tell him next will either make or break your deal. So explain it to him slowly and carefully. This is what you say.

"Mr. Smith, the chances are that because you are in a high income bracket you are left with only $3,000 of spendable money after you net, let's say about $10,000 from your apartment building. The government takes $7,000 of it. If you sell me the building, I can show you that you will have a spendable income of about $4,500. But more important, you would be relieved of management."

At this point, the elderly owner will probably interject:

"Could you explain how I get $4,500 of spendable income instead of $3,000?"

This logical question opens the door for a fuller explanation.

"Here is the way it works," you say. "Of the $10,000 net you now get from your building yearly, I would like to keep $2,000 overage for myself and pay you $8,000 a year until the balance of $95,000 is amortized. Over the life of the loan, the average principal payment will be about $5,600 and the average interest payment, about $2,400. And your tax consequences will be as follows:

"You will pay a long-term gain of 32½ per cent on an average of about $5,600 a year, leaving you a spendable tax-free income of about $3,780 a year. In addition, you will pay 70 per cent of ordinary income on an average of $2,400 interest a year, leaving you a spendable net of $720 a year. Adding the $3,780 spendable from the long-term gain and the $720 spendable from the ordinary gain, you will have a total cash spendable of $4,500 over the life of the loan, or $1,500 more per year than the $3,000 which you would be getting if you continued to own and manage your own property."

After the figures are corroborated by the owner's accountant, you must impress upon the elderly gentleman that your youth, managerial ability and integrity are his insurance for the preservation of his equity and the continuation of his annuity. That his estate will be protected by a responsible owner who has the years to see it through.

The advantages to you are manifold. First, you get an overage of $2,000 a year until the $95,000 is paid, plus any rent increment due to inflation. When the mortgage is paid up, you own a $100,000 building free and clear. Not bad for only $5,000 of seed money!

Obviously, a buyer who is the same age as the seller cannot make such a deal. Time is against him. This deal is logical only for one who is beginning his career and another who is tapering off. And if you're alert. you can find many such combinations.

When you turn 65, after consummating several of the deals I have described, you too should become amenable to selling your real estate on a conduit basis to able young men of tomorrow. It's a selling idea which makes a lot of sense for the old and the young. The reason more deals of this nature are not being made is because not enough young men know enough about it. And many elderly men sell their property for cash, to their own disadvantage.

It should not be difficult to implement this fascinating idea and buy a million dollars worth of property by the time you're thirty-five. In twenty-five years when you'll be sixty, you'll be worth $1,000,000. This is not pie-in-the-sky. It can happen, and it can happen to you. Let me narrate several deals which vividly illustrate the conduit idea, and how they changed the lives and fortunes of the people involved.

A SIMPLE CONDUIT IDEA CATAPULTS A YOUNG COUPLE IN A $300,000 EQUITY POSITION

Several years ago, I received a telephone call from a nurse in a small town of a nearby state.

I heard her say over the 'phone:

"Mr. Bockl, I read your book on leverage and it fascinates me, because you describe how people get into big deals with little money. Could you fascinate me a bit more by telling me how my husband and I can buy the nursing home where I work with a $10,000 down payment?"

During the twenty-minute conversation that followed, I ascertained the following:

1. The owner of the nursing home was an elderly man who was interested in retiring on the equity he had built up in his business.
2. The nurse was his right arm who practically ran the nursing home. He merely provided supervisory effort.
3. Its forty beds were operating at about 80 per cent occupancy and netting the owner a profit of about $25,000 a year.
4. The owner had a $50,000 mortgage against it, and he was trying to sell it for $200,000. His depreciated cost was about $75,000.
5. The nurse was receiving about $7,000 a year salary, and her husband was working for an accounting firm for $10,000 a year.

I suggested that my caller use the following arguments to acquire the nursing home from the elderly owner:

"Tell him," I told her, "that he can actually save money by selling his nursing home to you for $200,000 with $10,000 down. Here is how. If he sold it for cash, he would probably have to slash the price by $25,000, and he would have to pay a long-term tax on a profit of about $100,000 since his depreciated cost was about $75,000. Subtracting his $50,000 first mortgage balance and about $25,000 government tax from the $175,000 proceeds would leave him about $100,000 in cash. If he invested it at 6 per cent, he would get $6,000 a year.

"Now tell him that if he sold you the nursing home for $200,000, you would be paying him 6 per cent interest on $140,000, that is, the difference between his $50,000 mortgage and the balance of $190,000 you would be owing him after you paid $10,000 down. He would then be receiving $9,000 a year interest, after investing his $10,000 cash down payment, instead of the $6,000 a year from the cash sale. An additional advantage to him is that since he is selling his property with less than 29 per cent down, he would be paying his tax on the installment basis, as he gets it from you, instead of all at once as is required on a cash sale.

"Now after explaining all these concrete money advantages," I told her, "be sure to emphasize that he would be lending the money to someone he knows he can trust and who has the qualifications to continue to run the nursing home successfully To clinch the last point, why don't you tell him that in the event of a sale, you would have your husband quit his accounting job and join you in running the business—which, by the way, would be a good idea."

After we reviewed the facts and arguments once more, she thanked me profusely for the free advice, ending it with, "I'm grateful there are people like you around."

Two years later, her husband called me.

"Remember my wife calling you and asking for advice about buying a nursing home? Well, we've bought it on the basis you suggested, and we've added ten new beds and we're running 90 per cent occupancy. Our net after $10,000 salary for me and my wife is about $75,000 a year."

Then he ended his success story by asking:

"Would you like to sell our nursing home for $500,000?"

I told him I was glad he made a success of his venture, but that I would have to decline because our brokerage operations were involved with other ventures at the time. He said he called me in appreciation for the advice I had given his wife. He wanted to favor me with a brokerage commission. I suggested he call a local broker who could get him better and quicker results.

The conduit idea as a leverage tool helped the fortunes of a young couple and provided a safe annuity for an elderly man. And the chances are that the patients in the nursing home were helped too. The devotion of a young couple who own their business is bound to be greater than if the nursing home were sold to a chain, and run by remote control from another city by a local manager.

The conduit idea releases capital to flow from those who have it to those who need it and for the benefit of both. By telling this story clearly and simply, we can tap billions of dollars to finance deals that are locked up today because of lack of mortgage money. The conduit idea unlocks them.

The key in each of these deals is to delineate the advantages to both buyer and seller so that they are clearly understood. It doesn't work when the advantages are lopsided in favor of one or the other.

A SERVICE STATION ATTENDANT BECOMES A RESTAURATEUR—HERE IS HOW

A widow's restaurant was becoming too much for her to handle. She decided to sell. She asked $215,000 for the building, equipment and the going business. Her mortgage balance was $100,000 and she wanted the difference of $115,000 in cash. Two years went by without any takers.

What she didn't know was that she could count on her fingers the number of restaurant buyers in any typical metropolitan area of, let's say, a million people, who either had or were willing to part with $115,000 in cash. What she also didn't know was that there were few sources of secondary financing for restaurants because of their high mortality rate.

I pointed out to the widow's son who managed her affairs, that even if his mother was willing to sell the restaurant for $175,000 in cash she couldn't get it because statistically and realistically there were no such cash buyers available. Few people who have $75,000 in cash would be willing to invest it to make $15,000 a year working seventy hours a week.

"Then what's your plan?" he asked.

"Let me find a young man who could make a go of your restaurant and then I'll structure a deal which will make sense to you and to him."

I found a 32-year-old married man who, in my estimation, had many of the qualities to succeed in the restaurant business. He had leased a dying service station and turned it into a money maker, and now he felt he was ready to fulfill his life's dream—become a restaurant owner. But he had only $10,000.

"Dick," I said to the young man after he toured the restaurant and liked it, "$215,000 is a high price for it. But even if you could get it for $175,000, and even if you could assume the owner's $100,000 mortgage, and even if you could get a $65,000 second mortgage for five years at 12 per cent interest which is highly unlikely, your payments would be beyond your means, I would advise you against such a deal.

"However, the deal I would recommend would be for the widow to sell you the restaurant on a land contract with $10,000 down, and the balance of $205,000 to be paid off at the rate of no more than $1,400 a month, including interest and principal, interest at 5 per cent."

"A thousand four hundred a month would be fine. It's like a reasonable rental. I'd go for that," he said, "and I'm sure with those payments I could make a go of it."

Several days later, I went to see the widow.

"Mrs. Jones," I said to her and to her son, "let me explain something which I want you to think about for several days. If it makes sense, act on it, if it doesn't, well, at least you'll be a little better informed."

"No one gets hurt listening and learning," she said graciously.

"First of all, you've been trying to sell your restaurant for cash without results. Isn't that true? That ought to tell you something. There are few cash buyers—almost non-existent.

"And second, my young man who is interested in your restaurant is better than a cash buyer. Let me explain. He's willing to pay your price, but with only $10,000 down, and to protect him from failure, I want you to finance the balance of $205,000 on a land contract with payments of $1,400 a month to include interest and principal, interest at 5 per cent. By protecting him from unrealistically high payments, you are protecting your own annuity for about the next twenty years.

"And third, I want to tell you something about the young man. He's excellent collateral. He's willing to work hard, he's a devoted family man, and he's as stable as a rock. These may be old virtues, but they're money in the bank—your bank—if you put your blue chips on him. He'll prove a sturdy conduit through which you can pull out all of your $115,000 from the restaurant.

"Since you don't want to work anymore, and your son is not interested in taking over, I believe that my plan makes sense for everyone."

The widow accepted the deal as I structured it. The young man has been running his restaurant for three years now. He's as proud as all get-out, as he should be, because he's meeting all his bills promptly and making $25,000 a year for his family. He and his wife work seventy hours a week, but they're not complaining—they love it. And the widow is happy too, because she is enjoying her leisure—her annuity insured by the hard work and monthly payments of a capable young couple.

And I am happy too, because I've made three parties happy, the young couple, the widow and her son, and myself. I'm receiving a commission of $10,000 at the rate of $100 a month until paid. Not as good as cash, but what's good for the widow ought to be good for me.

CAN IT BE MORE ADVANTAGEOUS
TO CHARGE 4 PER CENT INTEREST
INSTEAD OF 10 PER CENT?

A friend of mine owned a community shopping center consisting of about 70,000 square feet of stores that netted him about $90,000 a year before debt service. His tenants were small local retailers. My friend had a $500,000 mortgage balance on his project at 5 per cent interest with an original 25-year amortization. He was in the 70 per cent income bracket due to his various other holdings.

One day he complained to me that he was getting tired of tenant complaints, and it was interfering with his golf, which he loved. I offered the most logical suggestion.

"Sell it," I said.

"I've tried, but no one is interested."

"What are you asking?"

He answered, "$1,050,000, and it's a bargain. If anyone really wants to roll up his sleeves, he can increase the income $25,000 a year, but I've lost my zest. Frankly, I'm more interested in breaking 90 than breaking my neck getting more net out of my shopping center. Fifteen years ago—yes, but not now."

"I know why you haven't been able to sell your shopping center," I said.

"Why?"

"Because you've been trying to sell it the conventional way. I suppose you're looking for someone with $200,000 down, who is able to obtain an $850,000 mortgage so you can cash out?"

"What's wrong with that?" he asked.

"Nothing, except you can't get it. It's not in the cards '

"Why?"

"Because an $850,000 loan at 10 per cent interest with a 20 year amortization creates a debt service of about $100,000 a year, or $10,000 more than your present stream of income. Can you tell me who'd be foolish enough to invest $200,000 for the privilege of being minus $10,000 a year for twenty years?"

"But my shopping center would cost $1,250,000 to reproduce," he argued.

"That's not relevant here. It's what makes sense to the buyer that counts. If you listen carefully, I'll formulate a deal which will make sense to you and to the buyer."

"Okay, I'm all ears, and I'm glad you put me first."

"First of all," I said, "I'll get your price—$1,050,000."

"That's a good start," he said. "I'm interested."

"I want you to sell your yearly $90,000 stream of income with $50,000 down, and the balance of a million dollars to be paid off at the rate of $70,000 a year, including interest and principal, interest at 4 percent."

"Four per cent interest!" he exclaimed. "Are you nuts or something?"

"Listen carefully now," I said. "I want to show you that you're better off taking 4 per cent interest, and getting your full price, than having to slash it in order to sell it conventionally with the present 10 per cent interest rate."

"Go ahead," he said, "show me why 4 per cent interest is better than 10."

"Okay," I said, "I'll show you. You are in the 70 per cent tax bracket. You probably have about a $400,000 profit in this shopping center when you sell it for $1,050,000. Now follow me carefully. When you receive $70,000 a year payment, $40,000 of it is interest on $1,000,000, and taxable at 70 per cent, leaving you $12,000 after taxes. Now of the $30,000, about two-thirds, or $20,000 is a return of capital on which there is no tax, and on the $10,000 there is about one-third long term gain, or about $3,300, leaving $6,700 tax free money. Adding the $12,000 from the $40,000, $20,000 return of capital and $6,700 after paying the gain on $10,000, you have a yearly cash spendable of $38,700.00.

"Now even if you found someone foolish enough to pay you 7 per cent interest on your million balance—10 per cent would be out of the question—both of you would lose. He would be paying $70,000 a year on interest and paying off nothing on principal. You would be paying 70 per cent income tax on $70,000 or $49,000, leaving you a net spendable of $21,000. Now compare this with $38,700 cash spendable which you would be getting based on my plan."

"I guess it makes sense," he admitted. "The only fly in the ointment is that by paying less interest, the buyer gets to own my property that much faster."

"But what would you rather have, I asked, "more spendable money for the rest of your life or a bigger balance on the land contract when you die, which I hope will be a long way off?"

"You've given me a new selling slant, and as far as I can see, it's sound. But $50,000 down, isn't it too low for a million dollar deal? And what about your commission, if I pay it to you in cash, I'll have nothing left."

"You can keep the $50,000 cash, and I'll take my commission at the rate of $5,000 a year for ten years. And I'll even go a step further. If for some reason the buyer can't make it, and hands the property back to you, mv commission ceases too. We both gain if I pick a good conduit, a stable young man with ability and integrity."

"Okay, my friend, find the young man and if I like him, I'll make the deal."

So far, I have not found the young man who in my estimation could take on the management of the shopping center, and who also has the $50,000 in cash. But when I find him, he will have a bonanza.

First, he will be getting an immediate overage of $20,000 a year—tax sheltered and with golden opportunities to increase it because the elderly owner allowed the rents to slide. Second, he will be paying off $30,000 on the principal the first year, and because of the low 4 per cent increase rate, the amortization will be increasing at a rapid rate. This is a new way of leveraging in a tight money, high-interest market. It's an innovative way of creating new buyers and sellers where none existed before. It's a sound approach in buying and selling commercial real estate.

HOW TO SELL A $1,000,000 BUILDING FOR $2,000,000

A trust officer of a bank called one day to ask me for advice on how to sell a 200 family apartment hotel which he held in an estate. He had a $2,000,000 appraisal on it in his file. It was a 40-year-old building on an entire square block of land, well-located and in excellent condition.

The trust officer's dilemma was that without a mortgage on it, the building showed only a $50,000 net and yet, based on the appraisal, he had to make an effort to sell it for $2,000,000.

"It's obvious," I said after we discussed the deal at length, "that the appraisal is incorrect. How can you justify a $2,000,000 price for a $50,000 a year net?"

"But the appraisal is based on a cost of reproduction of $5,000,000, so that $2,000,000 is on the low side even if you depreciate it 50 percent. The report makes the further point that the property has been mismanaged and that the $50,000 net could easily be raised to $100,000."

"I agree," I said, "but how is anyone going to pay off $2,000,000 at 9 or 10 per cent interest, even if the net could be raised to $100,000?"

The trust officer chuckled, "You're explaining my problem. I want a solution."

"We have here," I said, "an excellent illustration of how high interest rates, high real estate taxes and high operating costs erode the value of real estate. But if you insist on a $2,000,000 price, here is one way of getting it:

"Sell it with $100,000 down, the balance to be paid at the rate of $100,000 a year to include interest and principal, interest at 4 per cent. This will pay intself out in about 25 years. The estate will pay taxes on some $80,000 of interest, and $20,000 will be partially taxed capital gain, and the balance will be a tax-free return of capital. This ratio will change more favorably for the estate as the interest decreases and capital gain increases. But most important of all, you will convert the present $50,000 income to $100,000 a year for about twenty-five years.

"The key to this deal is getting a skilled, young property manager to assume the responsibilities of ownership. That's the other side of the coin in structuring the sale of this property.

Getting the right young man is more important than getting the $100,000 down, because if we find the young talent, it's easy to get an investor to back him for part of the action and the valuable depreciation."

"Do you have a young man in mind"? the trust officer asked.

"If your bank decides to adopt my plan, I believe I can produce several young men who will qualify."

This type of real estate reasoning has enabled me to put together many seemingly impossible deals. It is one way of beating the tight money market. For tax purposes, the government allows the seller to charge 4 per cent as imputed interest instead of the higher going rate.

As of this writing, the trust department is still thinking about my plan, and I think I know why. It can't reconcile itself to taking 4 per cent interest when the going rate is 9 to 10 per cent. It is difficult for those who live by interest to let go of 5 per cent on close to $2,000,000 for 25 years. It's a stupendous amount of money, and I agree. But what trust department thinking doesn't want to face is that if it insists on 9 per cent interest, then the building is only worth $1,000,000—its $2,000,000 appraisal notwithstanding.

They can't have it both ways—$2,000,000 and 9 per cent interest. They are asking for the impossible. They have to yield either on the interest or the price. If they don't yield on one or the other, the estate will suffer. Because as good as trust management is, it is rarely as good as aggressive young ownership control where imagination and innovation are more apt to bring a property to its highest and best use.

HOW THE CONDUIT IDEA AND OLD WORLD CHARM ASSURED TWO BROTHERS A LIFETIME OF SUCCESS

Everyone has a favorite restaurant. I had mine. It was an old farm house which had been turned into a restaurant a half century ago. It was now surrounded by luxurious homes in a fashionable suburb.

The food was both wholesome and low-priced. It was a favorite family eating place. Two brothers in their late 30's were its proprietors. They had inherited it from their mother who worked there until she died at a ripe old age.

It was a small restaurant, seating less than one hundred people. Nothing had changed in fifty years and that's what, in my opinion, gave it its charm. The floors slanted a little. The bar was old-fashioned. The window frames, if one looked closely, were weatherbeaten and cracked. But when the fluffy potato pancakes, or duck browned just right, or fresh pike tasting the way fishermen prepare it on shore were brought on, one didn't mind the dim glare coming out of old light fixtures, the drapes not matching anything in the room, or the antique wallpaper that must have delighted restaurant goers decades ago.

By quick reckoning I presumed that the brothers were doing about $400,000 of sales a year, and each was probably earning about $30,000. It was the most successful small restaurant in the area. But the brothers were straining at the leash. They felt too confined and limited.

One day at lunch, I noticed a big, tinted drawing of a new restaurant with a sign over it: "This is what our new restaurant will look like." It looked to me like a half million dollars.

I walked into the kitchen after lunch and asked one of the brothers, who was standing over a broiler in his big white hat:

"Are you going to tear down my favorite restaurant and build a new one, like the picture shown on the wall?"

"Yes," he answered without taking his eyes off the broiler. "We've just gotten permission from the village board to go ahead with our project. It took a lot of doing because the neighbors were against a large commercial building in the midst of a residential area."

"Do you think you're doing a wise thing?" I asked. "Have you stopped to figure out how much it would cost you a year in interest, principal and taxes to pay off about $500,000 over the next twenty years?"

"We haven't figured it out exactly, but we have no choice. We've got to expand."

I had a liking for this quaint little restaurant and I was fond of the two young proprietors. I remembered them when they were bus boys while I was courting my wife. Intuitively, I felt they would be making a mistake going into $500,000 of debt. I put my mind on their quandary.

I closeted myself for a half hour and tried to think of an idea that would solve their expansion problem. None came. But the next morning, while I was shaving, a solution lit up my mind.

A few miles away from my pet restaurant was another one run by a man who bought it for a lark to see if he would like it. In his travels, he had eaten in some of the best restaurants of the world, and he thought he knew enough about good food to run a restaurant of his own. He was wrong. He lost money the first year, the second year, and he was about to lose $75,000 the third year. The restaurant was about ten years old and would have cost about $400,000 to reproduce.

I called the owner and said:

"I have a young man who can bail you out of your losses, but you'll have to sell your place with $10,000 down and for about half the price you think it's worth."

I gave him the name of one of the brothers. He knew him.

"I like the buyer," he said, "but I'm not crazy about your price and down payment."

"Well, It's the only way my buyer can make a go of it. He has several children, and though he makes good money, $10,000 is all he's been able to save. But as you know, he's one of the best operators in the county. If you can see yourself stopping your losses by selling your restaurant for about $230,000 with $10,000 down, I believe I could get him a $150,000 first mortgage and turn over the cash to you.

"And if you will carry a second mortgage of $70,000 at some reasonable interest rate on a 20-year amortization, I can see my buyer being able to meet all his obligations, and save you from what must be unpleasant losses. Does all this make sense to you?"

"It's good for him, but is it good for me?"

"I think it is, because you have no alternative. You've been trying to sell it for . . ."

"Okay, I'll give him a break because I like him. Go ahead and see what you can do."

I had an unhappy seller, but it was the only way, I felt, to get a happy buyer. Though I would be getting my commission from the seller, my heart, I must admit, was with the buyer.

A day later, I was again at the broiler of my favorite restaurant, talking to the older of the two brothers.

"Fritz," I said, "I think I can get you out of your dilemma. Instead of going into debt for $500,000, which by the way, will cost you about $75,000 a year for interest, principal and taxes, I suggest that one of you brothers buy another restaurant, and I happen to have one."

I described the restaurant, which of course he knew, and the terms under which one of them could purchase it.

"The plan I have in mind is for one of you to stay here and continue as you have been without any changes, and the other to buy the restaurant on the terms I suggest. This, in my estimation, makes a lot more sense than borrowing $500,000 at today's high interest rates. I can assure you, your potato pancakes will not taste any better in your modern facility. In fact, I'd prefer them in your old-world, charming atmosphere.

"My plan for your expansion is safer, because you're assured of success—both of you. Tearing down your successful restaurant to fulfill your grandiose building plans could strain your resources to the breaking point. In fact, it could break you. My plan is failure proof—100 per cent."

After several weeks of discussion the two brothers decided to separate. The younger brother chose to stay with the old restaurant, and the older one chose to go along with my new idea.

As I anticipated, obtaining a $150,000 first mortgage required a major effort. It took a bank president who was a devotee of the brothers' farm restaurant, as I was, to chance a $150,000 mortgage in this risky loaning area. But the real persuaders were the $400,000 appraisal and the character and ability of the borrower.

This story has a very happy ending. The younger brother who kept the old restaurant is doing as well as ever, and making more money because he doesn't have to divide it with his brother. The older brother who bought the new restaurant turned it around in six months. Under the former wealthy owner, it was losing between $50,000 and $75,000 a year. The new owner is now earning between $30,000 and $40,000 a year.

And I gained, too. First, a commission of $10,000, and second, I saved my charming little restaurant from being bulldozed out of existence.

---

*George Bockl, *How to Use Leverage to Make Money in Local Real Estate* (Englewood Cliffs, N.J.: Prentice-Hall, Inc., 1965).

Chapter 9

Entrepreneurial Leverage

BUYING WHOLESALE AND SELLING RETAIL
ANOTHER WAY OF MERCHANDISING REAL ESTATE?

Selling real estate for a commission is an orderly and time-tested method of merchandising. However, although most real estate in our country is sold that way, it need not be the only way. Cars, refrigerators, boats and tens of thousands of other items are not sold on a commission basis.

Could homes, land, apartment buildings, or commercial properties be merchandised the same way? Could an entrepreneur inventory real estate in the same manner a retailer inventories goods, and then sell it to the public? It is not the prevailing practice, but I believe it could be another way of merchandising property.

Buying wholesale and selling retail is in the American tradition, and there is no reason why it cannot apply to real estate. It means taking greater risks than in brokerage, but with it come greater rewards. Setting up a buying and selling organization takes more knowledge and money than setting up a brokerage company.

There are two primary musts in developing a buy and sell real estate office: one, to establish credit with a bank, and two, to establish a relationship of trust with a savings and loan association. The first is for interim financing, and the second for permanent mortgages. The temporary or interim financing should be for about 80 or 90 per cent of the purchase price of the property, and it should be for a period between six months and a year. Such financing is usually costly, but necessary, and should be added to the purchase price of the property. This enables the entrepreneurial buyer to act quickly if a seller wants to get cash for his property in a hurry

A real estate company specializing in buying and selling should have a well-organized buying department. It should be subdivided into such specialities as residential, commercial, investment and industrial, with one or more buyers in each, and a manager supervising them. The manager should be a man of wide background and good judgment, a sort of liaison man between the buyers and his boss. His most valuable function ought to be the screening of purchases and submitting the good ones to the owner so he doesn't waste his time on "cats and dogs."

Buying specialists are a different breed of men than selling specialists. The producing guts of a buying and selling organization is to be found in the handful of super buyers. Super buyers are more valuable than super salesmen.

While vacationing in the West Indies one winter, I met a real estate operator from London who ran a classic buying and selling organization. He had four buyers and four salesmen, each on salary, plus bonus. The buyers combed the city of London for flats (apartments), land, office buildings, etc., and after he approved and purchased what he liked, the properties became merchandise on the shelf for the salesmen. My vacation friend became wealthy because his buyers knew how to find properties—he knew how to pick them—and his salesmen knew how to sell them.

I don't know of any firm in our area which merchandises real estate with the buying and selling precision of my London friend, and in talking to brokers from many parts of the country, they indicated they didn't know of any large organizations which merchandised real estate in this manner either.

However, I know of several small companies who buy and sell, but in each case the buying salesmen are also the selling salesmen. There is a lot to be said for that because a buyer of a property already has a good knowledge of it and, therefore, is in a favorable position to sell it.

Here is how these small buying and selling organizations operate. The owner sends letters to brokers in his area asking them to sell their properties to him for cash. Most of them will ignore him. They prefer to sell their listings for commissions. But a few will answer, especially if they have listings that are not selling.

Another source for purchasing properties is to circularize attorneys specializing in probate work who are looking for cash to close out an estate. If the price is close to the appraisal, the lawyers are likely to accept a cash offer rather than list the real estate with a broker, who may or may not sell it in six months.

Trust officers of banks in charge of liquidating estates are good sources for buys. They, too, prefer cash offers to listing property with brokers who may not sell in time to close their estates.

The most direct source for getting leads to buy real estate is to advertise in the local newspaper under the column marked, REAL ESTATE WANTED. The ad usually reads like this:

WE PAY CASH
for
LAND, HOMES and
INVESTMENT PROPERTIES
of all kinds.
NO WAITING
Get your cash
as soon as you present us
with a clear title.

John Doe   (phone)

After these buy and sell companies obtain their interim financing for their property purchases, the next step is to put a price tag on them. This, however, is more complicated that might first appear. Since the public is used to buying with small down payments, the markup has to be much more than the usual 6 per cent commission. For instance, the profit could be a lengthy amortized second mortgage or land contract equity. In either case, the amounts are not tantamount to cash. To protect themselves, the buyers must look for profits between 10 to 20 per cent so that if they have to sell their land contract equities or second mortgages at a discount, they will earn at least the 6% commission the brokers usually get, plus another several points for the risks involved.

Here is an illustration: The owner of a buy-and-sell real estate company buys a building for $50,000 in cash and sells it for $60,000 with $5,000 down. The new owner signs a $45,000 first mortgage and turns over the proceeds to the seller, plus the $5,000 down payment. The seller's profit now is in the form of a $10,000 second mortgage. If the cash flow is high enough, the investor-buyer could have his second mortgage amortized, let's say, over ten years. If, however, there is little cash flow in the property, the seller may have to be satisfied with interest only, or no interest, for ten years, and wait for refinancing before he gets his second mortgage paid off. The real estate entrepreneur must, in all cases, tailor-make his deal so it makes sense to the new buyer, otherwise he is jeopardizing his own position. But if enough second-mortgage profits of $10,000 come in, he can either accumulate a large second mortgage portfolio, or sell them at a discount.

I know several small real estate buying and selling entrepreneurs who earn more money with their small organizations than brokers do with their large ones. I know men who operate out of their homes without any salesmen who earn more money buying and selling real estate than some high priced professors, lawyers and doctors. Some of these "lone wolf" operators buy from brokers and have other brokers sell for them at a profit. Usually these men have an uncanny sense in seeing something in a property others miss. They also have a way of finding buys where others have looked and couldn't see them. In every branch of business, there are a few who have a sixth sense, an intuitive knack that sets them apart. In buying and selling real estate, having that gift is imperative.

A real estate buying and selling organization can be set up in two ways. If the owner of the business can give it his full and undivided attention, he should put his organization on a salary basis. And there are plenty of good men available who would prefer to work for a salary and bonus arrangement rather than on commission.

However, if the owner of a buy-sell organization is not able to give it his full time because of other interests, then he ought to set up his organization in this manner: Put a man in charge of operations on a salary with a bonus based on a percentage of the net profit, but enter into the following arrangement with the salesmen: Pay them one-half of the profit on any buy and sale they make, but also hold them responsible for any loss. In this way, every salesman is in fact, in business for himself. If he is on the ball, it is conceivable that he could make more money than the salaried men in a similar situation. I have known salesmen who consistently earned between $25,000 and $30,000 a year working under this buy-sell and half of the profit arrangement

Either way, whether the owner gives the company his complete attention and puts everyone on salary, or gives it part of his attention and puts more responsibility on the salesmen, the buying and selling way of merchandising real estate can be highly profitable.

I am not suggesting that speculative merchandising is superior to brokerage, I am only saying that it is a different way of selling. In fact, I can see hazards in it for the public as well as the broker. An aggressive buyer could take advantage of a little old lady who doesn't know much about real estate and doesn't hire anyone to represent her. Or a broker who doesn't know much about value and less about the art of financing and selling could easily go bankrupt. I have seen both situations happen.

HOW TO BUY AND KEEP A REAL ESTATE FORTUNE

In no other business can youth cash in on youth as in real estate. Any young man of thirty who becomes skilled in property management and learns how to borrow imaginatively, will be worth about as much as he can borrow after he amortizes his debts. If he manages to sign a million dollars worth of mortgages by the age of thirty, he will be worth $1,000,000 when he's 55. It's that simple, and as I've indicated in previous chapters, it doesn't take extraordinary talent to do it.

And if a young and capable property manager wants to extend himself and sign $5,000,000 worth of mortgages by the time he's 35, he will be worth $5,000,000 by the time he's 60. This assumes that the rate of depreciation will be matched by inflation. And that's a safe bet.

All right, you're 30 years old, you have a certified property management certificate, you're earning $12,000 a year managing one or several buildings for an owner, and you want to know how to borrow a million dollars. You want to be an entrepreneur instead of an employee

Well, if you have a passive personality, if owing a lot of money makes your heart beat faster, if a few reverses will throw your stomach into a tailspin, don't try to borrow a lot of money. If you don't think you have the mental maneuverability to keep the stream of income flowing, if you get easily frustrated and problems confuse you, then don't try to be a big decision maker. Let someone else with steadier nerves and better judgment decide for you. You'll be a lot happier—and that's worth a lot more than making a lot of money and playing coronary brinkmanship.

Know yourself, and choose your category carefully. That's why I wrote the fourth chapter, a guideline to help you match your psychological and intellectual resources with what the various real estate categories demand.

But if you are an active personality, if you know how to sublimate your restlessness into an even flow of energy, if you think you can manage property, and can honestly rationalize that borrowing money is doing the lender a greater favor than the borrower—then let me take you by the hand and lead you into making a fortune.

Remember, you must think positively. The lender is putting you to work to earn money for him, not the other way around. When you borrow a million dollars at 8% to be amortized over 25 years, he will be earning $1,500,000 in interest. So don't be timid about borrowing. He's making more money than you, with less work. But linked to bullish borrowing, you must have an unswerving confidence in your ability to extract the full potential income from a property. This must not be based on pie-in-the-sky optimism, but upon a responsible evaluation of your and the property's resources.

If you're ready for a bumpy 25-year ride, if you don't mind meeting crises, and lastly, but most important, if you are stable enough so that making a lot of money is not going to warp your values and personality (that's where many successful men fail), then here is the way to get started.

Get to know a dozen or more of the leading brokers in your community and announce to them that you are ready to buy some of their investment property for cash or on terms. Follow up every lead they give you, even if it means a lot of wild goose chasing. See twenty properties a week, thirty if necessary, study their statements, get a feel of comparative values. When you see one that has a lot of potential, move in on it. If you can get it for a low enough figure, offer all cash, with the hope that the appraisal will be 20 per cent higher so that you can buy it with an 80% of value mortgage.

Now comes the difficult part. You must convince the lender that although you are not putting in any of your money, the property has an untapped potential to make it a safe loan, and that you can tap it. Few will listen. Most will want front money. They don't like to see you move into a deal only with your elbows.

But just as you had to see twenty or thirty properties before you zeroed in on a good one, so must you see a dozen lenders before giving up. Remember, it only takes one to make a deal. He could be the 12th one. This is more easily said than done—and that's why only a few are doing it. If you don't have the perserverance to get up smiling after many, and sometimes rude turndowns, then this game of try, try again is not for you.

If you find a lender who sees things your way, then all your work of finding the property and the lender will pay off. But what if you're convinced you have a good deal, and there's no way of getting 100% financing? And the only way the deal can be made is to raise $25,000 or $50,000 of equity money? That's a problem more easily solved. Get a silent investor in on the deal by giving him 50% interest for putting up the front money. If you really picked a good buy, you should have no trouble in getting a partner with money to ride in on all of your work. If you can't convince any investor, then you've either picked a lemon or you're not communicating well.

If you're having difficulty finding good buys and financing them 100%, or getting partners with equity money, then take another route. Look for property that you can buy on terms. Pay a higher price, if necessary, if you can buy it with a low down payment. Use leverage, the conduit approach, the 4% vs the 9% argument where it applies, or any combination of these, to convince the seller that you're the logical buyer for his property. If you're not making any headway in acquiring property through any of these methods, then either you are too inexperienced in handling executive type sellers, or your presentation is not imaginatively conceived to build confidence. To overcome these possible handicaps, I suggest you expose yourself to more and more sellers until you find someone who will listen to your story. It's one of the ways to overcome inexperience.

To get more property and seller exposure, I suggest you place the following ad in your local newspaper:

I WILL BUY
Your Investment Property
Either for Cash
or on Terms

You are bound to get many calls from an ad like this. You will get calls from brokers as well as property owners who want to sell direct. Follow up every lead. Keep an orderly record of all the properties you have seen, the offers you have made, and who has turned you down. Be sure to follow up the properties which have a special interest for you. Perhaps there will be a change of mind. A warm up call will catch it. Within a year, you might have 300 or 400 pieces of real estate which have had your studied attention and whose owners have heard from you. This is an excellent investment. It would be most unusual if within a year, five or ten of the sellers did not call you back and ask to talk things over When that happens, you must prepare your strategy quickly, leaving no loopholes. You are entering an area of decision. Here is where the thousands of hours you've spent looking for properties, talking to sellers and trying to convince lenders, can pay off. As a result of all this work, you may buy one property, five, or ten. You're on your way.

If seeing brokers and newspaper advertising does not expose you to enough property, then go after bank trust officers, probate lawyers and foreclosure sales. Buying property is a full time job. As your investment portfolio grows you will have less time to search for buys because you will need more time to manage your property. When you've bought as many as you care to own, then consolidate your holdings by applying yourself to full time management. Rely on your native intelligence first, but always be ready to improvise on it by using the insights you can glean from reading books on management and attending seminars.

Side by side with looking for buys you should spend a great deal of time developing mortgage sources. Each successful acquirer of real estate has his favorite lenders. Never mind if twenty or thirty lenders turn you down, as long as you can cultivate four or five who believe in you, that's all you need. They become very important people in your life, and I advise you to study them because they will be studying you. Know what they expect of you, and live up to it, even beyond their expectations, if possible. Never, but never, be late in your monthly payments. Live up to every promise—without any exceptions. Never cross a lender. Never disappoint him. Never make him look bad.

When he is completely relaxed about your dependability, that's when it will be easier for you to get that extra 5% or 10% of mortgage which often is the difference between making and breaking a deal.

Good management adds value to property—keep that uppermost in your mind. Sometimes it can even double it. But bad management can reduce the value of property too. It can cut it in half. I have seen it happen both ways. I can't overstress the fact that unless you have managerial know-how and a rare sense of good judgment, you should not become involved in borrowing large sums of money. It is not nearly so difficult to get a loan as it is to keep property in the black and pay the loan back.

Not enough money lenders and elderly investors realize that they need youthful money-makers to act as conduits through which they can earn interest on their money or preserve the stream of income from their properties. It is up to you to convince them that they have a valuable vehicle in your 25 years of future earning power, and they can use it advantageously to earn money.

Remember, the earlier you start, the more time you have to pay off your mortgages, and the sooner will you have your properties free and clear. Youth is an asset. Begin using it as soon as possible so you can retire and do some of the things you've always wanted to do but didn't have time. If you plan your real estate buying career well, there should be no need for you to keep up the pressure to make money at 55. That's when you should begin to decompress. That's when you should sell your property to younger men so they can do what you have done—become the conduits for an older generation.

When you're between 55 and 60, and your properties are free and clear, that's the time to travel, attend seminars, read significant books, and generally digest your experiences by sharing what wisdom you might have accumulated with others who may need your help.

After 55, when you have enough, there is no point in pumping away to make more money. That's the time to pump some of your energies back into your community. Give yourself the luxury of becoming a philosopher king. Find something bigger to live for than making more money

HOW A 30 YEAR OLD BOUGHT A FARM AND BUILT IT INTO A $3,000,000 FORTUNE

Twenty-five years ago, a 30-year-old lawyer developed a property acquisition plan which was more ambitious and successful than any I have advanced thus far. He knew he couldn't make big money in law, but he had a hunch he could do it in real estate. He was right.

With the first money he earned from his law practice, he bought a 140-acre farm, paying $10,000 down and assuming a mortgage of $34,000 on the balance. It was located about 10 miles northwest from the center of the city.

After checking with the heads of the water, sewer and expansion departments, and combining their information with his own judgment, he concluded that his farm would be in the path of development, and that it would peak out in about 20 years.

Five years later, a speculator offered him $100,000 profit for his farm and he wisely refused it. He stuck to his plan of waiting, and it worked out beyond his wildest dreams.

Let's take a look at how ingeniously he cultivated. His farm happened to have a rich layer of topsoil. Some might say he was lucky. But he was more than lucky—he was smart. Before he was through, landscape gardeners had paid him $30,000 for his topsoil.

That wasn't all. His farm was about 5 to 10 feet above grade and his clay soil was excellent for filling. He called several dozen builders who needed fill, and over a five-year period, he received $50,000 from them while they removed the hills on his farm which would have cost him about $20,000 to level in preparation for building.

And that wasn't all. His farm was bounded by two narrow, lightly traveled streets. The county decided to widen them to handle more traffic. After a year of negotiating, he agreed to take

$90,000 for a narrow strip of land bounding both streets of his farm, but with the important proviso that his land be zoned commercial and light manufacturing. His farm was now astride two new and wide semi-highways, adding greatly to the value of his investment. With approximately $170,000 profit already in his pocket, and his farm still intact, he began to investigate the possibilities of putting it to its highest and best use, that is, getting the most money for it.

He sold the corner to a gasoline station for $100,000. Several years later he sold 15 acres at $30,000 an acre to a public utility company. A year later, he sold another 15 acres to a discount store for a half million dollars. He kept dividing and selling off more acreage to light industry and wholesale distributing companies until he accumulated $2,000,000.

And that wasn't all. The $90,000 that the young man received from the county for allowing it to widen his streets brought him another million dollars because of this unusual tax angle.

Under a clause known as the Involuntary Conversion Clause, if an owner receives an award from the government, in this case the $90,000, there is no tax on it if this award is used to purchase another property within one year. Our fantastic young man bought another piece of land with the $90,000, upon which he paid no tax, and ten years later, he sold it to a discount department store for $1,000,000.

This is but one of the unusual stories taking place in many cities where young men with imagination buy land in anticipation of development, and using their youth as a factor in the time-pricing equation, let it ripen, and reap the profit harvest when they're about ready for retirement. It's an easy way to become wealthy.

Socialistically inclined people might criticize the capitalistic system for allowing young men to make so much money with so little effort. Are they right? Let's see.

By earning $3,000,000, our young attorney has hurt no one. On the contrary, he has done a lot of good. He was the catalyctic agent which moved topsoil to where it was needed, turned hills into needed fill, indirectly helped build $10,000,000 worth of industrial shelter, created hundreds of jobs and widened his city's tax base. Without the incentive to make the $3,000,000, the 140-acre farm might not have been developed in this orderly and well-thought-out fashion. The incentive brought out the best in our young man, and although his aim may not have been altruistic, indirectly it redounded to the benefit of his community.

HOW TO BUILD A FORTUNE
BUILDING BUILDINGS

At a time of high interest rates, high real estate taxes and high building costs, it would appear impossible to build and have a cash overage. But it's not so.

There is still room for the innovative builder. When I was in a California town a few years ago, I saw two apartment developments in their initial stages. One had the amenities of yesterday—good, but not good enough. The other projected beyond what was good—it was innovative. The architecture was authentically Spanish, featuring a red tile roof, a sunken conversation area around the fireplace, heavy doors, arches, Mexican floor tile and other authentic special amenities.

When I visited the town again recently, the ordinary project was floundering, the innovative one was filled. The unusual amenities made the difference. Attention to unusual arthitectural detail which may have raised the cost of building 7% enabled the builder to charge 15% more rent. This gave him two advantages over the unimaginative builder—8% more profit, and the money saved through quicker renting.

There was a time in the late fifties and early sixties when almost any Tom, Dick or Harry built and made money. Those days are over. Only the innovative can survive today. It's a tight-rope building act, and only those who can balance themselves adroitly can cross over into the black where others fall in the red.

Building and keeping what you build was a great deal easier when the interest rate was 6 per cent, the amortization constant 2 per cent and the net on the project before debt service was 10 per cent. If you were able to mortgage 100 per cent, you had a 2 per cent cash flow, which on a million dollar project meant $20,000 a year.

A builder I know from the East built a number of bottling plants for a large beverage company. He had a very simple arrangement with the beverage company. The beverage company people drew the plans and obtained certified costs for their plants. Then, after selling them to my friend, they leased them back from him on the basis of an 8% return. Using the lease as collateral, my friend went to his favorite lender and borrowed the entire cost at 6% interest with a 2% amortization. While he had no cash flow, he had none of his money in these facilities, either. In 25 years, he will own millions of dollars worth of the company's plants free and clear, and when they renew their leases, he or his estate will be getting pure profit.

Can this be done today? Certainly! All you have to do is to change the formula to reflect the higher interest rates. For instance, if the interest rate is 9 per cent, then add 2 per cent for amortization and lease the facility on the basis of an 11 per cent return, so that instead of receiving $80,000 a year rent on a $1,000,000 plant, you will be getting $110,000. Sophisticated lessees, who know the economic facts of life, will pay higher rent if they find a reliable builder like my friend who will supervise the construction, arrange the financing and present his clients with a trouble free key job. There are hundreds of such opportunities available if you find the companies whose lease collateral is as good as that of the beverage company I mentioned.

The industrial giants are too sophisticated to let the builder make more than the 2 per cent amortization in a sale and leaseback. They know that they can get enough builders to take their deals without cash flow.

However, this need not be the case in small building ventures where the entrepreneur can make his 2 per cent amortization and 2 to 5 per cent cash flow as well.

Here is how one man I met at a commercial property clinic in Chicago built a multi-million dollar fortune in 25 years.

"There are big fortunes to be made in small projects," he told me. "The big companies pin you to the wall. Their big shots are too demanding. The little businessman, because his collateral is weaker, is less fussy.

"Here is how I got started and kept going. I solicited small commercial and industrial tenants and offered to build small buildings for them. 'Don't lose your identity in a large building,' I would tell them. 'Enjoy the prestige of your own name on your own individualized plant.'

"My projects were from 3,000 to 10,000 square feet. I was able to lease these buildings favorably to me, as well as my tenants, for these good and economical reasons. I bought lots for songs. That's because I looked at twenty before I bought one. I dealt with small contractors who were satisfied with small profits. However, I saw to it that my masons, carpenters, electricians and plumbers were reliable men. There are as many good and honest workers among small contractors as there are among large ones.

"Here, roughly, is the arithmetic of my deals. I would build a 5,000 square foot factory building in the 1950's for about $6 a square foot, or $30,000. The lot would cost another $7,000, miscellaneous $3,000—total $40,000. I would lease it at a dollar a square foot net to me, or $5,000 a year. My payments on a $40,000 mortgage, if I was lucky to get 100% financing, at 6% on about 20-year amortization was about $4,000 a year. I enjoyed a $1,000 cash flow. My equity money was my hard work.

"When I built a small office building on a long lease for a small user, the arithmetic was about as favorable as for a small industrial plant. My cost for building office space was about $9 a square foot, so that a 5,000 square foot office building cost me $45,000. The typical lot cost about $10,000—total $55,000. The typical loan was about $50,000, and my payments on interest and principal about $4,000 a year on a 25 year loan. My fixed expenses were about $1,000 for heat, $1,000 for light and air conditioning power, $3,000 for daily cleaning and repairs, $1,000 maintenance and about $2,000 for real estate taxes with the lessee paying for any increases. Total expenses and debt service $12,000. Rent was about $3.25 a square foot, or $16,250 a year. This gave me a cash flow of about $4,250 for a $5,000 investment. Usually I had no investment.

"Believe it or not," the grandfatherly gentleman told me during the luncheon break, "I built 50 of these small buildings during the last 25 years. I have a cash flow today of about $200,000 a year. And it was all done with small businessmen, God bless them. And they all got good deals."

"These big shots on the panel," I told my elderly companion, "use different criteria than you do."

"These big shots talk big, but I could buy and sell each one of them."

"Then why are you sitting here?" I asked. "You should be sitting up there, telling us."

"But I don't have their education. I can't talk like they do. I come here to relax, and once in a while maybe, I get an idea here and there."

Can young men still do today what this elderly gentleman did so easily in the last 25 years? Why not? If factory space costs $9 a square foot to build today instead of $5, if interest is 9 per cent instead of 6 per cent, then charge the user $1.50 a square foot for rent per year instead of $1.00, and the arithmetic can be as favorable today as it was yesterday. And the same goes for office space.

HOW 3 YOUNG MEN BUILT $30,000,000 OF APARTMENTS WITH OTHER PEOPLE'S EQUITY MONEY

Not long ago an architect came to my office and said;

"I've got a sure fire project for 70 apartments in an ideal location priced out at $1,000,000—complete. The best financing I can get is an $850,000 mortgage at 9 per cent with a 25 year amortization. I've read your book on leverage, but I've been unable to get 100 per cent financing. Can you tell me how I can get $150,000 in equity money so I can get this project off the ground?"

The architect had done some work for me, and some of my zest for entrepreneurial effort must have rubbed off on him. He wanted an ownership position in addition to his architectural fees.

"Zeke," I said, "just as there are certain fundamentals in architecture so are there certain fundamentals in approaching investors. Here a few of them:

"Approach number one: Offer your investor 50 per cent ownership in your project for $150,000 equity money. Agree to have all the overage go to him until half his investment is paid in full, after which you begin to participate in ½ of the overage.

"Approach number two: Offer the investor 50 per cent interest on the same basis as in approach number one but with this sweetener. Give him 90% of the accelerated depreciation. That's money in his pocket because he can use the depreciation to better advantage than you. He's presumably in a higher tax bracket. Not

many are aware of this clause in the law, and consequently few use this innovative selling point. I suggest, however, that you check with your tax attorney before drawing up this depreciation division agreement.

"*Approach number three:* Sell 75 per cent of your equity for the $150,000, and begin collecting your share of the cash flow on a proportionate basis immediately.

"*Approach number four:* Get all the contractors to take 15% of their bids in the form of second mortgages to be paid off at the same interest and amortization rate as the first mortgage. This approach is especially relevant when work is scarce and the project has a high degree of feasibility.

"*Approach number five:* Offer the contractors 50% ownership for their $150,000, payable by leaving 15% of their contract amount in the deal.

"*Approach number six:* Give 50% ownership to the lender and have him increase his loan from $850,000 to $1,000,000. Many deals are structured this way, but I advise it only as a last resort. I don't like the lender also becoming the entrepreneur. If this trend is allowed to continue, the mortgagee will elbow himself more and more into ownership, until the idea man will become a mere puppet. Eventually, the lenders could smother the entrepreneur's creativity by buying him off with a fee. If this happens, both will suffer—the imaginative borrowers and the hard-headed lenders."

My architect friend was visibly impressed by the variety of options.

"Now could you take me a step further?" he ventured. "Where do I meet these men to offer them these deals?"

"You meet them at service clubs, charity affairs, in political action groups and athletic clubs. And when you meet them, be original in your presentation, so they remember what you say. You've got a good start already. With a name like Zeke, they'll remember you."

He smiled, and we parted. I sized up his chances of getting the $150,000 equity money about one to three. When he called me three months later, he was still working on it.

In contrast to the architect's difficulty in finding an investor, I know three young men who are literally pursued by investors offering them equity money. Here's why.

These three young men formed a building corporation. One was a light construction engineer with a lot of practical building know-how. Another was a professor of mathematics with a flair for convincing lenders on the feasibilities of projects. The third was an expert property manager. And in addition to their expertise, they had integrity. And they were all involved in community affairs.

By merging their talents, the three men offered investors in high income brackets a responsible and dependable investment vehicle. By using approach number one and two—the builders didn't need to resort to the last four approaches—they gave their investors 50 per cent equity, 50 to 90 per cent depreciation and limited liability. The last benefit is a very important one, and the way they worked it was to sign the project's mortgage in a corporation, and then immediately transfer the property to a partnership between themselves and the investors, but subject to the mortgage. This gave each member of the partnership depreciation but without any personal liability.

The ingenious builders improvised on approaches number one and two. They charged each project a 5% entrepreneurial fee, so that they drew $50,000 in cash out of a million dollar project as part of its cost. And, in addition, when the builders were able to buy a lot for $50,000 and rezone it so it would appraise for $100,000, they would put the lot into the project for $100,000 and earn another $50,000. In spite of all these improvisations, the young men had money chasing them instead of the other way around.

In less than 10 years, they built a $30,000,000 apartment building empire without a dime of their own money. Each is already a millionaire, and by the time they will quit, which may be in 15 years, each may be worth about 10 million dollars.

These men are making a valuable contribution to our community. They have not only been innovative in using other peoples money, but in new building and managerial techniques as well. They have built high rise buildings, garden apartments and town houses, and have kept them all. They do not sell.

Affluence, however, is beginning to take its toll. I play golf with one of them. I have a feeling he is beginning to decompress to a point where he is more interested in breaking 90 than in his next project. He can afford to slacken, and if he were to ask for my advice, I'd say, go ahead, decompress.

THERE WILL ALWAYS BE ROOM FOR
SMALL FRY BUILDERS LIKE YOSSEL

Who said the building business has no room for the small fry? I'd like to offer exhibit one—my friend, Yossel. Of course, my example is an unusual one, but what one can do, others can do also.

By the time Yossel was 9 years old, he had already saved $1,000 by selling newspapers. When his indigent father needed money to buy a small grocery store, his nine year old son loaned him the cash.

Yossel knows nothing about algebra or geometry. He learned to add and subtract, and with difficulty to multiply and divide. If someone were to ask him if Spinoza was the name of a vegetable or a man, he would have a 50 per cent chance of guessing the right answer. Yet this unlearned and earthy man built, financed and leased $6,000,000 worth of shopping centers. And he's adding to them at a time when big time professional builders have been stopped in their tracks by high costs, high interest rates and high real estate taxes.

How does he do it? Here are a few examples:

While cautious builders are grinding their operations to a halt, and businessmen are wringing their hands in anxiety, Yossel added 25,000 square feet of office space in one of his $2,000,000 shopping centers. While the professional analysts were issuing reports that in today's high labor market ordinary two-story office space construction costs $16 a square foot, Yossel built it for $10 a square foot.

How did he do it? Yossel never uses a general contractor. He subs everything out. But the ingenious way he uses his subs makes the difference—the difference between $16 a square foot and $10 a square foot.

For instance, when it came to carpeting his 25,000 square foot office building, which he leased to a single tenant, and which the latter wished to have partitioned mostly into 10 x 10 foot offices,

Yossel hit on a spectacular idea. He went to a large carpet wholesaler and bought remnants of regularly priced $8 a square yard carpeting for $1.25 a square yard. The wholesaler was eager to clear his stockroom of the scraps. Yossel sold his tenant on having different colored carpeting for the different offices, and promised to paint the various rooms to match the carpeting. His prospective tenant was delighted with getting a variety of color schemes, instead of the usual monotone effect.

But that wasn't all. It generally costs $1.50 to lay a square yard of carpeting, but, of course, Yossel didn't pay it. He found a retired carpet layer, buddied up with him, and during evenings while Yossel regaled him with stories about his youth, he had his carpet laid for 50 cents a square yard.

Yossel's tenant wanted moveable partitions. The bid for fabricated dividers was $450 for each 10 x 10 office. Yossel wasn't about to be taken for a ride. He asked his tenant if he would mind the warmer look of wooden moveable partitions. The tenant agreed. Yossel found a small lumber company to pre-cut the material needed for these partitions, hired two retired carpenters who were willing to work at $4 an hour instead of the $8 an hour the professionals charge, and built the 10 x 10 cubicles for $100 each.

Throughout the 1960's I had been paying no less than 60 cents a square foot to install ceiling tile in office buildings. I took a half a dozen bids from ceiling contractors, and I wasn't able to beat that price. But Yossel did. He bought the tile at a lower price than the general contractor can, at a remnant sale, and hired some retired "buddy" ceiling hangers, and gave his tenant a modern 60 cent a square foot ceiling that cost Yossel only 38 cents.

Improvising on masons, engineering and architectural services in the same manner, he built his 25,000 square foot office building addition to his shopping center for $250,000. And he leased it for $90,000 a year. This was about $1 less per square foot than the prevailing rent, but as any neophyte in the real estate business knows, when anyone can get $90,000 a year rent for a $250,000 investment, it's a spectacularly successful venture.

By beating the high labor costs, Yossel indirectly beat the high real estate taxes as well. When he showed his costs to the real estate assessor, he had to be influenced by them. The assessor cannot very well assess Yossel's building for $400,000 (the cost to knowledgeable builders) when he can show him certified bills showing that the cost was no more than $250,000. So, in addition to saving money on building, Yossel saves money on real estate taxes as well.

Yossel did a snow job on paying 8 per cent for interim financing when the more sophisticated borrowers were paying 9 and 10 per cent during the same year. How did he do it? He got out of the large banks and "buddied up" with presidents of small banks. He persuaded them to lend him money at 8 per cent because, he told them, "there will come a day when you'll be looking for borrowers and I'll stick with you, if you will now stick with me." Was he successful? He has a total credit line of about $700,000 with a half dozen small banks. They love his earthiness. They have confidence in his basic common sense, and they are in awe of his ingenuity.

There are not too many Yossels around, but if a summa cum laude in finance wants some practical knowledge on how to make money, I suggest he follow a man like Yossel around for a month and see how it's done.

Chapter 10

Innovative Management Is

What Converts Ordinary Property

into Astute Investments

USING THE PUBLIC MEDIA
TO PROMOTE AN INNOVATIVE IDEA

Used innovatively, newspapers, magazines, television and radio can sell an unusual idea—at no cost to you—more effectively than an advertising campaign.

Remember, the public media must have grist for its mill—to keep the readers and listeners interested. If what you have to sell is newsworthy or has a human interest feature, then let the news media report it. People pay more attention to what others say about your idea than your own horn-blowing. You can get publicity for nothing if your stories are genuinely newsworthy.

Several years ago, one of my salesmen got a few lucky breaks and sold a million dollars worth of real estate in his first year. That's news for the real estate pages of any newspaper. I prepared a news story, salted and peppered it with a few interesting incidents, and the real estate editor was impressed enough to run it in his paper with a picture of my salesman. He caught the eye of Milwaukee real estate investors, and from then on he went on to become a huge success.

This salesman had natural ability, but it might have taken him several years to get where this article got him in six months.

Before the advent of low down payments, when buyers needed as much as 50% cash to purchase a home, my organization developed a plan enabling people to buy properties with $100 down. Our costly advertising told this interesting story, but it reached only a limited number of people. It was not until we managed to get a news article into the paper, explaining how our plan worked, that our idea caught fire. The real estate editor put legs under our plan and away it went. We couldn't do it through advertising—it was too slow and too costly

At a time when a six-month listing for a residential property was the accepted custom, I advertised that we could sell a property in 30 days. A few readers were mildly interested. However, when we explained in a news article that taking 20 prospects through a home in 30 days created more excitement and motivation to buy, than taking the same number through in six months, our idea became a success, not only for our organization, but for others as well.

In the latter part of the 1950's, I got a brain storm. I called it Back-to-the-Small-Town Realty Company. The idea was to interest people in large cities who were caught in an unhappy rat race to move back to the small town from which many of them came. With their big city know-how, my ads said, big city people could revitalize small communities by buying small businesses, running them, and improving their lives in the process. I got little attention.

But when our newspapers gave this idea front page publicity, worth tens of thousands of dollars, it became publicly visible. Although my rescue operation did not meet with great success (I only moved a handful of people from the big cities to small towns), it was not the fault of the media. The fault lay with me for not pursuing it more diligently. Also, perhaps the immense financial problems which surfaced blocked these transfers. Without the free public media, however, to back what I still consider to be the most exciting real estate idea in America, all of my paid advertising would have gotten me nowhere.

This idea took a different turn a half a dozen years later. The details are described in Chapter 14.

Using the public media imaginatively is part of astute management, as what follows next so dramatically illustrates.

HOW TWO INNOVATIVE IDEAS ADDED $500,000 TO THE VALUE OF AN APARTMENT HOTEL

Who would be foolish enough to pay $1,700,000 for a dying
hotel that was losing $100,000 a year? I was! And if you take
about ten minutes to finish this story, you may learn to be
"foolish" too.

The hotel was in an attractive location, and yet convenient to
downtown. It had charm and flavor. Half of the hotel rooms were
for permanent guests and the other half for transients. However,
the hotel was a bit off the beaten track for transient hotel trade. A
"jumping" restaurant and a discotheque were on the premises, but
these two operations only jeopardized the tenancy of the permanent guests. The hotel was neither fish nor fowl—neither permanent residential nor hotel transient. The restaurant and the
discotheque were also operating in the red.

Why then did I pay $1,700,000 for a building that was losing
money. Because beyond it's apparent disadvantages, I saw a
magnificent fireproof structure on one of the most ideally located
square blocks of our city, a property that would cost $5,000,000
to reproduce. I couldn't resist the challenge to put it to its highest
and best use.

But you must be careful when you become intrigued with
meeting challenges because sometimes they can inundate you. I
was inundated with $300,000 of expenses during my first two
years of operation, in addition to my fixed operating costs. This
$300,000 had to be spent to stave off the tentacles of creeping
obsolescence. The electrical, heating and plumbing systems had
to be overhauled; many of the apartments needed painting,
carpeting and new furniture; the creaky elevators had to be given a
new lease on life, and dozens of miscellaneous mismanaged items
had to be attended to.

I closed down the discotheque and restaurant and leased it to a
gourmet cafe type operator for $15,000 a year. I discontinued the
transient hotel trade and concentrated on getting permanent
guests to move back into the building.

After three years of operation, with the help of a $1,500,000 mortgage and $500,000 of my own money, I still was losing $50,000 a year. Some challenges can indeed try one's soul and pocketbook.

Why couldn't I make a go of a building that had so many amenities—architectural uniqueness, ideal location, 200 charming apartments and, at the risk of being immodest, good management? I did some research. I found that the four other apartments hotels in our city of about the same size, vintage and location were doing worse than I was. I managed to get their operating statements, since each one was for sale.

In each case, the causes for the poor financial showing were the same. Higher operating costs compared to newer buildings, lower rents and higher vacancy rates. I was caught in the vise.

I offered it for sale, hoping that someone else had a hankering to test his innovative idea. About a dozen buyers looked at the operating statement and said no—except one.

"Yes," he said, "I'll buy your apartment hotel, if I can buy it with nothing down."

I must have looked surprised because he said with a twinkle in his eye:

"That shouldn't startle you. I've read your LEVERAGE book, where you say, 'any damn fool can buy a building for a million dollars if he has a million dollars. The trick is to buy a million dollar building with no money.' Well, I have no money, and I'd like to buy your building."

I smiled.

"What you didn't read, apparently, is that if you don't have any money you must have unusual ideas, and a track record showing that you've made some of them work. What's your idea and what's your track record?"

"Turn this building into communal living for the elderly. I managed such a building in Florida, and I think this idea could catch on in northern climates as well."

"But you begin losing $5,000 a month the moment you take this building over," I said. "Where are you going to get the money to make up the loss? It has to take you at least a year to turn this building around, even if your idea succeeds. Under these circumstances, aren't you asking too much to have me hand you a $2,000,000 project with nothing down?"

If he had said something original, and with sincerity, I might have been tempted to consider his proposition. I was a ripe seller—overripe, in fact. But all he said was:

"Think about it and let me know."

I was unable to detect the slightest hint of originality, and I was less than overwhelmed with his sincerity. That killed the deal for him. But his idea, I must confess, lived on. The more I thought about communal living for the elderly, the more I liked it. I couldn't research the idea because there was nothing like it in the Middle West.

Communal Living for the Elderly

If you are between 75 and 85 years old, too mobile and healthy to live in a nursing home, but too insecure and weak to live all alone in an apartment, and if there is no place for you with your children, where should you live? I innovated a real estate idea around trying to answer this question

Every city has thousands of people like these. Many of them are at nursing homes against their will. And many others live alone, corroding in loneliness, often too weak to market for food, let alone prepare and cook it.

Before we began looking for these people, we converted one of the luxury 2,500 square foot three-bedroom apartments overlooking the lake, into a charming, homelike, little restaurant. We built a kitchen, hired a chef, a few waitresses, and we were ready to begin.

We formulated a price program. For an efficiency and three meals a day with minimal care (that is, if any of the elderly became sick, we would be responsible for calling their children or doctor), the price was $350 a month; for a studio $400 a month; for a one bedroom $450 a month; and for a two bedroom $500 a month.

We couldn't use the free public media because we had nothing to say, nothing to show. So we formulated the ad depicted in Figure 1.

We began to get one or two phone inquiries a week, and we responded by sending our brochure which described our program in detail.

Then we sent letters to every doctor in Milwaukee County, asking them if they had any elderly patients who should not be in

Figure 1

(Courtesy *The Milwaukee Journal*, Milwaukee, Wisc.)

a nursing home, or who were too fragile to live alone and should be living with us, where with minimal care, they could prolong the independent management of their lives. We received only a few inquiries.

It took several months before we signed up our first member. We took several one-minute spots on a local television station. The response was weak. By the fifth month, we had only five members. To give some identity to the elderly who were living with us communally, that is, American Plan, we made them members of the Juneau Club. I was now losing more money than ever.

One morning, while I was shaving, I hit on an idea that our ad ought to appear on the television page, since the elderly are avid T.V. watchers. I called my advertising man and asked him to place the ad there. We received 15 calls. And from then on, every time our ad appeared on the T.V. page, our calls multiplied. Within six months, we had 20 members in the Juneau Club.

Now, I said to myself, I'm ready to put the public media to work. I had something to say.

I called the real estate editor of one of our papers and gave him the story.

"Here is a way for mobile elderly people to prolong the independent management of their lives," I told him. That was the theme I tried to emphasize.

The real estate editor did a mangnificent story with pictures of the restaurant, typical apartments and club members at one of their meals. Within one month, as a result of this story, we leased more apartments to Juneau Club members than we did in eight months at a cost of several thousand dollars.

We began getting inquiries from small towns within a 100 mile radius. I wrote a feature story about the Juneau Club, enclosed several pictures with it and I sent it to every small town newspaper within a hundred mile radius. About 10 of the 20 newspapers ran it. Our inquiries, as a result, increased and new members were added.

Then I hit on another idea. Why not a documentary by our public broadcasting television station? Sure enough! The station manager thought it was an excellent idea. The station taped the Juneau Club story—in color. More inquiries and more members. Then our leading commercial television station ran about a three minute news feature on the Juneau Club, and our unique way of caring for the elderly became a household word in Milwaukee's metropolitan area. Then followed an interview with a radio reporter, and later a slick monthly magazine catering exclusively to Milwaukee readers did a feature on the Juneau Club.

What paid advertising couldn't do, the free public media did. They gave our idea visibility and success.

Graduate students in sociology and psychology became interested in our idea, and I gave several lectures on the new concept of caring for the elderly. Retired lawyers, musicians, teachers, businessmen, engineers, school principals began to fill the Juneau Club ranks—people from the middle class and up.

Many mobile elderly came from nursing homes where they had been only because they were too feeble to fend for themselves with all the myraid duties of housekeeping. Others who lived alone in apartments or homes which were more of a chore to them than a comfort, came to live with us, and left the cleaning, shopping and cooking behind.

The Juneau Club became permanent resort living for them— nutritious meals prepared by a fine chef, served three times a day by friendly waitresses, maid service, switchboard security, friendships if they cared to make them, entertainment several times a week, immediate reporting to their children or doctor when they took sick—all this indirect care in an uninstitutionalized atmosphere where they led independent lives just like any of the other tenants in the building.

The Juneau Club idea spread across the length and breadth of our metropolitan area. Senior clubs and retirement clubs from our city and suburbs not only requested our literature, but invited us to speak at their meetings. I hired an articulate housewife, with a natural empathy for the elderly, to fill these speaking engagements.

One day one of the officials from Health, Education and Welfare came to look us over, to study what we were doing for the elderly. She was immensely impressed. In parting, she offered this very wise advice:

"Don't make the mistake of institutionalizing your idea. That is, don't turn your 200 apartments into a Juneau Club. If you do, you'll turn it into an old home. Don't have more than 75 members. Let them be a part, not the whole, of apartment hotel living. That's when you'll do them the most good."

I never forgot this advice. I understand now what she meant when I see the octonegerians ogling the mini-skirted actresses who come through our lobby, make friends with the young couples who stay with us, chat with the visiting professors who come to lecture to our urban universities and visit with the executive trainees whose average two to three month stays give the elderly a chance to see new faces.

And this leads me into innovative idea No. 2—converting one-third of the apartment hotel into a Home Away From Home.

Home Away From Home

You are an executive trainee away from home being prepared to assume a new position in a new city. You have to be away for three months. Perhaps you have your wife along, or even your children. You can't rent an apartment because the owner or manager wants you to sign a year's lease. You don't want to live in a hotel because it is too expensive and too busy. Where shall you stay?

Or, you are a professor who has been invited to lecture for three months at an urban university. You'll have the same problem as the executive trainee.

In Milwaukee, you'll have no problem. You'll stay at our apartment hotel where we have set aside about 70 units for our home away from home tenants. We do not demand a year's lease, nor do we ask you to pay the high transient daily hotel rates. The average daily rental of an average hotel in our city is about $18, or $540 a month. At our home away from home, the monthly rate for a furnished efficiency is $225; a studio $275; a one-bedroom apartment $325; and a two-bedroom, two-bath luxury apartment $450. These monthly rentals reduced to daily rates amount to $7, $9, $11 and $15, respectively. We're giving them larger quarters, kitchens, quiet atmosphere and home charm for less than half what they'd have to pay for much smaller hotel rooms.

It's a pioneering real estate idea which has caught on because it meets the needs of a mobile society, of job training and retraining, and of the popularity of exchanging lecturing professors. And that's not all. Our home away from home is used locally by people whose homes or apartments are destroyed by fires, by those who need a temporary "home" between buying and selling a home, or by a new family moving into town looking for a home. And a month doesn't pass without at least one irate husband, after a spat with his wife, coming to our hotel to "cool off" for a month or two.

However, our main monthly users are industrial trainees from out of town, visiting professors, people who live in the south and come to Milwaukee for the summer, theatrical people, and families from foreign countries who have reason to stay in our city for several months.

Our home away from home idea succeeded because there is a definite need for a monthly transiency as there is for a daily transiency. Only it's on a smaller scale. That such a need is there is borne out by the fact that 60 of the large corporations in our city use our facilities on a regular basis.

But it wasn't an easy idea to sell because we didn't operate as a hotel, and the housing recruiting personnel of large corporations don't like to experiment with placing their out-of-town guests. They want to be sure, and the transient hotels or motels are the obvious answer. That we finally were able to prevail is an indication that this unusual market can be cracked—in any city in America.

The home away from home required different promotional techniques than the Juneau Club. First, we were unable to rely on the free public media. Both the financial and real estate editors of The Milwaukee Journal turned me down when I submitted an article on how the home away from home idea was meeting a new need in our mobile society—hotels by the month. I don't blame them—it didn't have the poignant human interest of the Juneau Club.

However, the Milwaukee Sentinel did run a feature article on how the home away from idea was meeting a hotel need, and I quickly followed it up by placing the following ad in the financial pages of both papers.

The inquiries from the ads (which were very expensive) did not produce the results we hoped for. The article did not stir up any interest either. Here was an innovative money-making idea, but I was having difficulty putting it across.

Sometimes we don't see the obvious. The housewife who did such an excellent job telling the Juneau Club story to the elderly was my answer. I called her in and said;

"I want you to print the same copy we ran in the newspapers on cards and send about 500 of them to every personnel director of all companies in our metropolitan area employing more than 100 people. Then I'd like you to follow up the mailing by making a personal call to each one of them, telling the home away from home story in your own inimitable style."

That did it—direct mail advertising, followed up by personal solicitation. What worked for the Juneau Club didn't work for home away from home. We had to devise something new—and it turned out to be obvious, inexpensive and effective. The leading industrial and business firms are using our home away from home regularly, and the number is growing. And why shouldn't they? They're getting better accommodations at half the price. It's one of those ideal deals, good for buyer and seller.

Efficiencies which used to bring $120 a month from permanent guests now rent for $225 a month to home away from home users. And that's only $7 a day, compared to $18 a day for a smaller room in a transient hotel. A visitor from another country with his wife and one or two children can stay with us in a two-bedroom, two-bath luxury apartment for $450 a month, or less per day than it costs for any ordinary room in any ordinary motel. Is it any wonder that one-third of our apartments are used by our grateful home away from home clientele?

This new idea was not only an economic boost for us, but a morale booster to the Juneau Club members as well. They saw new faces every week as new trainees, theater people and visiting professors came and went. The changing scene was one of their intriguing subjects of conversation. And sometimes one of the elderly struck up a conversation with one of the monthly tenants on the go—to their mutual benefit. Many of the Juneau Club members were the doers of their generation, and when a doer of the present generation took the time to talk, he was amply rewarded.

Our building now had an interesting mix, one-third Juneau Club, one-third home away from home and one-third permanent guests, and our operating statement was just as interesting.

When I purchased the apartment hotel, the yearly gross rent was $350,000, and my expenses, including the debt service on a $1,500,000 mortgage were $400,000— a loss of $50,000 a year. By adding the Juneau Club and home away from home ideas into the income picture, my gross rent rose to $550,000 a year, expenses to $475,000 a year, leaving a cash flow of $75,000. Without these two ideas, there was no way of keeping the 200 apartment hotel in the black under the constant payment pressure of a $1,500,000 debt service.

The chances of doing better are excellent because we're still in the initial stages of the home away from home idea. Once I can persuade the public media to recognize that we're pioneering something in America, and they begin to give it visibility, our ratio of occupancy could be 60% home away from home, and 40% Juneau Club. When that happens, our gross rent will jump to $650,000 a year, and our expenses, I believe, can be stabilized at $500,000.

We can give hundreds of dying hotels in America a new lease on life by implementing these two new ideas. But what is far more important, we can give a new way of life to deserving elderly who have made their contribution, and now need our help. And we can meet a new need for the busy people of America too, by offering them the quiet charm of home when they're away from home.

When we can make money and help people at the same time—what more can we ask?

CREATIVE MANAGEMENT IS A
POWERFUL MONEY MAKING TOOL

Creative management is many-faceted. It is knowing how to reconstruct an operating statement, when and how to change one use of property to another, and how to finance it astutely. Then come the more obvious prerequisites, that of knowing how to maintain buildings and satisfying tenants. In addition, there are all kinds of variables and nuances which can lead a property either to the brink of bankruptcy, or to profitable heights.

Some of the most knowledge-laden people flop at it while near illiterates make a success of it. Why don't people succeed in property management in proportion to their education? For the same reason that some people have good judgment and others do not, and education makes little difference. Unusual managerial ability is like having an almost computerized intuition as to what will work and what will not work.

I have seen a $400,000 property mismanaged into a $200,000 value, and a $200,000 property, through a creative change of use, double in value, and in each case, in a matter of a few years.

Putting a property to its highest and best use must always be linked to this corollary. That the owner also raises its net return. For instance, changing a warehouse to a medical building and losing money in the process is not changing the property to its highest and best use because it then loses its feasibility. It fails economically.

Creative management is highly profitable. An unsung property owner who hardly creates a ripple in his community can earn more money through astute management than many top-salaried sales executives, professors, lawyers and doctors. Of course, I am measuring success here in terms of money. In terms of service to their communities, the professional men may contribute much more.

I do not want to give the impression that wise managers of property do not need any knowledge. They should have basic building knowledge. However, acquiring that knowledge is a lot easier than acquiring the knowledge needed in medicine, teaching or law.

A property owner is always walking a tightrope of good and bad judgments. One wrong decision could bankrupt an investor. That's where he's more vulnerable than those in the professions

What are some of the factors that go into making a right or wrong decision? Let's take an example:

A fireproof, six-story steel and concrete warehouse, located near a hospital in a congested area, lost its feasibility as a warehouse. Its owner was losing money. The warehouse use could no longer support the building. What to do with it?

To reproduce the 100,000 square foot building would cost about a million dollars. The owner tried to sell it for $700,000, then $500,000. Several years later, I bought it for $200,000. But even that low price could have been too high, unless I found a new use to make a feasible project out of it.

To have turned it into an apartment building would have been a colossal error because apartment rentals could not have supported the cost of remodeling it. Renting it as loft space, or as a wholesale distribution center, was not feasible because of high labor handling costs in a multi-story building, and besides, it was the wrong location for it.

The key to a successful project was a 400 bed hospital a block away. I remodeled the warehouse into a modern medical office building and generated a rental of $250,000 a year. It was probably the only key, because office space can be sold for $1.50 per square foot more than apartment space. The cost of remodeling it was so high ($1,200,000) that anything less than high-priced medical space would have thrown the building into the red.

The Bread and Butter of Management

A careless owner can lose thousands of dollars a year by calling in high-priced contractors everytime something goes wrong with the mechanical nerves of a building. A good all-around maintenance man could easily plug up that needless drain of money. I have known managers who have been paying 10 cents a square foot to paint one coat on plaster or drywall year after year, when they could have had it done for as low as 5 cents a square foot. I have seen well-educated managers overpaying as much as 20 to 30 per cent by heating with oil, when they could have been heating with gas and oil standby, and thus save thousands of dollars. One sophisticated property manager of a utility company lost $38,000 in ten years because he wasn't aware of it. There are dozens of ways a property manager can lose or save money in heating, painting, laying floor tile, hanging ceilings, electric fixtures, cleaning, light bulbs, and the dozens of other maintenance problems.

Perhaps I can best dramatize the importance of cutting down expenses by pointing out that for every $1,000 saved we add $10,000 to the value of a building when we decide to sell it. And the same is true for every $1,000 raise in income. What quicker way to earn $100,000 than by a combination of minimizing expenses and maximizing income we increase the net income of a building by $10,000, and thus increase its value by $100,000?

Often a little wisdom is more effective than a lot of know-how. I bought an 80-year-old office building 20 years ago that was three-quarters empty. I had to do something to attract tenants. One of the problems was the lobby. It was of a forlorn, gay ninety-ish architecture. Do I powder the lobby's face for about $1,000, or give it a complete $25,000 face lifting? I remember doing a lot of financial soul searching. Fortunately, I decided to merchandise its old charm for $1,000. I filled the building with $1.50 a square foot paying tenants, and several years later a bank bought it as part of a site upon which it built a $20,000,000 bank structure. Had I spent $25,000 for remodeling the lobby, I would have had $24,000 less today.

Some years ago, I bought an old building where the key tenant was an art gallery. I called in an architect to give me some ideas on how to improve the entrance. The wooden doors were 15 feet high and the paint was peeling. I wanted something new and modern. After the architect looked at it for 15 minutes, at times closing his eyes in deep thought, he came up with the answer—a wise answer.

"Leave the door exactly as it is," he said. "However, I want you to remove all the old paint and antique it in a bluish-grey."

I was ready to spend several thousand dollars. His suggestion cost me $50. I gave him $50 for his half-hour's advice. It was the wisest $50 I spent because when the stately doors were antiqued they became the focal point of the building. I bought old world charm at a very low price.

An innovative owner will add special physical amenities to induce tenants to stay in his building. In apartment projects these range from roof gardens with natural grass, swimming pools and saunas to putting greens, party rooms, tennis courts, and even an exclusive little restaurant catering primarily to tenants and their guests.

These special amenities attract renters and reduce tenant turnover. They more than pay for themselves, because they justify higher rentals and reduce the cost of painting and maintenance through reduction of tenant turnover. And special amenities always produce more appreciative occupants.

How To Get And Maintain Near 100% Occupancy

Keeping the occupancy close to 100 per cent is an indispensable factor in astute management. The operating cost of an 80 per cent occupied building is almost the same as one that's 100 per cent occupied. The top 20 per cent rental is, therefore, pure profit. It's a cardinal point to remember.

The relevant question is, how do we attain and keep 100 per cent occupancy? A few hints and insights.

In industrial and commercial leasing, and especially in office leasing, it is not wise to wait too close to lease expirations before negotiating renewals. In 3-to-5 year leases, begin talking about renewal no later than six months before expiration, and negotiations to renew a ten-year lease should begin about the end of the 9th year. If you don't think early enough about renewal, the tenant will, and if some alert salesman gets his ear by the time you get to him, you may be too late. Hundreds of leases and millions of dollars are lost every year in every city through apathetic lease follow-up.

Getting new tenants is as innovative as dreaming up feasible projects. Among the commonly used methods to ferret out tenants for commercial and industrial buildings are: cold turkey calls, direct mail, newspaper ads, free public media and word of mouth. But each of these can be effective, or ineffective, depending on how we use it.

Cold turkey calling must be selective. There is no point calling $3 a square foot office space users when you have $7 a square foot office space for rent. Don't try to sell Cadillacs to Volkswagen customers. Don't spray your shots on random calls. Spend as much time thinking about the kind of call you're going to make as the time to make the call.

Use the same target approach in direct mail advertising. One hundred personalized letters with names carefully chosen can bring a higher response than 1,000 impersonal letters thoughtlessly broadcast. And it's less expensive.

Newspaper advertising can drain your budget in a hurry if you continue to use copy that lacks imagination and response. When I built a 200,000 square foot building in 1956, I wasn't making much headway with my advertising until I signed a large automobile company as a tenant and placed an eye-catching ad that played up a glowing endorsment of the building by the company's branch manager.

That ad did it. Two more AAA companies signed up as a direct result of this ad. A dozen others followed suit when I used the same format and quoted the managers of the AAA tenants in the same manner. A great deal of the success of filling the building was due to this type of effective advertising.

Of course, innovative use of the public media is a must in the promotional management of a project. If you don't know how to dovetail free advertising with paid advertising, you're only cooking on a rear burner, and if the paid advertisement is weak, it could be on a low flame, to boot. When you're not innovative, you become the fodder out of which opportunities are created for others.

Word of mouth advertising is the least expensive and often miraculously effective. I use the word miraculous to dramatize the importance of "planting seed" as a means of advertising. If you have office space to rent, tell people about it—at Rotary, at parent-teacher meetings, at political rallies, at church, yes, even to cleaning ladies. A charwoman of a building I owned was told by my manager that we had a beautiful office suite that was vacant. She told it to another tenant in the building, who mentioned it at bridge to a doctor, who was looking for office space. The doctor in turn asked his insurance man what he thought of our building. This insurance man happened to be an acquaintance of mine. He told me several weeks later about the doctor's inquiry. I immediately called the doctor. I had exactly what he needed. We signed a five year lease for $6,000 a year.

Hundreds of leases are consummated as a result of word of mouth for millions of dollars every year in every city. I call it serendipity.

I have stressed that property management is many-faceted. You can be an astute financier, an expert in getting tenants and have expertise in maintaining property, but unless you develop the host-guest relationship between landlord and tenant, you have not put the blue ribbon on the complete package of ideal management.

Host-Guest Relationship Between Landlord and Tenant Is Practical

Only the innovative property owner sees the practical potentialities of implementing the host-guest relationship between landlord and tenant. It is not only commercially sound, but personally fulfilling.

For instance, only a thoughtful, host-like manager will write a welcome note to a tenant who is moving into his building. It is so easy to do and yet so few do it. After spending a great deal of money to get a tenant, we certainly ought to protect our investment by making the initial move to keep him.

In one of our apartment projects, when about ten tenants moved in on the first of the month, we took them all to lunch because they were harried from the chores of moving. These tenants never stopped talking about it. The goodwill we built with this gesture was priceless. It cannot be bought It can only be earned through caring.

The understanding owner knows that there can be a few snarling tenants, but there should never be a snarling landlord. Empathy is a cardinal virtue.

One property manager I knew happened to be brilliant. He had all the technical answers. He knew buildings and he knew prices, but he lacked empathy. He **paid** the price for it. Instead of becoming a top-notch property owner, he sank into managerial mediocracy and finally phased out of the management business altogether.

We should not treat all tenants alike. It is not realistic because they are not all alike. Some don't want to be catered to, they like their privacy. Others love it. If we're perspicacious, we will treat tenants differently to fit their varying personalities.

If someone falls behind in his rent for a good reason, that's not the time to push him and make him uncomfortable. Listen to his story sympathetically. Give him understanding, instead of, "Everybody here pays on time." A struggling artist tenant of mine fell behind several months in his rent. And because I didn't crowd him, he became one of my best friends. He went on to become one of the leading artists in our state.

If someone demands a little extra care, a little extra attention, give it to him. Wouldn't you do it if he were your guest? And you don't have to assume that others will want the same extra attention because most tenants will leave you alone. When you care for the few, the many, who don't ask for the extra care, will appreciate it too.

A Young Man Uses the Logic of Philosophy
To Assemble a $100,000,000 Real Estate Empire

A young man who majored in philosophy but was not good enough to get a teaching job, turned to property management and assembled a $100,000,000 real estate investment portfolio. He started as a $75 a week rent collector, but soon his uncanny ability to size up the potential of a building became visible. He made others see it, too, because they were eager to back him with mortgage and equity money. Eventually, he made millionaires out of them and himself.

His brilliance in upgrading buildings to new uses and increasing their net was phenomenal. Within six years, the young man had purchased an assortment of apartments, office buildings, hotels and shopping centers—always with an equity position for himself— and he became one of the real estate wonders of New York.

I asked him at a commercial property seminar where he was one of the speakers:

"How did you make the transition from philosophy to property management?"

"Logic, my friend," he answered. "Philosophy is sheer logic and so is property management. Creating real estate wealth is targeting the wisdom of philosophy on property problems. It's that simple."

I know a young man who did, on a small scale, what our philosopher friend did on a grand scale. His specialty was buying sick buildings and making them healthy, which in turn made him wealthy. He was not interested in new buildings, nor in well-managed buildings. Someone else's headaches became his opportunities. He snooped the city for poor managers and ailing buildings, and they usually went together. He was a small operator. He dealt in small buildings—four families, eight families, a twenty-family building was the largest he owned.

Using his own money and sometimes that of his relatives and his friends, he managed to put together deals which in 10 years provided him with a net of about $35,000 a year. This is an excellent earning record compared to the average lawyer who nets about $20,000 a year and the average doctor who clears about $30,000 a year. And since this young man had only a high school education, it points up that creative property management offers unusual opportunities for making money.

There are few businesses where there is more room for innovation in creating wealth than in real estate management. In a complex society, new needs are constantly arising which have to be met by new real estate thinking. As we moved from the cave, to the hut, to the home, to the castle, to the cathedral and to the skyscraper, it was always the innovator who was at the forefront of change. He thrilled to the vibration of new ideas as he set out to meet new needs of people.

We can live more vibrantly too, if we look at property management not as a mere rent collection exercise, but as an exciting, many-splendored activity in which we can make a relevant contribution to society, and earn a lot of money as well.

---

*Courtesy of *The Milwaukee Journal.* Journal Square, Milwaukee, Wis.

PART III

THESE IDEAS
BUILD FORTUNES

Chapter 11

Ideas that Change Ordinary Men into Super Salesmen

**HOW THE FOUR-WAY-BENEFIT TEST
INCREASES INVESTMENT REAL ESTATE SALES**

The rule of thumb in evaluating a real estate investment is: Subtract annual expenses from gross rent and then capitalize the net income. For example, if the gross rent of a certain property is $20,000 a year and the expenses are $10,000 a year, the net income is $10,000. If you want a 10% return on your money, you should be willing to pay $100,000 for the property. It's that simple.

But it gets complicated and crucially important when you consider the mortgage variable. That's because by borrowing money you can raise the rate of return from 10%, as in the above illustration, to 20% or 40%, depending on how much equity money is invested, and the amount of cash flow it generates.

Suppose you borrow $90,000 on a $100,000 property, and develop a $1,500 a year cash flow—the amount left after all fixed expenses and the debt service on the $90,000 mortgage. Then the return on your $10,000 down payment is 15%.

But that's only the beginning. There are three other items that swell the rate of return on the $10,000 down payment: (1) The value of the yearly amortization on the $90,000 mortgage; (2) The value of tax sheltering income through accelerated depreciation, and (3) The yearly value that inflation adds to the property.

Unless we can explain in simple terms how a real estate investment works for us in these four ways, we are not telling the full story. What looks on the surface like a 10% return can indeed be a 25% or 45% return

The capitalized rate of return is only the visible part of a real estate investment. Like the visible part of an iceberg, it only reveals the obvious. To sell investment real estate, we must be able to explain the invisible part of the iceberg—the larger part that the average investor does not see, does not take into account and, in many cases, does not understand.

To explain the advantages of a real estate investment in depth, it should be presented in what I like to call the "four way benefit test", or the four sources of income which make up the full rate of return. Let me elaborate

EXAMPLE NO. 1–RESIDENTIAL INVESTMENT

Let's suppose you want to sell a 16-family apartment building priced at $170,000. The gross rent is $25,000 a year and the fixed expenses are $8,000, leaving a net income of $17,000. If the buyer paid all cash, he would realize a return of 10%.

Now let's see how the rate of return increases when the buyer borrows $140,000 at 7½% on a 25-year amortization. The buyer's $30,000 down payment, if he's in the 50% tax bracket, can be shown to earn 44%. Unbelievable? Not at all. Here it is.

Benefit No. 1–Cash Flow Return

Gross Income	$25,000
Fixed Yearly Expenses	$ 8,000
Yearly Debt Service on $140,000 (rounded out)	$12,500
Total expense and debt service	$20,500
Cash Flow	$ 4,500
$4,500 cash flow divided by $30,000 investment =	15% return

Benefit No. 2–Amortization Return

Average yearly amortization of principal during the first 10 years of payments on $140,000 mortgage is about $2,840 a year. $2,840 divided by $30,000 = ... 9.4% return

Benefit No. 3—Gain From Tax Shelter

Straight line depreciation on 40-year life is 2½%. Accelerated allowable depreciation to second buyer is 125% of straight line or 3.125%. Assuming a $10,000 land value and $160,000 building value, the first year depreciation would be 3.125 x $160,000, or $5,000.

This would tax shelter $5,000 of $7,340, the latter being the sum of the $4,500 cash flow and $2,840 of average amortization. Thus, if the buyer is in the 50% tax bracket, the tax sheltered $5,000 is worth an extra $2,500 in tax savings, which is an 8.33% return on his $30,000 investment, that is, $2,500 divided by $30,000 = ...8.33% return

Benefit No. 4—Return From Inflationary Gains

Assuming that the 16-family depreciates at 2½% a year, and assuming that our inflation continues at 4¼% a year, it is safe to assume that the value of the 16-family would increase at the rate of 2% of $170,000, or $3,400 a year. This increase of $3,400 divided by $30,000 = ...11.33% return

The sum of the rates of return *44%*

Thus, the buyer of the 16-family can be earning 44% a year on his $30,000 investment.

This is not an exaggerated representation. And if the buyer purchases the same 16-family while it is under construction, he's allowed 200% accelerated depreciation, instead of 125%. Keeping all the other facts constant, his rate of return would then be increased by about 5%, for a total of 49%. This sounds unbelievable, but it is out of an understanding and implementation of these specifics that ordinary salesmen become super salesmen, and those who take their advice become astute investors.

Let me cite personal proof as to the soundness of the four-way benefit test. In 1960, I built a 94-unit apartment building at a cost of $650,000, and mortgaged it for $500,000. I have averaged a 43% return a year on my $150,000 equity through 1970 because the cash flow during the 10 years amounted to about $15,000 a year, or $150,000, and because most of it was tax sheltered, it was worth about *$250,000* to me. Also, at the end of 10 years, the difference between the approximately $400,000 mortgage balance and the selling price of $950,000, if I wanted to sell it, was

$550,000. The amortization and inflation did their jobs—
$400,000 worth—the sums of $100,000 profit through amortization and $300,000 profit through inflation. I, therefore, earned $650,000 during 10 years, or $65,000 a year, for the stupendous rate of 43% return per year on my $150,000 initial investment—if I chose to sell the property.

I can point to dozens of similar cases. In the face of this information, why should anyone want to invest in 4% municipals, 6% savings and loan certificates, or even in 8% bonds? The answer, I suppose, is that the four-way benefit test of a real estate investment was never properly explained to him.

EXAMPLE NO. 2–COMMERCIAL INVESTMENT

Let's see what happens to the rate of return on a building leased to a large supermarket chain which an investor purchases during construction so he can take the allowable 150% accelerated depreciation. A second purchaser is allowed only 100% depreciation.

Let's assume these facts; the gross rent is $40,000 a year and the net rent is $30,000 a year, with the lessee absorbing all the real estate tax increases. Also, the length of the supermarket lease is 15 years, the price of the building is $350,000, the down payment is $100,000 and the mortgage is $250,000 at 8% interest with a 20 year amortization.

Without the mortgage variable, it is merely an 8½% return deal. That is, the $30,000 net return divided by the $350,000 price. But now let's inject the mortgage factor, and give it the four-way benefit test and see what the rate of return really is when all benefits are added—when the hidden part of the iceberg is brought into full view:

Benefit No. 1–Cash Flow Return

Gross rent	$40,000
Expenses:	
Real Estate Taxes & Miscellaneous	$10,000
Debt Service on $250,000 loan at 8%	
20 year amortization	$25,000
Total Expenses	$35,000
Cash Flow	$ 5,000
$5,000 cash flow divided by $100,000	
investment = ...	<u>5% return</u>

Benefit No. 2—Amortization Return

The average yearly amortization of the principal during the first 10 years of payments on the $250,000 mortgage at 8%, 20 years, is about $8,000 a year, divided by $100,000 investment = ... <u>8% return</u>

Benefit No. 3—Tax Shelter Depreciation Gain

Straight line depreciation on the 20-year life of a one-purpose building is 5%. Since accelerated 150% is allowable to first owner of building, the depreciation rate would be 7½%. Assume that the land cost is $50,000 and the building cost is $300,000, then the depreciation the first year would be $300,000 x 7½%, or $22,500. Since the depreciation amount would decrease each year, let's figure that the average depreciation for the first 10 years would be about $13,000 a year. This $13,000 average depreciation during the first 10 years would tax shelter the $8,000 average amount amortized each year, as well as the $5,000 cash flow for a total of $13,000. If the buyer is in a 50% income tax bracket, he would save $6,500 in taxes, which is tantamount to a 6½% additional return on his $100,000 investment. Thus, his benefit from tax shelter depreciation is . . . . <u>.6½% return</u>

Benefit No. 4—Return From Inflationary Gain

Assuming that the property depreciates at the rate of 2½% a year, and again assuming that inflation increases at the rate of 4½% a year, this would increase the value of the A & P store 2% of $350,000, or $7,000 a year. This is worth 7% on the $100,000 investment, or . . . . <u>7% return</u>

Total rate of return per year on $100,000 investment = ... <u>26½%</u>

This is not bad for a no risk, trouble-free, backed by a multi-million dollar lessee, investment. The only risk is picking a location that is going to have good residual value. With our population explosion, however, most food store locations become better rather than worse, which means that at the end of 15 years, the rental could increase due to the double stimulation of increased population and inflation.

It takes more time to prepare a sales presentation showing the invisible parts of a real estate investment, but it pays off. It stimulates recalcitrant buyers to act because they see the full anatomy of a deal for the first time. When the four-way benefits are out in the open, they think twice before they turn down a 44% or 26 1/2% real estate investment in favor of a 4% municipal, 6% certificate or 8% bond.

This four-way benefit test is a dynamic selling idea which can transform ordinary men into super salesmen. It works because its selling magic is supported by indisputable facts

A BOLD TROUBLESHOOTER BUYS A $5,000,000 PROJECT WITH A $25,000 NOTE

Occasionally, the bigger the operator, the bigger his mistakes. In this case, an experienced developer messed up a five million dollar project and provided an opportunity for an inexperienced salesman to capitalize on his mistake.

The developer had been extremely successful in several office-building projects in another part of the country, and decided to build one in a midwestern city.

When I read in the newspaper where he was planning to erect his 200,000 square foot office building, I was amazed. He made several glaring judgment errors.

He obviously did not have the "feel" of the city. First, he chose to build his office building on the west side of a river where the demand for office space was less and the rate about $1 per square foot lower than similar office space east of the river. Second, he picked a time when the city was overbuilt. He apparently didn't know that we had about 250,000 square feet of vacant Grade A space. Third, he overpaid for the land by about $500,000. And, fourth, he had a weak sales force selling space in a weak market. To make matters worse, the building was architecturally ordinary.

Two years after the building was ready for occupancy, only one of its twenty floors was occupied. When the project was offered to me for sale, it was in deep financial trouble. The interim loan of three million dollars was in default with about $300,000 of unpaid interest. About a dozen contractors were looking for $700,000 of unpaid bills. The real estate tax arrearage was about $200,000. It was rumored that the developer had $250,000 of his own money in the sinking project.

However, the point of the story is not how a large developer fumbled a project, but how a young man picked up the ball and scored on an idea which turned him into a super salesman.

The young man, let's call him Austin, learned about the foreclosure-ripe project, and made the following offer to the harassed owner:

"It's obvious you're about to throw in the sponge on your deal. Let me show you how you can recoup $25,000. It's not much, but what's more important, I might be able to pacify your creditors by bailing the building out of a hole

"What's your great idea?" the developer asked.

"Quit-claim the building to me for $25,000. Since I don't have the cash, I'll sign a note, payable upon my successful disposition of the building. Whatever profit I make over $25,000 is mine. I'm ready to move my family to this city for as long as it takes to either fill the building, or sell it."

The developer sold him that quit claim deed for the $25,000 note, and, of course, for the more important possibility that the bright young man might tidy up the many loose ends of his abandoned project.

When I met Austin, he had already leased three floors of the building, and was developing interest for several more. And he was using the rent money, not to make payments to the bank, contractors or toward delinquent real estate taxes, but to complete interior partitions so he could rent more space. The creditors were grumbling, but none made a move toward foreclosure.

"Why should they try to move me out," Austin was telling me at lunch one day. "I'm putting the building on its feet. If I stop, nothing will happen. Also, a judge may not be in such a hurry to get rid of me if he sees I'm the only one breathing some income life into the building."

"But the real answer to my problem," he continued, "is to find a wealthy businessman who is in the half a million dollar a year ordinary income bracket. The building now loses $300,000 a year, but if someone with that yearly income takes it over, in two years, with the help of Uncle Sam, who would be picking up the losses, this building could be filled. Then this wealthy angel could become wealthier because, instead of losing $300,000 a year, he could earn $100,000 a year and have it all tax sheltered. Know any man like that?"

I smiled and looked at the young man in amazement. What a long shot he was taking. The seasoned developer gave up—he had no time for a hopeless situation. He was exploring new fields to conquer. But our hero had nothing to lose—only his time.

I suggested several names which he cross checked with a list he was accumulating from others like me. Methodically and unhurriedly he was presenting his multi-million-dollar project to the financial "Who's Who" of the city. Some wouldn't see him; others paid little attention to him; some were intrigued, but all said no.

A door finally opened. A wealthy oil man became interested in Austin's proposition. He had the ordinary income to shelter the loss. He paid Austin $125,000 for the deed.

The "angel" paid the real estate tax arrearage, and made more than a fair settlement with the contractors. Some of the smaller ones were saved from bankruptcy by his generosity. He was in a position to wipe them out if he wanted to. He paid off the interim bank loan and arranged for permanent financing. He hired a capable young man (who used to work for me) as his property manager and leasing agent. Within two years, as Austin predicted, the building was filled and it became a financial success.

We need catalytic agents like Austin. They make things happen. They become the super salesmen through the force of their innovative ideas. Look at the good he has done.

He shored up a sagging deal where everybody was losing money—the developer, the banker, the contractors and city hall. A vacant building is wealth going to waste. His innovative idea made a wealthy man wealthier, but in the process, others gained too.

Austin gained $100,000. When he said good-bye to me, I asked him:

"Got anything on the hook?"

"I've got something in Florida that sounds like a whopper. I'll be there for about a year. If you've got something interesting, call me."

The only danger Austin and others like him face is that in taking wild chances they're likely to become wild gamblers. That's when they're apt to lose their integrity and with it their stability. And that's when their innovation, no matter how unusual, can begin to lose credibility. They often become the "rolling stones" of their profession. It's a rootless and insecure existence.

A NEW ANGLE TO THE CONDOMINIUM IDEA
TURNS AVERAGE MEN INTO SUPER SALESMEN

I thought of it, my salesmen pounced on it, and we all cashed in on it. Here is the idea in a nutshell.

Every city has thousands of parcels of real estate with two or more properties on one lot. They can be cottages, or duplexes, or a combination of both. In some cases, we've found as many as a dozen properties on one lot having one legal description. They were sold as investment properties because no one thought of subdividing them and selling each parcel separately.

I backed into this idea by accident, and when I saw its potential, I went after it with gusto. As a result, our organization earned hundreds of thousands of dollars, and several of my ordinary salesmen became super salesmen in the process.

In 1950, I bought 6 cottages on one lot for $3,000. Each previous owner had milked it as an investment, putting in a minimum of repairs, and extracting the maximum rent. By the time I bought the cottages, they were wrecks. They had wooden basements and outside plumbing.

As I was modernizing them, building new block basements and installing inside plumbing, an idea struck me. Why not sell each cottage individually? At that time, I had never heard of the word "condominium" but that's exactly what it developed into—the "horizontal condominium."

I split the legal decription into six ownerships, and sold each cottage separately. I sold them within 30 days for a total of $5,000 profit. And the new owners subsequently resold them for additional profits.

Here was an idea that stopped blight and created more individual ownerships. I praised this profit-making idea at one of our sales meetings.

Most of my salesmen let the idea slide off their orthodox heads. They were doing well selling properties the old way, and didn't get excited about splitting properties and making money a new way. But I noticed far away looks on the faces of three of my salesmen. After the meeting, they circled me and I could almost feel their excited "let's go to it" vibrations.

We went on a buying spree, paying good prices for three, five, eight or any number of properties on one lot, remodeling them, subdividing them, and then selling them at good prices to individual owners. But even with good profits to us, the purchasers were still getting good buys.

We had to do an educational job with the savings and loan associations in financing these horizontal condominiums. Sharing common land areas was strange to them, and they penalized the loans by cutting down the appraisal value. This hurt our profits, but the buyers got better buys.

What a difference 20 years has made. The most sophisticated lending agencies not only mortgage horizontal condominiums today, but vertical condominiums as well. Today condominium owners not only share land areas, but apartment halls as well.

After we had split or subdivided about 100 parcels into about 500 ownerships, one of the three salesmen who was implementing the buying, splitting and selling program for me, came into my office.

"George," he said, "I'm leaving your organization and going into business for myself. I'm going to concentrate on nothing else but splitting properties. It's the greatest idea I've come across in this office."

"Good luck," I said. "I'm sorry to lose you, but I can't say I blame you. It is a fantastic idea."

He was an easygoing, average salesman before he learned about the horizontal condominium. But it transformed him. He pounced on it with a vengenance. It seemed to awaken all of his sleeping ego-packed energy.

Of course, he became a huge success. He hired several salesmen and subdivided just about everything that was divisible in our town. The innovative horizontal condominum idea turned him into a wealthy man.

Of course, I didn't exactly stand still either. I began to improvise on the idea. I bought 12 new eight-family units on several acres of land. I carried the horizontal condominium one step further. If it worked with old properties, why couldn't it work with new properties as well? I paid a good price for the project, but when I sold them to individual owners, with each sharing the walks and the common parking area, I made a $5,000 profit on each eight-family. And all this happened before I knew what condominium meant.

The idea is relevant today. It's as simple as buying wholesale and selling retail. There are fewer buyers for 96 unit apartment buildings than there are for eight-family units. And it's only logical that an eight-family buyer should be willing to pay a little more than one who risks buying an entire project.

AN UNUSUAL MAN,
A UNIQUE PROBLEM
AND AN INNOVATIVE SOLUTION

Geniuses have created many wondrous things, but in the process some of them develop uncontrollable intensity, and somctimcs become illogical and unreasonable.

What has this got to do with real estate? Well, my story is about a real estate genius, who I will call Mitch.

Mitch was not an architect; yet he knew more than architects. He was not a contractor; yet he knew more than contractors. Nor was he a designer; yet he knew more than designers.

He bought a thousand acres of wooded land that was a acres of raw land and built thousands of residential units, and he was reputedly worth many millions of dollars.

Then a new idea surged within his prolific brain. He wanted to build one of the largest, one of the finest and one of the most unique resort-hotels in his section of the country. And he had the wherewithal to do it—the money, the genius and the drive.

He bought several thousand acres of wooded land that was a veritable wilderness paradise. A river coursed through the verdant land. There were also spring fed, fish-stocked lakes to titillate the ardcnt fishermen. Through the virgin forest, he cut over twenty miles of country road, leveled land for an airplane runway, and added several unique amenities—golf courses, ski runs, etc.

Now he was ready to build his masterpiece. Working every day for a year far into the night, he designed and drew every line of his gargantuan hotel—the hundreds of rooms, the restaurants, the shops, the large hall, and the immense lobbies. And with meticulous care, he specified all the woodwork, the stone, the brick, the fixtures, and the extravagant landscaping.

When Mitch took me on a tour of his resort, it had already been up two years, but not one guest had yet stepped through its doors. By then, he had already poured years of labor and ten million dollars of his own cash into the fabulous resort. Why didn't he open? He had run out of money.

The architectural planning and its execution were magnificent, but the financial planning hit a snag—a serious one. He needed $3,000,000 worth of furniture and equipment to complete his project, and because money was tight, he couldn't borrow beyond his $3,000,000 first mortgage. Several years earlier, Mitch could have had an $8,000,000 mortgage. But instead of accepting the insurance company's terms, he laid down his own terms, and they parted. Now Mitch couldn't borrow what he needed, although he had a bona fide appraisal of $18,000,000 based on the cost of reproduction.

Mitch, unfortunately, ran into a double buzz saw. One was psychological and the other real. The psychological one was that the longer his resort stayed empty the more difficult it became to sell or mortgage it. The other problem was that the financial climate in the country was becoming foggier every year.

So here he was, "fogged" in—stranded in one of the largest and most beautiful of empty resort hotels. He was paying his taxes and the interest and principal on his $3,000,000 loan by selling off some of the land he still owned.

Mitch solved his most important problem; he didn't buckle under the pressure even though his entire fortune lay fallow in the ground. With a lifetime of work and $10,000,000 hanging in the balance, he was cheerful, witty and cocky.

"Why do you look so glum?" he asked teasingly as we were touring his big white elephant.

"I'm thinking," I said, furrowing my eyebrows to accentuate his remark. "I'm trying to figure you out. If I can do that, perhaps I can solve your financial problem as well."

"Don't try. I'm too complicated. Just get me $10,000,000 for my resort and that'll solve all my problems."

"Mitch," I said, "I have read your $18,000,000 appraisal. I know the value is there, but there are so many minuses. No one is going to bail you out with $10,000,000. You're dreaming. I've got to come up with something more innovative. You've had about 30 turndowns. I don't want to lead you to number 31."

"As long as your solution calls for $10,000,000 in cash and not a cent less," he answered ebulliently.

It was the most challenging real estate problem I had ever encountered. I became absorbed in it. After many meetings and many plans which he turned down, I came up with an idea which I thought made a lot of practical sense. I met a man who had an entree to one of the largest furniture manufacturers in America. I told him Mitch's story.

"George," he said, "I think I could get this manufacturer to invest $3,000,000 worth of furniture and take over the running of the resort, if he could be shown he couldn't miss making a success of the venture."

My financial plan was as follows: The furniture manufacturer was to furnish and equip the resort, and take it over, subject to the outstanding $3,000,000 first mortgage. For five years, the furniture manufacturer would pay nothing to Mitch on the $10,000,000 cash he had in his hotel. After five years, he would begin paying him $430,000 a year, which would amortize $7,000,000 at 4 per cent in approximately 25 years.

In my opinion, this made sense for both buyer and seller. In the first difficult five years, the buyer could make ends meet even with 30% occupancy because he would have only about $250,000 a year debt service on the $3,000,000 first mortgage, plus the payments on his own $3,000,000 worth of furniture. With every raise of 10% above the 30 per cent occupancy, he could make about a half a million dollars profit. By the time he had to start meeting the debt service on Mitch's $7,000,000 second mortgage, he could be well on his way toward a 40% to 50% occupancy. And who knows, perhaps 60%, and then the facility would indeed be worth the $18,000,000 appraisal.

This would be a good deal for Mitch too. Now he was languishing in limbo; not only having to come up with payments on his $3,000,000 first mortgage and the real estate taxes, but also earning nothing on his $10,000,000 investment. And more serious, the facility not in use deteriorates with accelerating speed.

In my plan, Mitch would have the following benefits: He would be rid immediately of having to pay taxes and making payments on his $3,000,000 first mortgage. In five years, he would start receiving $430,000 a year for 25 years. His chances of getting it would be excellent because the furniture manufacturer could hardly miss putting the resort in the black under the extremely favorable financial terms. And even if the buyer for some unforseen reason couldn't make it, Mitch would be getting a going business with $3,000,000 worth of furniture—much easier to sell than what he had now.

As I carefully explained this deal to Mitch, he listened politely, and then with his usual bravado and a wave of the hand said;

"George, 1 can't buy that. Why should I lose $3,000,000 right away, and then wait five years before getting the balance at 4% interest? It's as bad as your deal."

I smiled. His answer didn't surprise me.

"But it's not bad when you measure it against the fix you're in," I said. "I know you're not easily defeated, but there comes a time when it's illogical to resist any further. This deal could get you out of your financial quagmire. For years now, you've been nursing a loser. There comes a time when you must admit a mistake and face the consequences. Let your ego hurt a little. It's big enough and strong enough to survive. My plan will give life to your dream. People will begin enjoying what you've worked so hard to build."

"George, you're wasting your time."

As of this writing, my furniture manufacturer is still waiting in the wings, or at least I think he is. And Mitch's resort and dreams are still empty of realization. Was it because a genius decided to remain stubborn? Or, am I stubborn, too, in believing that I was right and he wrong?

IT PAYS TO GET UP AT FIVE IN THE MORNING
IF YOU HAVE A GOOD IDEA

Adriel's shyness hid a desperate drive to succeed. Behind his pale blue eyes, I saw a bottled up ego drive. I knew that if I could release his potential with an unusual idea, he would race to success. This happened years ago, and this was the idea which turned him into a super salesman.

"Adriel," I said, after he resigned his shoe salesman job and joined my organization, "I want you to concentrate on the type of clients who are looking for low-priced homes. And here is why.

"There are brokers in our town who are not interested in dealing in low-priced properties. They list them but they do not make much effort to sell them. Follow-up these brokers' ads and buy their rundown duplexes and cottages in need of repair. Here's how to buy, finance and sell them."

Years ago, it was difficult to buy homes with small down payments, especially in poor neighborhoods. The idea was to overcome this difficulty.

"Let's say we buy one of these properties for $10,000," I explained to Adriel, "and mortgage it for $8,000. We advertise it for $12,000 with $500 down and sell it subject to an $11,500 land contract. Now, we'll sell our $3,500 equity in the land contract subject to a 30% discount and get $2,450 in cash. This, plus the $500 down payment will net us $2,950. From this, we subtract our $2,000 outlay, the difference between the $10,000 purchase price and $8,000 mortgage, leaving us a profit of $950."

It was a roundabout way of earning slightly more than the usual 6% commission.

Adriel got the point quickly and moved in to implement this plan with an enthusiasm that was a contrast to his shy, pale blue eyes. He was an instant success for two reasons. His introvertive personality created trust and acceptability among the low income families, but more important, he filled a pent-up demand among people who wanted to buy homes but didn't have large enough down payments.

Soon the story of his success spread, and salesmen in my organization and other real estate organizations began to compete for this business. About a dozen men were now combing the city to buy low-priced properties. Adriel came to me and said;

"What do I do now?"

"Get there first. Get up five in the morning," I said flippantly.

Sunday is a big day in the real estate business. That's when brokers advertise the heaviest. Adriel took me literally. He got up at 5:00 a.m. and circled the ads that looked promising. That took about two hours. Between seven and ten o'clock he made sidewalk appraisals of all the encircled properties. Then he would immediately get on the 'phone and make offers to the brokers, subject to interior inspection. By noon, he often had two or three of the properties bought.

Adriel became a super buyer. The ordinary salesman saw the properties on Sunday afternoon or Monday. By that time, Adriel had already bought the good ones or was in the process of negotiating for them.

Adriel made a science of this idea. He became king of the low-priced property buyers. He had been earning $75 a week selling shoes. He averaged $25,000 a year during the 20 years of his association with my organization.

Because he found his slot and filled it, he became a super salesman. I doubt if he would have become a success in the high priced real estate category. He was a natural dealing with brokers who wanted to make a quick sale of problem properties, as well as with the low-income people who could only afford to buy low-priced homes with small down payments. Dealing with executives in commercial real estate would have turned him into a failure.

MATCH-MAKING—
THE RIGHT WAY TO GET STARTED
SELLING COMMERCIAL REAL ESTATE

There is a wrong way and a right way to get started in leasing and selling commercial real estate. Even if you have the prerequisite for it (discussed in Chapter 4), you can still fail if your planning lacks sales power. For instance, it is folly when getting started to latch onto one listing and work it to death in the hope of making a quick killing. Even if you sell it, it won't do you any good because you will have created a wrong pattern. And if you don't sell it, you're bound to become discouraged. You lose either way.

The right way has the selling power to launch you into the super salesman class. What is the right way? It is to put inventory on the shelf. It's simple enough, but so many fail because they start off with too little merchandise to sell.

To get started right, you should do nothing for three or four months but obtain information on what is for sale or lease in your city. Don't try to get exclusive listings because the serious sellers will only give them to producers. Visit several dozen owners of office buildings in your city and find out what they have for rent. Almost every building owner will have space available—few buildings are always 100% occupied.

Develop a plan to catalogue and arrange each of the buildings' available space in a quick, easy to explain manner so that both you and your prospects will know what is available. Be sure to get all the facts—the rental per square foot per year, the special amenities of the space, the term of lease, when it's available, what remodeling the owner will do and what remodeling the tenants must do, the available parking, etc.

Becoming familiar with about 50 different suites in about 15 or 20 office buildings is a good start.

Now do the same thing with industrial space. There the information to be gotten is: floor load, loading facilities, access to expressways, is the building sprinkler equipped (that affects insurance rates), type of elevator service if it is multi-storied space, types of tenants in the vicinity, parking facilities, etc.

Next, you should spot about 50 land sites that are available for apartment or commercial projects. Ascertain the zoning, the prices, whether the owner wants to sell or lease, whether he would be willing to build to suit, and perhaps a dozen other pertinent points of information.

Do the same with apartments and commercial buildings that are for sale. Their statements should be crystal clear to you. That's the only time they'll be clear to your prospects.

Inventorying this information for future use should take a minimum of three or four months, working ten hours a day. During that time, you ought not make any move to contact prospects. This is a time for studying, absorbing and digesting information about what you will have to sell.

Now you're ready for the next step—getting prospects. This, of course, requires more ingenuity than inventorying information.

Some ways of getting prospects are better than others. One very logical way is to run a small ad in the daily newspaper, under the classification of office space for rent, reading somewhat as follows:

East of the River
Beautiful, Air Conditioned
1700 sq. ft. Suite
Under Cover Parking
50 Other Suites to Choose From
In 15 Different Office Buildings
From 400 to 10,000 sq. ft.
Call for Details
(Name)   (Telephone)

And the industrial ad would read as follows:

10,000 sq. ft. at $1.00 a sq. ft.
Sprinklered, Tailgate loading
Unlimited Floor Load, N.W. side
50 Other Choices Available
In Many Price Ranges
For Details Call:
(Name)   (Telephone)

And the land-site ad could read as follows·

Northwest Side
Zoned for 30 Luxury Apts
50 Other Land Sites Available
All Over Town
Suited for Apartments
and Commercial
For Details Call:
(Name)   (Telephone)

It's not necessary to run big costly ads. A six to ten line ad run consistently in the proper classification will outdraw the big ads run infrequently on the basis of per dollar return.

Another method for getting prospects is direct mail. Find an inexpensive direct mail service, and periodically send cards or letters on a selective basis to potential office and industrial space users. Your responses will be in direct proportion to the care with which you select the names.

Another way of getting prospects is to join as many service, communal, and charity organizations that your time permits, and then very diplomatically but persistently let your friends and acquaintances know that you sell and lease all types of commercial real estate. If some of them should ask you for specifics, be sure you have enough information memorized so you can give the answer on the spot, and not say, "I'll look it up and let you know tomorrow." That's losing a golden opportunity. Instant information is a great help in getting the sale started.

All my suggestions are predicated on the proposition that you risk your time on non-exclusive listings. Some owners may cheat you out of your commissions, but it's a risk you have to take to get merchandise on your shelf. Fortunately, those who deal behind your back are few. Most owners of property are honorable men and are only too glad to pay you a commission when you lease or sell their properties. Anyway, it's more fun trusting people. And from my personal experience, I can report that it's not only more fun, but more profitable as well.

What I have just described is a lot easier than solving geometry problems, writing a learned paper on the causes of the Civil War, or learning a passage in a foreign language. It's merely solving the basic problem of supply and demand. It's simple matchmaking.

You become a super salesman not because of your superior mannerisms, but through the momentum of a good idea.

A NEW USE FOR AN OLD HOTEL
PROVIDES THE SELLING MAGIC
TO TURN LEAD INTO GOLD

Thousands of old hotels are losing out to the younger motor inns of today. Only a few, like the Drake of Chicago, The Plaza of New York, or the Chateau Frontenac of Quebec, which have turned the half-century mark, are still making it competing with the modern inns.

In one city, a prestige 200 room hotel of the 1920's is fighting a losing battle with modern motor inns located in the same area. When I recently looked at the dying hotel's operating statement, its revenue from all sources was $600,000 and its expenses a few thousand dollars more. Fortunately, its proprietor owned it free and clear.

The hotel was in a good location. A highly-credentialed appraiser valued its land and improvements at $1,800,000. I smiled when I put its operating statement alongside the appraisal. Something was wrong. Either the appraiser was wrong, or the owner didn't know what he was doing.

Here, I thought, was an excellent opportunity to move in with several new ideas—leverage; the conduit concept; 4% interest is better than 9%; and a new use for the building—all rolled into one plan to solve this real estate conundrum.

I arranged a meeting with the owner of the aging hotel. To prepare for it, I applied innovative step number one: I found a young man who was ready to lease the hotel from me for a youth treatment center, specializing in the care of retarded, dull and brain-damaged teenagers. He had a record of success in that field.

The hotel was too big, and the fixed expenses too high, to profitably house only 50 of these unfortunate youngsters. Since caring for more than 50 youngsters would depersonalize individual care, I asked my lessee a few questions about his patients in the hope of finding a complementary use for the balance of the rooms.

"I need about 25 sleeping rooms for my 50 kids, a restaurant and about 10,000 square feet of classroom space," my lessee told me. "For the boys I need training areas for auto mechanics, welding, small motor repair, building maintenance, food service, etc. For the girls I need workrooms for instruction in sewing, food service, nursing aides, housekeeping, store clerking, switchboard operation, etc."

As he was talking, an idea was formulating in my mind.

"What you're driving at is that work is the main therapy for these youngsters and you need lots of space for the social workers and psychologists to train them. And now for an important question. How much help do you need for their total care?"

"One to one," he answered. "About 50 full time and part time help for the 50 boys and girls."

"Do you think any of your help might be willing to stay at the hotel?" I asked.

"I suppose," he answered. "You see, many of the part time people will be graduate students working for their master's or doctor's degrees."

I quickly calculated that his help might rent 15 to 25 rooms. But that was only the beginning. Now I was ready for the main thrust of my idea.

"What if about a hundred rooms were to be used by retired, low income elderly—let's say at $250 a month, including meals and lodging? (I had in mind a lower priced version of the Juneau Club discussed in Chapter 10.) Could your youngsters, under the supervision of a maintenance man, housekeeper and chef help with painting and minor repairs, cleaning and making beds, help in the kitchen and wait on tables?"

I saw a light in my lessee's eyes.

"You mean I could fill the hotel with some of my part time teaching help, the 100 elderly, and have my youngsters experience meaningful work while they help in keeping my expenses down at the same time?"

After several days of negotiating we tentatively agreed that he could afford, and would pay, $65,000 a year net rent for 25 years with an option to buy the hotel for $850,000 within five years.

Now I was ready to meet with the owner of the hotel who I learned was an astute and intelligent man.

"Well," he said abruptly when we met, cutting my attempts at small talk, "are you going to use leverage on me? I read your book, you know."

"I'm not only going to use leverage, but I've evolved something new—the conduit idea."

"What's the conduit idea?" he asked.

"It's to convert your profitless hotel into an annuity to stabilize your estate."

"And what else are you going to use?" he asked smilingly.

"We'll probably disagree on price, so I've devised a plan whereby I can pay the price you might have in mind providing you agree that 4% interest will do you more good than 9% (the going rate at the time), and I can prove it."

"You're an intriguing fella, but let's stop playing games and get down to business. What do you think I ought to get for the hotel?"

"Seven hundred thousand," I said.

"In cash?"

"No, $100,000 down and the balance of $600,000 to be paid off at the rate of $45,000 a year, to include interest and principal, interest at 4%."

"Do you realize that $700,000 at 4% is the same as buying the hotel for about $350,000 at 9%?"

"I do. But the main point of this deal is that getting $45,000 a year is better than nothing, which is about what you're getting now. And to protect this flow of income, you have my reputation, my $100,000, and an added layer of protection, a young man, who simultaneously with my purchasing the hotel, will lease it from me for twenty-five years as a child treatment center and for communal living for the elderly. Now you'll have two people worrying about making payments to you—he and I."

"You've thrown some new ideas at me and I have to admit they make some sense. Let me think about them."

Though the hotel appraised at $1,800,000, the owner was seriously thinking of accepting my $700,000 offer at 4% as this book is being written. It is important to point out that I risked buying it even under these favorable terms because, although my young lessee had big ideas, he had little money. Should he falter, I would have to step into the elderly owner's shoes—and take over a loser.

My plan was a practical one. The owner, stuck with a deteriorating investment, could enjoy a $45,000 a year annuity. The young lessee who did not have the financial heft to buy the hotel, could acquire rights tantamount to ownership, with an opportunity to obtain the fee within a short time if all went well. Based on our combined projections of gross income from all sources, and $65,000 a year net rental, he stood a good chance of clearing $50,000 a year. Not bad for a young man who didn't have to put a dime of his own money in the deal.

And although I took some risk, the $20,000 a year differential, and the $150,000 profit potential upon my lessee's exercising his option, are big enough plums to warrant the risk.

In addition to changing a loser into a winner, with three men gaining financially, the 50 retarded youngsters and the 100 elderly would be gaining too—a friendly place to live.

Thus, the selling power of an innovative idea can solve financial problems and help needy people at the same time.

Chapter 12

How to Use Leverage Salespower
in a Tight Money Market

During the halcyon days of 1965 when I wrote my book, *How To Use Leverage To Make Money in Local Real Estate,* interest rates averaged 6%. It was not difficult to buy or build a real estate project that netted 10%. All an enterprising investor had to do was to mortgage it for 100% at 6% interest, and adding 2% for amortization, he was left with 2% cash flow. That meant that when he bought or built a $100,000 building, he enjoyed an overage of 2% or $2,000. In the case of a million dollar project, it was not uncommon for the entrepreneur to be left with a $20,000 overage. And because these overages were tax sheltered by depreciation, they were worth twice as much to anyone in a 50% tax bracket.

No wonder the real estate developers of the 1950's and early 1960's made millions. Fortunately, there were concomitant benefits for others, for in the process of making millions they created billions in new real estate wealth. And the workers who built the buildings and the ultimate consumers who used them benefited too, because as a result millions of new jobs were created and new and better residential and commercial shelter was built.

But today, we have a new set of conditions. In just a matter of seven years, the monetary environment has changed completely.

It's true that rents are higher, but not enough to absorb increases in interest rates, construction costs and real estate taxes. It is no longer easy to buy or build a real estate project which will net 10%. With 8% to 9% interest and 2% amortization, an investor is only likely to break even or dig into his pocket. No wonder real estate construction through private financing has fallen off drastically.

Is there a way out? I think so. We have to develop a new financial philosophy. Equity holders of existing properties and owners of land will have to bridge the gap between higher costs and what makes projects feasible. They will have to become the adjunct financiers. Here are a few examples.

HOW A SMALL TOWN GAINED
BY TAKING A $60,000 LOSS

Few builders in the country can afford or want to invest 25% equity or seed money in a project; in a million dollar project—that's $250,000 in cash. Plus, perhaps another $50,000 to $100,000 until it jells—the time it takes to rent and move it out from the red into the black.

How can we bridge this 25% gap and jelling time? Here is how one builder did it.

A small town in the midwest owned a vacant square block of property on its main street—a perfect site for a forty room, mamma-papa motel. The land was worth about $100,000. Lenders seldom like to risk more than 70% of value on motels, and paying $100,000 for the land would have meant that the builder, based on total cost projections, would have had to invest about $125,000 in cash to complete the project.

The builder was Bockl Development Corporation. I own 25% of it, and a former salesman of mine is its president and majority stockholder. I drove out with him to make the presentation to the small-town mayor and his aldermen.

"If you want a modern, forty-room motel," I told them, "with meeting rooms and restaurant which your town badly needs, you can get it if you're ready to sell us your land for $40,000. I know it's worth $100,000, but we're hemmed in by high construction costs and high interest rates, and frankly, we're looking to you for help. In return for your assistance (subsidy would have been a bad word in a small town), your main street will be rejuvenated. And remember, in three years our $20,000 annual real estate tax will make you even, and for many years thereafter you'll be receiving $20,000 a year which you're not getting now. Gentlemen, unless you see it our way, we cannot build."

And we wouldn't have because we couldn't have come out.

The mayor was for it, some alderman grumbled, and one prominent citizen concluded, "Sure it would be better to get $100,000 than $40,000. But we've tried and no one wants to risk building a motel here. So I say let's take the $60,000 loss and gain a hotel. I think Bockl makes sense. In three years we'll be even, and thereafter we'll get $20,000 a year we're not getting now."

We bought the land at our price, and by the time this book will be published, our mama-papa motel will be built.

Variations of this concept are available in hundreds of cities across the land. Innovative builders can continue to create wealth by appealing to the municipalities for help. And when the city fathers analyze it carefully, they realize that by helping the builder they are really helping themselves.

HOW A BANK LOST
BY REFUSING TO TAKE A LOSS

A suburban bank acquired a piece of land across the street for $190,000 for parking. When it was able to buy adjacent land more suitable to its parking needs, the bank put the first parcel back on the market. But there were no bidders.

The half-square block site was zoned for stores, apartments or a combination of the two, but in 1970 when the interest rates climbed to 10%, real estate entrepreneurs simply could not pay the bank's price and make it a viable project. Since the mortgage people would not yield from their interest rates, the building crews from their high wages, nor city hall from its burgeoning real estate taxes, the bank had to yield in some innovative way to make the land usable.

I met the president of the bank at lunch one noon and said to him:

"I would be willing to build 100 efficiency apartments on your site if you subordinated your $190,000 land cost to a $1,000,000 first mortgage. I can only pay 4% interest and no principal for the next 25 years. Then, when the first mortgage is amortized, your $190,000 will become due and payable."

He smiled a cool banker's smile.

"I see in your proposal a lot of advantages for you," he said, "but none for us."

"But that's only on the surface," I answered. "You'll find it has merit if you're willing to look deeper. First, the dandelions across the street don't exactly help your bank's image. Second, you'll be getting about $250,000 in interest during the next 25 years. Third, since your lot is only worth about $100,000 in today's hard to build market, you're actually getting about 8% on your money. Fourth, subordinating your position isn't so risky when you consider your site is a hot apartment location, and your helping with the financing as I suggest would make this a very feasible project. And fifth, having 100 apartment dwellers across the street could mean 100 new accounts, and you know what that's worth better than me."

"You've said a mouthful, George. Let me talk it over with some of my board members."

"Here," I said as we were walking toward our cars, "I have a colored rendering showing how the project would look across the street from your bank."

"It's a beaut," he said.

A month later the bank's board of directors met, considered my offer and turned it down.

When I saw the bank's president at a Rotary meeting several weeks later, I asked him for the rationale of their board's turndown.

"We didn't like the 4% interest, the no principal payments, the subordination, and especially your apartment idea. We think the land is more suitable for commercial use."

"My idea then rated a big zero," I said.

"I'd say that's an accurate description," he answered with geniality.

Two years later, the board of directors was still looking at the dandelions across the street. It has now owned its vacant land for ten years. The directors are still clinging to their unrealistic dream of getting a commercial development and a return of their $190,000 in cash.

In my opinion, they made a mistake in turning my project down. I believe a few of the directors realize it now. Just as municipalities, towns and villages will have to become resiliently innovative in order to attract builders, so will private owners, like

.banks, have to bend a little too, if they want to get out from under.

Bankers may not like it but they'll have to learn.

HOW TO USE LEVERAGE SALESPOWER
TO PUT OVER A $6,000,000 PLANNED DEVELOPMENT

To innovate is not only being different, but being better. That's why innovative ideas make super salesmen out of ordinary men. It transforms leaden facts into golden opportunities.

Innovative ideas melt sales resistance. This is what the next story is about.

A suburb of about 17,000 population owns ten acres of vacant land located near a university and main shopping area. It is looking for an unusual idea to develop this land. Whoever comes up with an idea that's right and different will become a super salesman.

Here's a plan I have submitted which I hope will get me into the super salesman category. I concentrated on two goals: how to best meet the suburbanites' needs, and how to stay in the black. In Russia, someone would simply be concerned with the first goal. In private enterprise, however, we have to do better—we have to meet the people's needs as well as stay in the black. That's why ordinary planning under capitalism is not enough. It has to be extra-ordinary. That's why consumers under capitalism get an extra margin of excellence.

The more innovatingly we meet people's needs, the better our chances of staying in the black, is a safe business axiom to adhere to. So taking my cue from Constantinos Doxiadis, the world famous town designer who believes that ideal urban planning is having work, school, home and shopping within walking distance, I devised the concept of a village square.

The central thrust of the idea is to have a mixture of uses catering to a mixture of people. At the grand gate entrance is a large motor hotel, with appropriate parking, and some 40,000 square feet of office space and stores. Off to the side, beyond a landscaped grassy field, I planned 100 one-bedroom apartments for the elderly. A stone's throw away were a dozen townhouses for the low income, large families. About 500 feet to the west, away from the village's hustle and bustle, overlooking a park and a river, I planned four 32 family units of semi-luxury, one and two bedroom apartments. And to round out the diversity, I allocated the most scenic area of the ten acres to a dozen luxury condominiums.

To give unity to these diverse elements, I instructed my architect to design a "Williamsburg" architectural motif for the entire village square—with country lanes, quiet grassy fields, and rustic landscaping to match. And in the center of all this, the frontispiece of all the planning, I suggested a winter and summer ice skating rink designed to accentuate the village mood.

To conceive a beautiful plan is one thing, to make it economically feasible is another. In presenting this development to the village board of trustees, I underscored the feasibility of each of the component parts. The motor hotel, I pointed out, was an economically sound venture because of the university a few blocks away and because of the scores of industrial plants to the west. The stores and offices made economic sense because the village's stores and offices in the immediate vicinity were second rate and starved for parking. The planned commercial area would be a striking improvement over anything in the village.

The 100 apartment complex for the elderly was a natural because 25% of the village's population was over 60 and many of its retired citizens would qualify for the low interest and rent subsidies which Title 236 provides, and under whose auspices we intended to build. A moderately incomed, elderly couple under the program could rent a one-bedroom apartment worth $165 a month on the conventional market for $110. And a low-income couple, or widow or widower, could qualify for 20 out of the hundred apartments, for as low as $50 a month.

And to help disperse some of the low income, large families away from their congested project housing, I suggested that the village play a responsible social role by opening its zoning to include a dozen townhouses financed under Title 235. This is an interest subsidy plan which enables these families to own their new three and four bedroom homes and pay as little as $110 to $130 a month to include interest, principal, taxes and insurance. To move a hundred large families in these townhouses would be wrong—it would change the character of the neighborhood. But a dozen—yes. It would help disperse some of the low income people from our central metropolitan area. Or there might be enough low income, large families living within the suburb who might qualify. In either case, deserving families would benefit.

The feasibility of the semi-luxury, one and two bedroom apartments was not hard to prove. Their scenic location would have a magnetic pull for faculty members who would be within walking distance of their apartments—a quiet retreat from the hubbub of university life.

The dozen luxury condominiums were somewhat risky, but my rationale for including them was to balance them off with the dozen low income families so as to get the ideal Doxiadis' mix. And besides, if I could not sell them to wealthy families who wanted trouble-free living, overlooking a breathtakingly beautiful view, I could always rent them at $350 a month and stay in the black.

The year 'round ice skating rink, I pointed out to the village trustees, could prove to be a bonanza for the village as well as the village square. The suburb had $250,000 to spend for some public recreational facility, and what better place to locate it in than in the center of the development. Its attraction and our "Williamsburg" development could spill over both ways.

So much for the plan. Now how to finance it. I decided not to offer it to an insurance company because I was looking for 100% financing, and for that kind of mortgaging an insurance company usually asks 50% participation. To avoid it, I decided in favor of splitting the mortgage into seven parts with a different lender for each building. Since the feasibility of each was well grounded economically, I had no difficulty in getting seven savings and loan associations to advance tentative loan commitments, the final amounts to be subject to final plans and specifications.

To give the village an additional measure of safety, I planned to lease the hotel to an experienced operator, and the office space and shopping area to a shopping center expert who in turn, would lease it to retail and office space users.

The arithmetic of the village square was somewhat as follows: I estimated the cost of building the three-story, unequipped and unfurnished 75 room hotel at $900,000 without the land. I intended to get a $900,000 mortgage, including the land, and lease it to an operator for $100,000 a year rent, net to me, or $10,000 above the debt service of $90,000 a year, based on an approximate 25 year amortization mortgage at 8% interest. This would enable the operator to earn about $50,000 a year, after he furnished it, if he was able to maintain about a 75% occupancy.

I estimated the cost of building the 40,000 square feet of office and retail space at $700,000 without the land. I hoped to get a $700,000 mortgage including the land and lease it to the shopping center expert for $80,000 a year, net to me, or $10,000 above the debt service of $70,000 a year based on an approximate 25-year loan at 8% interest. After the shopping center expert paid about $20,000 a year for real estate taxes and $20,000 for miscellaneous, for a total expense of $120,000 including debt service, he would earn $40,000 a year if he leased the 40,000 sq. ft. of space at $4 a square foot.

I estimated the overage from the elderly housing units, semi-luxury apartments, and the luxury condominiums, if we had to rent them, to be another $30,000 a year. This would give me a total overage of $50,000 a year.

Now for the pivotal point of my financial plan—upon which the entire deal hinged. The village paid $1,100,000 for the ten acres. I suggested to the trustees that I would pay 4% interest to the village on $750,000. I subtracted $350,000 for the land we were setting aside for the year round ice skating rink. It was my understanding, I pointed out, that the federal government made grants to villages for setting aside open areas.

Based on the assumption that the village could borrow at 4%, I offered to pay $30,000 in interest. annually for 25 years, and then pay the $750,000 in cash when the 25-year mortgages on the project were amortized.

Still one problem remained. Since I didn't think I could get the village to subordinate its $30,000 a year interest to the first mortgages, I decided to ask each of the savings and loan associations to allow a portion of the $30,000 a year interest to remain a first lien ahead of its mortgage. To induce them to do it I planned to pay this interest in advance to the lending agencies, (like real estate taxes) who in turn would pay it to the village. Since the interest amounts allocated to each building would be relatively small, I didn't think it would present a problem to the mortgagees.

Based on my preliminary calculations, the economics of the project shaped up about as follows:

My overage from all sources would be about $50,000 a year, and subtracting the $30,000 a year to the village, my overage would then be approximately $20,000 a year.

Since it is always difficult to get firm cost figures from preliminary plans, I allowed myself a half million dollar swing—that is, I was prepared to invest $250,000 above the mortgages if necessary. But with a bit of luck and a lot of careful subcontracting, I also had a chance to build for $250,000 below the some $5,000,000 of mortgages. My risk and problem, in an era of rapidly rising prices, was to stay within the 10% fluctuation range.

I volunteered all this information in my presentation to the village trustees. Letting them in on my step-by-step thinking and planning was using a combination of sincerity and innovation which I had learned early in my career was an effective use of sales power.

As an added sales fillip, I invited my son-in-law, a professional builder, into the deal. With his know-how and my know-why, I stressed, we formed a responsible team to carry out our ideas.

With all this elaborate, logical and feasible planning, the village could hardly ignore me, unless someone offered to buy its land for $1,100,000 in cash and build something more innovative than what I had proposed.

But in the absence of such a proposal, the village has a lot to gain from my plan. It will add $200,000 a year to its real estate tax base, give its citizens something new and different, and get an ideal location on which to build its $250,000 recreational facility.

And although it is not going to get its $1,100,000 in cash, making it possible for me to use leverage in a tight money market, the village will not lose either. It has a good chance to recoup the $350,000 loss from the federal government through an open-space grant, and whatever interest it has to pay on the balance of $750,000 it will receive from the project.

It will probably take a year after this book is published before the village will make an award to the successful bidder. If I get it, it will not be on the basis of my sales personality, but on the selling power of my ideas. That's what sells. The personality is but a small adjunct.

I suggest that this type of a development is applicable to many cities and suburbs in America. These ideas, or a modification of them should help your plans and the use of leverage in a tight money market.

WHAT TO DO
WHEN A LENDER BLOCKS YOUR PLANS

Tight money and high interest rates which we experienced in the late 1960's and early 1970's create new problems for which we have to devise new solutions. One of the problems for both buyers and sellers of real estate is the thorny clause in many mortgages that upon sale of a property, the mortgagee has the right to terminate the loan.

For instance, if you arranged a 5½%, 25 year amortization, $100,000 loan in 1964, and you now have a buyer for your property who is willing to pay $150,000 for it, the mortgagee can kill your deal by declaring the loan due. Here is the way he stops it. If the buyer is forced to get a new loan at, let's say, 8½% interest, his net return will decrease by 3% and, of course, he would then not be willing to pay $150,000 for the property. The buyer and seller are stuck. Thousands of such deals have been stopped in their tracks. Is there a way out?

The first thing to do is to examine the note and mortgage and see if the mortgagee does indeed have the right to terminate the loan. Many mortgages do not contain the termination clause, and then of course, buyer and seller can take advantage of the low interest mortgage balance. But what if the clause is there—plain and foreboding?

Sell your property on a land contract. A land contract transfer is a conditional sale, and completed only when the fee is conveyed upon meeting certain conditions in the future. For instance, the owner of the property who was stopped from selling it for $150,000 can sell it on a land contract with let's say, $50,000 down, and receive his payments from the buyer on the balance of $100,000 on terms agreeable to both, while he continues to make his payments at 5½% interest as he has done before.

However (and read what follows carefully), be sure that the loan language reads that the lender has the option to terminate the loan *"upon transfer of title"*. Then selling on a land contract is safe because such a conditional sale is not a complete transfer of title. However, if the mortgage clause reads something like, *"upon transfer of title or any interest therein, legal or equitable,"* then the mortgagee has the right to recall the loan or escalate the interest rate to the new buyer.

Generally, the mortgage clauses up to the year 1967 read: "upon transfer·of title". But after 1967, when the interest rates began to mushroom, the mortgagees' protected themselves by inserting the more comprehensive clause which closed the land contract loophole.

The above is the legal opinion of an attorney who has closed thousands of deals, yet I suggest you consult your own attorney before taking the risk of selling your property on a land contract in order to retain your low interest advantage. Local legal climates may vary.

Suppose your loan is locked in with the clause: "Upon transfer of title or any interest therein, legal or equitable". What then? Net lease your property to the buyer, giving him an option to buy it at any time during the lease when borrowing times become more propitious.

Let's assume you have a lessee-buyer for your 12-family unit for $150,000 and an $80,000 mortgage balance at 5½% with a debt service payment of $7,500 a year, including interest and principal. The balance of the loan pays itself off in 17 years. Also, assume that gross rent is $22,500 a year and fixed expenses are $7,500 a year. The overage would then be $7,500 a year.

Lease it to the lessee-buyer from $12,500 a year net, for 17 years, giving him an option to buy for $150,000 at any time during the lease, but with a security deposit of $25,000 (the amount to be invested and earnings to accrue to lessee). You will then have an overage of $5,000 a year ($12,500 less $7,500 debt service) and the prospective buyer or lessee would have an overage of $2,500.

The advantages to the lessee-buyer are: he earns $2,500 a year for his managerial responsibility and has the option to purchase it. His disadvantages: he does not have tax shelter depreciation and he loses control of $25,000.

Your advantages are: you have transferred responsibility of ownership, you are guaranteed $5,000 a year by an adequate security deposit and you increase your equity through yearly amortization.

It's as close to a sale as you can get without stirring up the lender to block it. It's making a legal end run with the buyer leading interference. The leasing approach is not taking advantage of anybody, it's simply using innovative, pragmatic means to meet the needs of a seller who wants to sell and a buyer who wants to buy.

A Rarely Tried Leverage Idea Where Lender Gets 17% Interest While Borrower Pays Only 8%

Here's a little known idea where you can get 100% financing when you show the lender how he can earn 17% interest while you're paying only 8%. Sounds improbable, doesn't it? Well, it isn't when you can find this set of circumstances, and it's not difficult to find, because it's fairly prevalent.

Let's assume you're a competent young man with a good record in property management. You've found an owner of a 16-family apartment building who wants to sell it to you for $200,000, subject to a $150,000 mortgage balance at 5%. But there is that clause that the lender can terminate the loan upon transfer of title, legal or equitable. It's a deal stopper.

Of course, you can't blame the lender for not being happy with the 5% interest, but there is nothing he can do about it as long as the original borrower owns the property. But here's where you can put an innovative leverage idea to work that is favorable to you and the lender.

Find the mortgagee who has the authority to make decisions, show him your managerial credentials, and tell him you're willing to sign a new $200,000 mortgage at 8%, the going rate, and cancel the $150,000 mortgage at 5%. What that means, you tell him, is that the effective rate of interest for the $50,000 he'll be advancing will be worth 17%. You don't need to explain too carefully that getting 8% on the $150,000 instead of 5% means 3% more interest on three times $50,000, plus 8% on the additional $50,000 adds up to 17% on the new $50,000 advance. The chances are he'll have it computed before you get through explaining it to him.

The only problem you may encounter is that he may not want to stretch his loan $10,000 or $15,000 to reach the $200,000 you request. But if you can convince him of your reliability and of your willingness to ride the loan without cash flow because of your prime goal to have a free and clear property by age 60, then he would indeed be short-sighted if he turned you down. The chances are that raising the interest and the amount of loan will dry up all of the cash flow.

Your only risk is that you will have given the mortgagee a new idea and he may steer the deal to a friend of his who he may think is a more reliable vehicle for your idea. It's a risk you have to take, but it's not a great one, because most lenders are honorable men. If you convey a sense of integrity, he'll hold on to you because he'll respect you for your innovative idea, and because when he sees 17%, he'll act quickly.

Search for these situations. Every city must have hundreds of them. When you find a 2% or 3% interest spread which will give you an opportunity to leverage innovatingly in a tight, high interest money market, move in on it. It's one of those remarkable ideas which enables the seller to sell his property, the lender to increase his interest yield, and you to ride in on a 100% financing plan.

Even if you consider yourself an ordinary salesman, if you can pull it off, it will turn you into an extraordinary one.

AN INGENIOUS WAY OF RAISING MONEY
THROUGH SELLING PROPERTY AND HOLDING ONTO OWNERSHIP

Here is a way of getting your cake, eating it, and having it. You build apartment buildings, sell one half interest in each at a profit, and retain the other half ownership without any investment. Sounds good? It is! All because of an innovative idea which is logical and benefits all involved.

It all started when a salesman of mine who had been earning $20,000 a year for many years said to me one day:

"George, I want to build apartment buildings in small towns. I want to pick up where you left off with your Back To The Small Town Realty Company."

"Great," I said. "How can I help?"

"You can help by letting me use your name for my corporation. In return, I'll sell you 25% interest in my company at cost."

"Sounds fair to me," I said. "What do you want to call yourself?"

"Bockl Development Company."

Using $250,000 as seed money, we built 40 apartment buildings worth about $7,000,000 in more than 30 small towns during the first seven years of operation. In 1970, we ran out of equity money and devised the following sales plan to continue building, selling and keeping what we built. Here's how it's working.

Let's say the Bockl Development Company starts building a 16-family apartment building costing the firm $150,000, upon which it obtains a $140,000 mortgage commitment. Before the building is completed, it sells a half interest to some professional man who is in a 50% income tax bracket for $180,000 subject to the $140,000 mortgage. When the investor pays $20,000 down for his half interest, the firm has already gotten the $10,000 it invested over the $140,000 mortgage and a $10,000 profit to boot.

In return, however, the buyer is guaranteed 8½% return on his $20,000 down payment in the following manner. He receives the first $1,700 overage from the 16-family, that is, 8½% of $20,000, and Bockl Development gets its $1,700 next, and if there is additional overage beyond the $3,400, it is divided equally between the two parties.

But what makes this plan innovative and salable is this very important provision: The partnership provides that if the cash flow on the 16-family should fall below $1,700 or even if it should show a cash loss, the investor still gets his $1,700 a year return. This part of the contract is backed by all the assets of Bockl Development—its $250,000 original investment, its equities in the properties it has built (probably worth about $1,000,000), and its future earnings.

If the reader will follow my reasoning carefully, he'll see how this sales idea benefits the investor, Bockl Development, and the small towns involved.

First, the advantages to the investor: (1) His 8½% return is trouble free (Bockl Development does the managing without charge). (2) The return is reinsured by the assets of the company. It is obviously safer than relying on only one building which could turn out to be a "lemon". (3) When we apply the four-way benefit test discussed in Chapter 11, that is, when we add the rates of return from overage, amortization, tax shelter through depreciation and inflation, our investors can potentially realize a 25% to 30% return on their investments.

Second, the advantages to Bockl Development: (1) We earn a small but immediate cash profit upon sale of our half interest. (2) Our remaining half interest costs us nothing. (3) We can continue building indefinitely because of the constant flow of equity money.

Third, the advantages to small towns: (1) Elderly couples who had been living in large old farmhouses welcome our new, easy to care for small apartments. (2) Our new apartment buildings in the old small towns initiate a revitalizing process. They trigger construction of other new buildings. (3) It broadens the small towns' tax base.

Six months after we started this unique partnership program, we had sold six half-buildings. The buyers were doctors, lawyers, insurance executives—all in the 50% income tax bracket or better. It's a bonanza for them and for us. It has solved our cash problem.

A word of caution. Any good idea can be abused, and even if it isn't, economic circumstances beyond the builder's control can throw it into a tailspin.

Of the some 40 apartment buildings the Bockl Development Company constructed in some 30 small towns, only about six of them took longer than eight months to fill, and we are enjoying a 95% occupancy rate. This did not just happen. It is the result of careful selection of sites, building the size and number of apartments each town needed, eliminating short cuts to quality, meticulous maintenance of grounds and buildings and friendly, competent management.

If we cease being as careful as we have been in the past just because we can now sell these half-partnerships and get all the money we need, we will dilute our corporation with unprofitable ventures. Then our investors and we could be in trouble. The value of our guarantees could erode and our assets with it.

So even if our innovative ideas brings us "easy" money, it will not pay Bockl Development to fall into "easy" ways of overpaying and undermanaging. For our sake and for the sake of our investors, it will behoove us to remain on our toes—alert, selective and careful.

However, if economic conditions beyond our control sends our country into a depression, high vacancy rates could force us into the red, putting our investors and ourselves in jeopardy—with many other businesses, I might add quickly. That's why we carefully avoid soliciting buyers from among people who would be investing their last savings. We prefer buyers who can afford to take a loss without getting hurt. We're not looking for a widow with $20,000 to her name. We want a doctor who is earning $75,000 a year.

When money is difficult to borrow, when your plans are stymied for lack of cash, an innovative idea making sense to lender and borrower alike, can break the log jam.

At least, that's what happened at Bockl Development.

A LITTLE SEED MONEY CAN PRODUCE
A LOT OF HOUSING FOR LOW INCOME FAMILIES

If you're not looking to make a lot of money but to help a lot of people, here's an idea where you can get all the money you need providing you use it where it'll do the most good. It's building homes for low income large families under the federal interest subsidy program Title 235.

You have no problem obtaining 100% mortgages. You apply to your State Federal Housing Administrator for the number of homes you want to build under 235. He'll grant your request, or a part of it, depending on his available money and the number of builders making such requests.

Let's say you've been allocated ten homes. You then go to a mortgage broker and arrange for ten mortgages. The lenders could be insurance companies, savings and loan associations or banks. They advance the money. The government merely insures the 100% loans, and pays the difference between the going FHA interest rate of 7%, 8% or 8½% (it fluctuates like conventional mortgage rates do), and as low as 1% interest, depending on the income of the large family buying the home.

Now you're ready to submit your lots and plans for FHA approval. In 1971, the appraisal limits were $24,000 for a four-bedroom home and $21,000 for a three-bedroom home. They were lower in 1969. When the FHA appraises each of your homes, it is in effect saying it will insure these amounts to qualified buyers. The interest subsidy is then pegged according to need with hardship cases bringing it down to as low as 1%.

The FHA adheres to a formula that a large hardship family should not pay more than 20% of its income for the total payment on its home—such payment to include interest, principal, taxes and insurance. There are some minor modifications to this general rule.

I want to warn the prospective Title 235 builder that qualifying a buyer is not a simple matter. A buyer can be rejected if he's making too much money or too little, if he has too few children or too many, or if his credit is riddled with judgments. For instance, FHA will not qualify a family with two children for a four bedroom home, or a family with seven children for a three bedroom home.

I have built 20 homes for the low-income large families and lost $10,000. But that need not be your experience. I gave myself the luxury of hiring a young man with a master's degree in real estate for $10,000 a year to cut the FHA red tape, supervise the building contractor, negotiate with the mortgagees and sell the homes.

By being your own contractor, however, and eliminating the luxury of having someone do the detail for you, as I have done, you can easily make a profit of about a thousand dollars a home. But you'll have to have a lot of patience. You're dealing with buyers who had never owned a home. Some of them qualify only after you've spent weeks and months clearing their judgments. Others, because of language barriers need interpreters to intercede for them.

My real estate representative with the master's degree and I worked with Neighborhood House and the Spanish Center—Red Feather agencies in the business of helping people. They interpreted our building program to the needy families. This was our assurance that we were reaching deserving hardship cases. Without the help of these social workers, our work would have been more difficult and the homes might have been sold to less deserving families.

For instance, an American-Mexican widow with seven children moved into one of our spanking new, four-bedroom homes where her total payment for interest, principal, taxes and insurance was $115 a month. Under conventional financing the payment would have been about $225 a month.

But getting her qualified was indeed a "federal case." A widow's pension enabled her to pay $80 a month for a basement, rat-infested flat. FHA would not qualify her for the $115 a month new home until it could be shown that she could get an additional $35 a month income. We suggested that she apply to the Welfare

Department for the additional income, but she refused. She was too proud to ask for public help. We explained the problem to the Spanish Center social worker and after months of negotiating with the Welfare Department and the widow, the aid was granted and accepted.

I visited her after she moved into her new home. I was overwhelmed with a feeling of pride for having done something worthwhile. The 32-year-old mother proudly showed me through her new home.

"I like home," she said in her halting English, "and my children . . . they like it too."

Building these 20 homes was a rewarding experience for me. And it can be rewarding and profitable for you. I suggest, that if you find it difficult to buck the hard conventional building market, turn to Title 235. You can not only make a good living at it, but do something worthwhile as well.

And if you'll permit me to preach for just one more paragraph, I'd like to suggest that businessmen ought to sponsor ten or more of these homes. They could hire builders who would do all the work, if they provided the seed money. This advance money is needed to buy the lots and pay for the interest and real estate taxes during construction. However, when the homes are sold, their money would be refunded. It can easily be arranged in advance that the sponsors will not have any losses or gains.

Whether you're a builder looking for a small profit, or a businessman-sponsor looking for a way to help deserving low income large families—Title 235 is the answer.

Chapter 13

Borrowing Money Imaginatively
Is Super Selling at Its Finest

Borrowing money requires more ingenuity than lending it. That's why borrowers are more interesting people than lenders.

The borrowers more than the lenders built the railroads, airplanes, skyscrapers, shopping centers and our modern apartment complexes. They had the ideas, the lenders merely approved the loans.

The borrower lives vulnerably. His red blood is warmed by excitement. The lender is cooler; his blood is a bit bluer. The borrower is an optimist. He says, "I can do it." The lender is a pessimist. He says, "What if you don't?"

It's more fun to be a borrower because that's where the action is. He makes things happen. The lender weighs and judges, and that's not as much fun. The only time a borrower doesn't have fun is when he can't pay it back. That's when the lender takes the joy out of borrowing. This is not to condemn the lender. It's his job.

The first cardinal principle of borrowing is to take every precaution to pay back the loan. Since a borrower is by nature a better salesman than a lender, he must be careful not to oversell, because if he does, his zeal will come back to plague him.

Lenders are expert plaguers, especially when we make them look bad. That's when their reservoir of good will dries up quickly.

On the other hand, when we borrow carefully and pay back on time, we must guard against a new danger. We're apt to get loans on half-baked projects just because of our past successes. The lenders drop their guards. But that's no reason for us to drop ours and start borrowing without caution.

When our reasons for borrowing are sound, we should ask with confidence, never with hat in hand. We are the buyers of the use of money, and if anyone is to be solicitous, it is the seller not the buyer.

During the late 1960's and early 1970's, a new business phenomenon has arisen—lenders getting into borrowers' hair. Envious of their successes lenders are horning into borrowers' projects for a piece of their action. If they'll continue to take advantage of a tight money market and elbow their way into equity positions, they will raise up a crop of entrepreneurial eunuchs.

If the borrowers are forced to succumb to the lenders' equity demands, the latter will get half-baked projects because the entrepreneurs, being more ingenius than the lenders, will find ways to compensate for this horning in. Equity demands strain and complicate normal borrower-lender relationships.

Such a climate of borrowing is not good either for the borrower or lender. It waters down private enterprise.

THE ART OF OVERCOMING LENDERS' OBJECTIONS

Lenders are agile at finding reasons for turning down loans, and borrowers must be equally agile in changing their minds. Logic is always an effective persuader, but sometimes we have to go beyond the reaches of logic and use more subtle means.

SPIRITUAL CONSIDERATION
MOVES A $500,000 LOAN OFF DEAD CENTER

In the early sixties, I decided to build an apartment complex for the elderly. I picked an ideal site, secluded, yet only a block away from transportation, and a few blocks away from shopping.

I had an architect draw plans and an artist paint a beautiful rendering of the project. I prepared a feasibility study and began shopping for a loan. Lo and behold! I was turned down by the first five savings and loan executives. Their reason? "We're afraid the elderly will not be able to meet their rent payments because of limited incomes."

"But the rent for a one-bedroom," I said, "is only $75 a month and that is about $20 below the market."

"Yes," they said, "it's true, but we'd rather gamble on higher rentals catering to tenants with higher incomes."

I didn't think they were logical because most of the elderly were on social security or pensions and were practically depression proof. In fact, they were better risks at $75 a month with their limited incomes than those who paid $100 to $125 a month with their fluctuating incomes.

Logic was on my side. Nevertheless, I did not prevail. I had the good concept but they had the money. I needed $500,000 and wasn't getting it.

I applied the "quiet time" method to resolve my problem. I closed my office door and told my secretary I wanted no calls or visitors for two hours. I quietly waited for an answer to my mortgage dilemma. Gradually, the chattering of my thoughts subsided. My mind became still. Then the answer came. Why not call on a friend of mine who is a devoutly religious man and head of a savings and loan association?

"Al," I said, "you've got to help me get a $500,000 loan for my senior citizens project. I've been turned down by five lenders but I think they're all wrong."

After I explained the project to him I said:

"Al, I want you to consider this loan on its merits. But if for some reason you don't see them, then let's go beyond them. The elderly in our city who have already made their contributions to society need housing badly and deserve to be helped. Responsible lenders like you and practical builders like me can raise the quality of their lives if we extend ourselves, that is, if we live vulnerably. That means mixing a little generosity with practical business. Isn't this what religion is all about?"

Al stirred in his chair and I could see a far away look in his eyes.

"I'll give it my best," he said almost absent-mindedly.

A week later Al called me and said:

"George, I have good news for you. The board has approved your $500,000 senior citizens' loan."

The apartments were built and the project became an outstanding example of how private enterprise can care for its elderly. Not only did it give impetus for others to build similar projects in our city, but at least five other senior citizen projects were built in other states as a result of the national publicity the apartments received after it was built.

Because building for the elderly was new, the lenders shied away from it. That's because most of them hesitate to stray from the beaten path. But if we are to borrow imaginatively, we must excite them to lend adventurously. If appealing to their transcendental natures will warm their blood and make it flow more abundantly, then let's do it.

The mortgage was an unorthodox loan. It broke new ground. And if I am allowed to crow a little in behalf of the borrowers, it took the imagination of a venturesome borrower to do it.

THE ENTREPRENEURIAL JUICES
OF AN 82-YEAR-OLD MAN
FLOATED AN IMPOSSIBLE $2,800,000 LOAN

In the mid fifties, I decided to build the first large, centrally air-conditioned office building in our city. It was a bold venture since it was predicated on my being able to obtain a $2,800,000 loan and build 200,000 square feet of office space for $3,100,000. My equity in the deal was a free and clear lot worth $200,000 and about $100,000 of working capital.

My loan odyssey took me to twelve lenders. Each turned me down. A year later I was still without a loan. Here was the nub of the problem.

"How can we loan you money," the lenders stressed in their cool, logical manner, "when you don't have any tenants?"

"But I know I can get the tenants," I answered confidently. "There is such a crying need for new, air-conditioned office space in our city."

"How do you know that?" they asked.

My answers didn't move them. I reversed my tactics. I tried to get tenants to commit themselves first, before asking for a loan. Their answers were just as discouraging.

"Why should we sign up with you," they questioned, "without having a guarantee that you'll get your loan and build your building? We don't want to find ourselves in the fix of giving notice to our present landlord, and then not having a place to move to."

It was a variation of the old conundrum: Which came first, the chicken or the egg?

A combination of luck, pluck and an 82-year-old man solved my problem. He was chairman of the board of one of the largest savings and loan associations in our state. But his entrepreneurial instincts were stronger than his loaning propensities. He was a wheeler-dealer at heart, and when I explained the logic of a new office building to him, I perceived an eager gleam in his eye.

When I appeared before his board of directors to make my $2,800,000 loan request, things looked dismal. After I made my presentation, all I could see, as I peered at their faces, were benign smiles. I didn't detect a nuance of enthusiasm.

But my 82-year-old friend felt differently. My presentation warmed his entrepreneurial blood. We vibrated on the same frequency. If he had been younger, he would have built this office building himself. I could see he wanted the vicarious thrill of being part of this project. After a month of negotiating and throwing his weight around with the board of directors, he made me the following proposition—a hard one, because he was also a lender, but a fair one.

His association would advance $1,500,000 so I could start building and begin soliciting tenants. If by the time I had drawn the full $1,500,000 I was successful in leasing 50% or 100,000 square feet of office space, they would advance the balance of $1,300,000. However, if I did not reach 50% occupancy, then they wanted, as additional collateral, two buildings which I owned free and clear worth about $300,000. I had to give them the right to sell this real estate and use the money before they advanced the balance of $1,300,000 to complete the building. These two buildings were my last reserves, and they knew it.

It took me eight months to spend the first $1,500,000, during which time I rented 70% of the building. I did not have to use my additional collateral, and by the time I finished the building, I was not only 100% occupied, but I had a waiting list of another dozen tenants.

What was the magic that worked here? First, it was finding an idea that was ripe for action—in this case, erecting a modern office building. And second, finding someone who believed in me.

For several years this loan was the talk of the town. It was understandable in view of the fact that this association had heretofore not made a loan in excess of $300,000. It was one of those miracle loans which went beyond the reaches of logic because an octogenarian dared to be innovative.

My elderly friend certainly went out on a limb, as did I. I borrowed boldly, and he loaned dangerously. We risked together, and we won together.

HOW I IGNITED A MAN'S ENTHUSIASM
TO MAKE AN $850,000 MORTGAGE ON A DUST-LADEN WAREHOUSE

Many feasible loans are not made because they are not presented imaginatively. Men too often present only hard-headed facts and fail to use the motivational keys that open lenders' hearts.

Several years ago, I bought a 100,000-square-foot empty warehouse with the idea of converting it into a modern medical office building. I needed an $850,000 mortgage to modernize it into first class medical office space.

After being told by several lending institutions, something to the effect of, "Who ever heard of changing a warehouse into a medical building?" I finally got the attention of a mortgage correspondent who showed some interest.

"Of course, I can't approve your unusual loan," he said, "but I think I can get one of the loan executives from the East to fly in and take a look at it."

I showed the loan executive through the dust-laden warehouse and explained the feasibility of the conversion.

I stressed these selling points: (1) The remodeled medical office space would be within walking distance of two large hospitals. (2) The location was a key bus-transfer corner. Patients could get there from all parts of the city. (3) The undercover parking garage would be a desirable special amenity for the doctors and their patients. (4) Since I had built and leased an office building before, my chances for a repeat performance were better than average.

The loan executive had mixed emotions. He saw the logic of the loan, but its unorthodoxy bothered him.

"But will the tenants be able to visualize a modern medical office building emerging from a dust-laden warehouse?" he asked.

"You know, my job is to make safe loans, and this isn't exactly one of them.

"If this were a safe, cut and dried loan, your company wouldn't have to send a man like you to investigate it. Any clerk could approve it. This is a character-loan supported by practical common-sense feasibility. It's a loan in search of the unusual. Why not match my adventurous spirit with a little adventuring of your own? You know, America wasn't built on safe loans. It was built on innovative ones. If together we can convert a dying warehouse into a modern medical office building, we'd be doing the unusual, and I believe, with a great deal of safety. Let's adventure together."

Several days later, he called me.

"George," he said, "I've decided to go along with you. But don't fail me, because if you do, I'll be the laughingstock of my associates here. I've gone way out on a limb for you. To use your adjective, this is probably the most adventurous loan I've ever approved."

The warehouse medical building is now grossing $275,000 a year rent. It has turned out to be one of their safest loans.

What was the key to making an $850,000 mortgage on an old warehouse? First, an innovative use; second, supporting data to make it feasible; and third, finding a man who had the vulnerability to have his enthusiasm ignited.

Borrowing with exceptional skill is making the exceptions work.

HONESTY NOT ONLY HAS A MORAL VALUE BUT A COMMERCIAL ONE AS WELL

One of my real estate departments was known as the "cats and dogs" division. It dealt in dilapidated cottages and duplexes which we would buy, refurbish and resell. Getting loans on these properties was sticky because appraisals could vary from 30% to 50%. The reasons for these fluctuations were the variables of location, their state of obsolescence and the difficulty of financing them.

A savings and loan official who had a prediliction for these loans, said to me one day:

"I'd like to use the banking commission appraisals only as guide lines, because I don't believe they're as reliable as knowing what you pay for these properties, what it costs to remodel them and what you sell them for. I don't want to find you paying $8,000 for a property which the banking commission appraises at $12,000, giving you an 80% loan of $9,600, and then seeing you walk away with $1,600 at the closing of the deal. I want to be sure that you have at least 20% of your money in each of these deals."

"All right," I said, "let's do it this way. In each case we will tell you exactly what we paid for the property, the cost of reconditioning it and its sale price. Then check us out against your authorized appraisals, and pick any of our loans you like on the basis of 80% of our cost."

This sounded fair to him, because being a cagey loan man, he knew that the chances were good that what we paid for the property would generally be less than the appraisals. Loan men are by nature a questioning lot, and they should be, to protect themselves. And so, I was not surprised when every now and then he would come in at the closing of a deal and carefully check our figures. I didn't mind because I knew what he was up to. He wanted to be completely sure that we were completely honest. He did this for a year. Once we established our reliability, he stopped checking us. It saved him a lot of time because we didn't have to wait days or weeks for appraisals. We knew exactly the loan amount we could get at the time of our purchase and at the time of sale.

We enjoyed this arrangement for 30 years, during which time we originated about $20,000,000 of loans for about 2,000 homes. It was a relaxing way to do business under this spirit of complete trust. His firm must have earned over a half a million dollars in interest from the loans we helped him originate, and we must have earned as much buying, rejuvenating and reselling these "cats and dogs" properties.

The factor of honesty, aside from the moral value, quickened a commercial relationship and cut the usual red tape and strain of borrowing.

Honesty could be said to be an innovative way of oiling the money-borrowing-and-lending machinery.

TAPPING COMMUNITY RESPONSIBILITY IS A PROLIFIC SOURCE FOR LOANS

Two of my friends came to my office ten years ago and said,

"George, we've got the finest lot for a motel in our city, but we can't get financing. We've tried for a year and the answers are always no. If you can arrange a loan for us, we'll cut you in for a third interest."

The location was indeed a dandy. It was a stone's throw from a state center for conferences and seminars where businessmen and academicians from various parts of the state and country congretated for two or three days, several times a week, to discuss and solve business and university problems.

I went to the largest savings and loan association in that city and put my cards on the table.

"My friends here have been trying to get a loan for the motel from the savings and loan associations, but all have turned them down. I think you're the most logical association to make this loan. And here's why. First, it's in your city and you ought to support it. But more important, the motel has built-in business generators to make it an outstanding success, and consequently, a safe loan.

"When my wife and I come to visit our daughters at school, we have to get a room at one of your antiquated downtown hotels, two miles away. This motel will have modern rooms just a few blocks away from where our daughters stay.

"And I understand that the university is contemplating adding rooms to the center because of the shortage of modern rooms for the conferees. It seems to me, private enterprise ought to do the job, not the university. Don't you think so?"

Fortunately, the secretary of the lending institution was a rugged individualist. He believed that private enterprise could always out-do public enterprise because it was more efficient.

"I heard it too," he said, "and I don't like it. Let me check with the university officials to see how far they've gone with their plans and see if they'll drop them, if we offer to build 75 rooms on your site."

Fortunately, the university officials preferred our motel to adding rooms to the center. We could do it more quickly, perhaps within a year, while getting their plans approved by the legislature could take several years.

The secretary of the association was as sold on our motel as we were. The problem was the amount of the mortgage. Our request for a $750,000 loan was by far the largest he ever encountered. To make him stretch to the limit, I told him that we would give the building contract to a local builder. It was to be a community project.

A month later we received approval for the loan—the full $750,000. And to sweeten our deal, we were able to get the appreciative builder to lend us $75,000 for five years. Since our total cost was $850,000, we only had about $25,000 in the deal.

Did we oversell the loan? No! The motel was a high occupancy success right from the start. Within two years, it was sold for $1,000,000. The contractor was paid in full, and the new owner has been netting about $50,000 a year ever since.

Had this loan not been made, the university, the visiting parents, the center's conferees, the lender, my friends and I would not have reaped its benefits. It's a case of an imaginative lender joining hands with imaginative entrepreneurs to make a mutual contribution to each other and to a community.

Chapter 14

How to Make Money

Selling Losses and Depreciation

Interim construction losses and accelerated depreciation are the entrepreneurial motivations today for sheltering income and making sales. But before I explain this, let me point out that the wave of interest in interim losses and depreciation is already cresting, and by the time it rises to the top and falls, a cycle that may take it through the 1970's, millions of dollars will be made by those who analyze its money-making potentialities.

The interim losses and depreciation benefits lie in two sectors of our real estate economy: (1) The rent subsidy programs applicable to moderate and low income housing of which about 40% of our population now qualify, and (2) The conventional multi-family, non-subsidized housing, involving the non-subsidized sector of our population.

THE MONEY-MAKING POSSIBILITIES IN SUBSIDIZED HOUSING

In my opinion, the FHA Title 236 offers the most direct route to helping moderate and low income families with their much-needed housing. That's the end product and the ultimate fruit of the program. But to motivate builders to create this high demand housing, the Federal Government has had to offer these carrots: (1) Little risk to the builder, (2) Interim financing losses and depreciation benefits to shelter the high income of investors, (3) The builder's ability to sell this loss and income benefits for cash.

Let's take a typical Title 236 one-million-dollar housing project, consisting of 70 one, two, and three-bedroom apartments. Let's assume that the physical improvements exclusive of land are $900,000. The FHA allows 10% of the $900,000 as a sponsor's risk and makes it an allowable cost of the project. Thus, the cost components of the project could be $900,000 for improvements, $90,000 for sponsor's risk, and $70,000 for land, for a total of $1,060,000. The allowable loan is 90% of $1,060,000 or $954,000, and the builder's equity is, therefore, 10% of $1,060,000 or $106,000. Since $90,000 is the allowable sponsor's profit, the builder would then have an investment of $106,000 less $90,000 or $16,000 in this slightly over a $1,000,000 project.

A few additional details. The builder is allowed a 6% rate of return on his $106,000 equity or $6,360 a year. He is also allowed a management fee of 5% or 6%, or whatever the local management fee happens to be.

Here are the advantages to the tenants. A typical one-bedroom apartment renting for $165 a month on conventional financing could conceivably rent for about $115 a month to a qualifying moderate or low income renter. And a two or three bedroom apartment would rent for proportionately less compared to the unsubsidized housing.

So much for the advantages to families who cannot afford the high rental conventionally financed apartments, but qualify for subsidized housing.

Now for the advantages to the builder. The 6% return on his $106,000 equity which costs him $16,000 and his management fee is just the visible iceberg of his reward for putting this deal together. Under the iceberg are the money-making possibilities of selling the losses incurred during construction and the double depreciation, for cash.

Here is approximately the way it works. The interest cost for the interim financing during construction for a million dollar project could be from $50,000 to $75,000, depending on the interim interest rate and the length of the construction period.

The real estate taxes levied during construction could be about $20,000. Then there are appraisal, survey, title and a dozen other fees which are a onetime cost and deductible. That could be another $5,000. And then there are "points," the fee the lender charges to make an FHA loan whose interest rate might be lower than that of a conventional loan. These may vary from 4 to 8 "points" so that on a $900,000 loan, they could be from $36,000 to $72,000. This is also a one-time expense and deductible.

The total loss during construction of a million dollar building project could be as high as $150,000, spread over one or two years, depending on the length of the construction period.

These losses are saleable and worth a lot of money to the builder. Let me illustrate: A friend of mine was an insurance salesman, covering the small towns in his state. He was offered a building site in one of the towns, for $75,000. It was a bargain, but he had no money. He heard about FHA Title 236, but when he obtained a pamphlet and read its rules and regulations, he became discouraged. He found a $15,000-a-year accountant as a partner, and together they went to a banker to help them formulate a Title 236 deal on this site.

The banker went with them to the local FHA office to help them sort out the important from the unimportant bureaucratic jargon. Slowly the deal began to take shape.

First, the two partners put a $5,000 down payment on the land, and agreed to pay the balance of $70,000 in cash when the entire deal was consummated. The owner of the land had it for a long time and didn't know what to do with it. He welcomed the possibility of getting his cash, and didn't mind waiting until the project was finished.

Then the partners found a retired contractor in the small town where the site was located and offered him 5% equity in the deal, a fee for supervising the construction, and the management fee which the FHA allowed. They also made him the general partner and they became the limited partners. There was no personal liability to either the general or limited partners since government insured mortgages have no recourse except to the collateral of the project.

The insurance salesman and accountant now had 95% of about $140,000 of interim losses and many years of double depreciation to sell. Since neither of them earned enough money to take advantage of these losses, they wisely at the very inception of the deal, offered it to four doctors whose earnings were in the 60% income tax bracket. The physicians, after conferring with their attorneys and accountants, paid the partners $120,000, payable at $40,000 a year. Quite a windfall for two years of part time work while they were holding down their jobs.

But the doctors did even better. Here is why. Each of the doctors was credited with approximately one fourth of the $70,000 losses or $17,500 during the first year of construction, and with the same amount during the second year of construction. Thus, each doctor saved 60% of $17,500 or $10,500 in taxes in each of the two construction years. In addition, he could carry the remainder of the $7,000 loss three years back and get a tax rebate, beginning with the last of the three years, and that's another 60% of $7,000 or $4,200.

Each doctor, on an investment of $10,000, saved $14,700 in income taxes during the first year, and the same during the second year. And in the third year, their losses dropped, but using 200% accelerated depreciation, they still remained at $40,000. Of course, this loss diminished by several thousand dollars every year so that in seven or eight years, if the doctors' earnings remain high and their depreciation losses disappeared, they could sell the project.

As can be seen, this Title 236 project created many benefits. A retired contractor now has a pleasant management job, the two partners earned $120,000, and the doctors have found a depreciation haven for their high earnings. But those who benefited the most are the large and small families of moderate and low incomes who probably moved from substandard housing and are now living in new, modern apartments within their limited budgets.

ANOTHER EXAMPLE OF TITLE 236 HOUSING
WHERE THE DEVELOPER DIDN'T REAP ITS FULL POTENTIAL

A policeman in a small town built 45 apartments under FHA Title 236 with the help of his local banker. Not being aware of the cash value of interim losses and double depreciation, he kept the project himself.

He could have sold his $75,000 construction loss and ensuing depreciation for about $60,000 in cash, but he wasn't aware of the opportunity.

But even then, it was a good deal for him. He built the project on a lot he had inherited from his father which was lying fallow, and for which the government allowed him $60,000 in cash. He also received $3,000 a year, which is the allowable 6% return on his $50,000 equity, and a $3,600 management fee. All this for very little effort, very little risk and very little money.

The government has come up with a winner in Title 236. Without question, it offers great opportunities to alert entrepreneurs.

And what's unique about it is that you don't have to be in the real estate business to take advantage of it. All you need is a little money and a lot of patience. And the results, as you have read, can be dramatic.

THE JOINT REAL ESTATE VENTURE–A FLEXIBLE MONEY-MAKING VEHICLE

Investors who put their money in public realty corporations have learned their lessons. They didn't do well. They were locked in with no depreciation benefits, and the low dividends they received was ordinary income to boot. For this and many other reasons, publicly held realty companies phased out of popularity. The growth factor which appealed to many sophisticated investors didn't pan out.

When real estate developers began to see the shortcomings of real estate corporations, they looked around for a better vehicle, and came up with real estate trusts. Its superiority over the realty corporation was that 90% of its earnings had to be passed through to its investors, and including the depreciation benefits. Many real estate trusts have gone public and the typical returns to their investors are about 7% to 8% with 50% to 60% of the income tax sheltered by depreciation.

However, the real estate trust requires complicated legal and accounting handling, and an organization of experts. Also, investors with millions of dollars. Something more flexible and less complicated was needed. The joint real estate venture is the answer.

It has the advantages of a real estate trust, it avoids the disadvantages of a real estate corporation and its investment opportunities can be designed to serve small groups of people—as few as two if necessary.

Let's say you own, or can buy, a piece of land upon which you want to build a 16-family apartment building for $200,000. You have two doctor friends who are each earning $75,000 a year and are looking for depreciation losses to shelter their incomes. You form a partnership or joint venture between yourself and your friends, in which you become the general partner and they, the limited partners. You, as the general partner, will arrange for a $170,000 mortgage, sign it, supervise the construction and take charge of management when the building is completed. The limited partners each put in $15,000. They have no further liability.

The division of ownership could be as follows: You, the developer, take half ownership for putting the deal together, and your friends 25% each. Let's analyze the advantages to each and see if it is a fair deal to all concerned.

Since your friends have gone into this deal primarily for interim losses and depreciation, it would be wise to give them 75% of the interim losses and depreciation, but only half of the cash flow. The chances are that the interim financing costs including interest, real estate taxes and other sundry items will be about $12,000, all deductible during the construction period. Each of the doctors can take half of 75% of $12,000 or $4,500 in losses, which is worth $2,250 in tax savings if they're in the 50% income tax bracket. That is equivalent to 15% return on each of the doctor's $15,000 investments. The developer keeps $3000 or ¼ of the $12,000 losses.

When the building is finished and the cash flow is about $2,000 a year or $500 for each doctor, that's worth about another 3.3%, which when doubled because it is tax sheltered, is worth 6.6%. Now add another $750 which is the average sheltered amortization for the first ten years of the loan, and that's worth another 5% return.

And that's not all. Since the doctors are the first users, they're allowed 200% depreciation. Let's assume that the land in the project is worth $20,000. The government would then allow 5% of $180,000 or $9,000 depreciation. Since the average sheltered amortization for the first ten years would be about $3,000 and the cash flow about $2,000 a year, there will still be a loss of about $4,000 a year; which, of course, will diminish some every year. Since the doctors by agreement, will be getting 75% of it or $3,000, each will then get a tax loss of $1,500. This is worth $750 in tax savings to each doctor, or 5% on his $15,000 investment.

I have described the real estate joint venture advantages in general terms, but the essence of the interim loss and depreciation motivations are there. However, I suggest that whether you are a developer or an investor, check out the specifics of each deal with your attorney and accountant.

Joint ventures in real estate are becoming popular for many good reasons. It is a flexible type of partnership which can take many forms, have varied arrangements, and be tailored to the few or the many. And it has appeal to the small as well as the large investors.

The joint venture or partnership can be between one developer and one or more investors; between a developer and an institution, like an insurance company; between a corporation and any number of limited partners; and many other variations.

The joint venture arrangements can vary to accommodate the goals of both the developer and the investor. The control of the venture can be vested in the developer who has the know-how, with the investors relying heavily on him for guidance. But, as between the developer and the institutional investor, control could be left with the latter, because it puts up all the money. Or there can be equal control as between developer and investors, alloting specific areas of control to each.

Interim loss and depreciation advantages can be divided on the basis of where they will do the most good. Investors, such as doctors or other high ordinary income producers need them the most. In fact, in today's market, it is the major motivation for investing, since it is difficult to get both cash flow and tax advantages.

Arrangements can be worked out to shift most of the loss and depreciation to the high income investors in exchange for a higher proportion of the equity or cash flow to the developer.

In structuring the venture agreement, it is important to get the best tax attorney available because unless he spells out in detail the several dozen variables as they affect each of the partners, it could mean trouble for all of the partners.

A few fine points before leaving the fortune-building opportunities that are now available in joint real estate ventures.

If several limited partners invest $30,000 in a $200,000 project as in the foregoing example, and the general partner assumes the $170,000 mortgage, the limited partners' depreciation is limited to their $30,000 investment, while the general partner can depreciate his share of the equity using the mortgage indebtedness as a base. However, if the $170,000 mortgage has an exculpatory clause, that is a mortgage without recourse, then both the general and limited partners can depreciate each share of the entire indebtedness.

In the typical real estate venture, the developer is usually looking for cash flow and the investor is usually looking for tax depreciation. The developer is in an enviable leverage position, because the venture usually involves the developer's know how and the investors money.

Tax shelter is really an indirect loan from the government. The object of the investor is to get his money back in tax savings in the shortest possible time—then all the remaining benefits are gravy. However, it is good to remember that at some time you have to pay it back, because depreciation reduces the base and when you sell, you pay it by way of gain (even if you sell for no more than the original price paid). And what's worse, if accelerated methods of depreciation are used, and most do, the accelerated portion is recaptured by the government at ordinary income rates.

But I want to add quickly that during an investor's high earning period, he should by all means use the tax advantages of sheltered income, that is, "borrow indirectly from the government," because when he has to pay it back, the chances are that he will be working less, earning less, and needing less.

A final note of caution. When you get involved with several joint ventures (and there's no need to stop at one or two) involving more than a dozen people, it is best to register with the government so you're not in violation with the Securities and Exchange Commission. There are criteria which apply to a private offering, which need not be registered, and to a public offering, which must be registered. But sometimes the lines are blurred.

My advice is to leverage with free abandon, but play it safe with the government.

THE CONDOMINIUM CONCEPT—TROUBLE FREE
APARTMENT OWNERSHIP AT LESS THAN RENT

A friend of mine was debating between building a 50-unit luxury rental project or selling it as condominiums. A condominium is a legal concept, where a person buys an apartment in a project, legally shares all common areas, and all expenses in maintaining them.

His wooded land was on the outskirts of a city, overlooking a lake, a few blocks from the highway, and a few minutes from the center of the city. He was planning garden, villa-type apartments of about 2,000 square feet each, consisting of living room, dining room, kitchen, two bedrooms and two baths.

In order to get at the heart of a feasibility study of a project, one must be able to step into the tenants' shoes. My friend did this, and decided in favor of selling the 50 condominiums for $48,000 each, instead of renting them. This was his reasoning:

First, he knew that in order to make it a feasible rental project, he had to charge $5,000 a year per apartment. The rent was too high, he thought, yet he had to get it because in a luxury complex, it is not uncommon to experience a 10% to 15% vacancy. Also, lenders being wary of luxury rental developments usually demand larger owner equities, higher interest rates and often, a piece of the equity. All this had to be reflected in the high rent.

In addition to the high rental of $5,000 a year, was the disadvantageous fact that none of it was deductible to the tenant. About the only advantage he had was that he could move if he didn't like his apartment.

Against these disadvantages to sell it as a rental project were the following advantages for going the condominium route: First, the buyer of a condominium could purchase it for $48,000 with 10% down, and pay off the $43,200 mortgage balance in 25 years at an interest rate that was about 1% less than the lender demanded for the entire project. The reason for the lower rate is this. The risk involved in having 50 substantial citizens signing individual mortgages is far less than a promoter signing a single large $2,000,000 mortgage.

Second, the total yearly cost to a condominium owner would be less than $5,000 for the following reasons. The 25-year amortization of a $43,200 mortgage at 7% would be about $3,600 a year. The real estate taxes are about $1,200; insurance, $400; miscellaneous repair, $300; his share of the maintenance of the grounds of the project, $500. The total would be $6,000 a year as against a rental of $5,000 a year. But wait!

If the condominium owner is in the 50% income tax bracket (and most of them in the project would be) then here is why the $6,000 condominium cost would be less than the $5,000 rental charge. Of the $3,600 yearly mortgage payment, in the first year, about $600 goes toward principal which the owner saves, and about $3,000 goes toward the interest which is deductible, making it worth about $1,500 in tax savings to the owner. The $1,200 real estate taxes are also deductible and that's worth another $600 in income tax savings. When we add up the principal, interest and real estate tax savings, we have $2,700. Now, subtract it from $6,000 and we have a net condominium yearly cost of $3,300 a year compared to a rental of $5,000 for the identical unit.

Aside from these economic advantages, there are special and personal benefits: (1) Owning is superior to renting, (2) Owner will have voice in management, (3) Owner can remodel and individualize his apartment to suit his tastes.

For these and other reasons, the condominium concept has become very popular in the south, especially in Florida and California, but it is now beginning to take hold in the temperate climates as well. So far, it has been a vehicle to save money for the classes, but I'm sure it will be innovated soon to save money for the masses. The advantages applicable to a $48,000 unit can, with a few financable refinements also be made applicable to a $25,000 unit.

I have dealt with the general characteristics of the condominium concept. There are many variations and improvisations which can be added to it. The trend toward condominium building is worth watching.

My friend is on the right track. When he sells the project to the 50 owners, he will not only give each of them a better deal, but he will make a profit of about $4,000 a unit for himself. He will thus pocket $200,000, instead of worrying whether he can rent the apartments at inflated prices.

Packaging a condominium project is no longer the money-making vehicle of the sophisticated few. It can now include you.

Chapter 15

The Small Towns of America--
Secret Goldmine of the Future

Take my word for it. There isn't a more rewarding way of securing your future than becoming a small town real estate specialist. There are not only millions to be made in this economic wave of the future, but equally important, there is a country to be saved—from dehumanized chaos.

Just as ·there has been an exodus from the small towns to the large cities during the past 100 years, so will there be a return exodus from the megalopolises back to the small towns. The wise real estate men of tomorrow will lead this movement, and make a lot of money doing it.

Here are four money making opportunities in small towns: (1) Selling small town businesses to big city people; (2) Building apartments; (3) Building mama-papa motels; (4) Getting industry to disperse their plants into the small towns of America.

Selling Small Town Businesses to Big City People

Every small town has several businesses for sale. It could be a gasoline station, a hardware store, a friendly inn, a restaurant, a beer depot, or a small bank. List a few of these businesses and place an ad in one of the large city daily newspapers to read as follows:

ARE YOU TRAPPED
IN THE BIG CITY?
BUY A HARDWARE STORE
IN HEAVENVILLE, WIS.
BEGIN A NEW LIFE
WHERE AIR IS FRESH
AND LIFE IS LEISURELY.
COME TO HEAVENVILLE,
ADD 10 YEARS TO YOUR LIFE
MANY OTHER BUSINESSES TO CHOOSE FROM
IN MANY OTHER CHARMING SMALL TOWNS
BACK TO THE SMALL TOWN REALTY CO.
Address   Phone

I realize it's expensive to place an ad like this in a daily newspaper, but it brings results. Probe and test other less expensive advertising media. Try the same ad in church periodicals. Spiritually inclined people are good prospects to get away from it all and spend their remaining business years in small towns.

A similar ad in a trade association newspaper or magazine, featuring a business to match the association, is another way of flushing out people who are champing at the bit to escape from their depersonalized big city existence. And, of course, I would check with advertising agencies for other innovative ways to get at the rat-race-trapped megalopolite who is looking for a way out.

To really zero in on letting people know that you have interesting little businesses in charming little towns is to get the real estate editor or a large daily newspaper to run a feature story about your first human interest deal. Let's say you've sold a friendly inn located in the heart of pine country at the edge of some small village. Their buyer is a carpet layer from Chicago, who was making $20,000 a year in his big noisy city, but is now happily working with his wife in his friendly inn and barely making $8,000 a year. But they are both ecstatically fulfilled.

See to it that a quote from the former carpet layer, something like, "I wouldn't trade the leisurely life I have now, where I can fill my lungs every morning with fresh pine air, for a $50,000 a year job in Chicago," gets into the story. If you can manage a picture of the harassed megalopolite bending over his carpeting in contrast to a picture of him and his wife in front of his idyllic inn, so much the better.

The impact of such an article would be far greater than a hundred ads. It could revolutionize your business. And equally important, you become a vital factor in revolutionizing lives and rejuvenating small towns.

Small town owners will gladly pay 10% commission for selling their businesses. Selling a hardware store in Tippecanoe, Missouri, to a hardware man in St. Louis for $20,000 will yield a $2,000 commission—and a grateful seller and grateful buyer. But the benefits do not end there. You have set a sociological force in motion.

The elderly seller, who might have been forced to close if you hadn't found a buyer for him, now enjoys some extra income as a result of your efforts. The buyer with his big city know-how will no doubt inject new life into the dying hardward store, and in so doing help rejuvenate the town. You have begun to play an important role in strengthening your country by moving people from congested areas into the roomier small towns.

When a big city businessman on the verge of a nervous breakdown told me after I sold him a small town store, "George, you've made me the happiest man in the world," I felt mighty happy too. When I put my head on my pillow that night, I felt a rewarding sense of accomplishment, in addition to having made a handsome commission. Can men in other walks of life enjoy that same wholesome feeling?

There Is Big Money in Small Town Apartment Building

The money-making rhetoric of the 19th Century was, "Go West, young man, go West". In the latter part of the 20th Century, it will be, "Go back to the small town, young man, go back." There are not only fortunes to be made there, but a new country to build.

One of the pioneering ideas is to build apartments in small towns. It's an idea with which I've had considerable experience. As stated elsewhere, a former salesman of mine and I have built about 700 units in some 40 buildings, ranging from eight's to 27's, in some 30 small towns in Wisconsin. The villages and towns ranged from 800 to 30,000 people.

Here are a few pointers.

The ideal location for an apartment building in a small town is a residential area—but it must be only a few blocks from the center of town. If you find a site that answers this description and the zoning is different from what you need, don't give up. Rezone it. The chances are the town fathers will go all out to give you the zoning you need if you can show them a quality project. You don't have to convince them of the need. They know that better than you.

You should not pay more than $1,000 per apartment for land. We have built many units where our land cost was as low as $500 a unit. In a large city, the cost can fluctuate from $2,000 to $4,000 a unit.

Your apartment building should have character—it shouldn't be garish or sleek, but rather functional and countryish. The project can usually be financed by local small-town savings and loan associations. They will go out of their way to give you high percentage, low interest loans because of their fierce pride and loyalty to their communities. If the project is too large for any one of them, they will cooperate in setting up a participation loan.

Here are several other advantages in building apartments in small towns.

Besides lower land costs and more favorable mortgage terms, the real estate taxes are lower, by 40%, compared to Milwaukee's metropolitan area. The small town properties are easier to maintain. Some 75% of our tenants are over 60 years old, and with few exceptions they care for their apartments as they did their own homes. And they do not like to move. As any informed manager knows, this cuts down expenses and adds profits to the bottom line.

I take a trip through the state now and then to talk to our tenants. They are the most appreciative lot I've ever met. Instead of complaining, they express appreciation and gratitude. It's a heady feeling.

Two elderly sisters in their seventies cornered me on one of these trips, and one of them said:

"You probably don't realize how much good you're doing building apartments in our town. My sister and I were too old to take care of our big house, but this little apartment—it suits us just fine. We're grateful."

You will very seldom hear such talk in the large cities. Complaints are the rule rather than appreciation.

Our ratios of efficiencies, one-bedroom and two-bedroom apartments are 10%, 80% and 10%, respectively. Only about 5% of our 700 units are furnished. The rentals range from $115 for an unfurnished efficiency, $135 for a one-bedroom and $165 for a two-bedroom. Our occupancy rate is about 95%.

There are also disadvantages in small town apartment building.

Building costs are somewhat higher because it is more difficult to get efficient contractors in small towns. Expediting is more costly because there are long distances to cover from one building job to another. Some of them are as far as 400 miles away from our small town base of operations located about 25 miles from Milwaukee.

Obviously, the management of these properties is more costly than if we were to have all our 700 units in Milwaukee. We appoint a local real estate broker in each of the towns to do the leasing, and a handyman to take care of the lawn and minor repairs. The new building expediters fill-in to oversee the general maintenance of the finished buildings in their parts of the state.

Do the monetary advantages and disadvantages of building in small towns even out? I'd say so. Our overages in small town projects are about the same as in large cities. We average about 11% on our equity investment, which is probably close to the overage in many large cities, as it is in Milwaukee, for instance. However, there is this big difference. The rental income and the tenant turnover fluctuates less in the small towns than in the large cities. This makes small town apartment buildings a more durable and stable investment.

Our small town building organization is small, compact and hard-working. One of my former salesmen is president. His main duties are to find the land, rezone it, and finance the apartment buildings. His brother-in-law is in charge of general construction, and another former salesman of mine is in charge of awarding the mechanical contracts—for plumbing, wiring, heating, etc. In addition, we have two expediters in the field and two women in our small town office. Of our $100,000 a year overhead, 75% is capitalized as a building cost, and 25% is allocated to management. We have been building at the rate of about 100 units a year, and in the last several years we have stepped it up to 200 a year.

Small Town Motels Will Be
The Little Bonanzas Of The Future

The small towns today are ready for small motels, and Bockl Development Corporation is doing something about it. In fact, we've already begun.

We've started four of them in four small towns with 40 rooms each.

Based on our research, which is more intuitive than factual, we feel that a 40-room motel will prosper in a small town if it has the following business generators: (1) 20 or more manufacturing companies; (2) a local college not more than three miles away; (3) a religious school or seminary where parents come to visit the students; (4) a special hospital such as one for retarded children or some institution specializing in some form of mental health; (5) a highway out front that leads through the main part of town, and (6) a site either in the heart of town or not more than a few blocks away.

A 40-room motel is an ideal size for a mama-papa operation. The wife with the help of a friend or her daughter can be responsible for cleaning and making up the rooms. The husband can be in charge of reservations, accounting, reports and general supervision. Or it can be a different combination of these work responsibilities, depending upon the husband's and wife's abilities.

A 40-room motel can break even on the basis of 50% occupancy and a debt service of about $35,000 a year based on a $350,000 mortgage at 8%, amortized over 25 years.

For every 5% rise in occupancy over the 50% break-even point, the owner can make $5,000. Thus, at 75% occupancy, not unusual, the owner of the 40-room motel could net about $25,000 a year.

Here are the economics of a 40-room motel. It costs about $8,000 to build the typical and adequate 300-square-foot room. The land should not cost more than $1,000 a room, and the furniture about the same. A modern two-story, 40-room motel completely furnished can be built for about $400,000 and mortgaged for about $350,000.

There are three ways to entrepreneur these mama-papa motels— sell them, lease them or own them.

There is a well known real estate adage—"you can't go wrong taking small profits." This is particularly applicable to building small town motels. What's wrong with putting up the right size motel, in the right location for the right man, in the right town and making a profit of between $25,000 to $50,000 doing it? There are thousands of competent big city buyers who are anxious to start new lives in small towns. These motels would be ideal for them.

If the down payment of between $75,000 to $100,000 to buy one of them is beyond the reach of a big city prospect, lease it to him. The deal would stack up about as follows: if you have a $50,000 cash investment in a 40-room motel, subject to a $350,000 mortgage upon which your debt service is $35,000 a year, leasing it for $1,100 a room, net to you, will bring a return of $9,000 overage (subtracting $35,000 from $44,000), or 18%. This is a highly desirable trouble-free rate of return, plus the benefits of amortization, depreciation and inflation.

And it's a good deal for the lessee too, because with a little investment (perhaps a $10,000 security deposit) he acquires the rights to a brand new motel which requires little manpower to manage, and offers the opportunity to earn $15,000 to $20,000 a year in an interesting, leisurely environment. And to sweeten the lessee's deal, give him an option to buy the motel for $450,000 at any time during the first ten years. This is an added incentive for him, and a built-in profit for you.

Whether you sell it or lease it, it's wise to direct the buyer or lessee to join a referral and counseling service so he can have expert help in setting up and running his inn. The charge is minimal, usually a small percentage of room rental.

It should not be difficult to get buyers or lessees for these small town motels. An ad in a daily newspaper, reading something like this will bring dozens of calls.

40-Room Motel
In Peaceville, Wis.
Buy It Or Lease It.
If You're Tired Of City Living
And Hankering
For a Slower Paced Life
Call Us.

Earn From $15,000 to $20,000 a Yr.
And Have Fun Doing It.
Name of Firm   Address   Telephone

The third entrepreneurial approach to mama-papa motel profits in small towns is running them yourself. The risks increase, but so do the profits.

As of this writing, we're planning to own and run our four motels, and also those we plan to build in the future. The majority stockholder of Bockl Development and I have a basic and friendly· disagreement about this. I'm for selling or leasing them. He's for running them. I think he's mistaken because our hired help will never be able to do as good a job as the owners or lessees. If that's true, and I think it is, then owning these individualistic businesses is going against the grain—economically and philosophically.

This personal reference is not a desire to air corporate differences in public, but a means of highlighting a practical problem and offering, to my way of thinking, a practical solution to those facing similar options. My parting argument to my majority stockholder was: "A little wisdom will take us much farther than a lot of ambition." It's particularly applicable as to what approach to take with mama-papa motels.

There Is Money In Getting
Industry To Move Into Small Towns

Industrialists, as a rule, are politically conservative people. They are as zealous for Capitalism and Democracy as they are adamant against Socialism. This can be converted into dynamic selling power for dispersing industry to the small towns. Challenge the industrialists to put their money where their mouths are. Use today's potent and visible argument that Democracy dies in megalopolises and thrives in small towns. Point out to them that by dispersing their industry they will shore up America, and in the long run, save themselves. Most of them will agree that rugged individualism has a better chance of surviving in 5,000 vital small towns of 40,000 each than in 20 megalopolises of 10,000,000 each. After you've prepared the philosophical and political groundwork, zero in from the general to the specific. Make the pitch that you have several small towns which would be ideal locations for one of their divisions. Or, if it's a smaller plant, suggest a complete "home" move.

Be sure you're prepared with facts and figures, in addition to your love for small towns. The profile of each town in your dossier should have its size, age groups, ethnic backgrounds, labor market,. religious orientation, access to highways, railroad and airplane connections and something about the local institutions and political climate.

Having established these facts, you are now ready to talk about the concessions the town is ready to make to a prospective wholesaler, blue collar manufacturer, or white collar large office space user. Small towns will give a lot to get new jobs for its people, and new people for growth. Concessions can vary from selling land for less to re-zoning it to suit. But the pivotal points will always be the cumulative charasteristics of the town's culture, and its accessibility to the user's transportation needs.

How does the real estate man make money in finding industry for small towns? First he can sell the land to the industrialists and he can build their plants. But more important, and here is an idea that has not been used too often, it is to educate the town officials to pay the real estate man a commission for each job he brings to a community for a certain number of years—similar to the commission he receives when he procures a long-term lease tenant. Give the real estate man specializing in breathing new life into small towns an incentive, and watch him go. As every small town mayor knows, for every ten new jobs created, another two or three jobs are added to sell and service the job holders. Production jobs are growth multipliers.

There are millions of dollars to be made dispersing industry and business into the hinterland. It's a mammoth job, but not too big for real estate pioneers who want to change the business and political climate of America. And it needs changing!

THERE'S MONEY AND FULFILLMENT
IN PLOWING UP THE GHETTOS

Replacing old ghettos with new and more congested ones has been tried and found wanting. That's because we were more concerned with economics than with people. Yesterday's planners were wrong on two counts. They were wrong in not anticipating the stress of people's psyches when too many low income families are confined to too small an area. In one of Chicago's public projects as many as 18,000 people were living on 60 acres—that's 300 people per acre—in acre after acre.

They were even wrong in the economics. While they were able to build each living unit for less, the taxpayers in the long run paid more. That's because congestion breeds welfarism and crime—two awesomely expensive social costs.

It's bad enough to sardine wealthy people in fashionable skyscraper apartments. At least their congestion is ameliorated by the fact that they use their apartments mostly at night—during the day they are out on the town, working or having a good time. But it's not true for the poor with their large families who have no place to escape their claustrophobia. Walls and people close in on them. Lacking psychological and spiritual resources to rise above their fate, they burst into abberative behavior and violence—into gangs and muggings. Is it any wonder that stark fear stalks their corridors instead of neighborly friendliness?

The planners have made some awesome mistakes. But that's the past. What about the future? What can we do to correct their mistakes?

Real estate salesmen of tomorrow can make a lot of money in replacing ghettos with modern factories, wholesale distribution centers, new post offices, parks, office buildings and new decongested housing. This would not only be a radical departure, but a practical way, once and for all, to do away with slums and build something entirely new and different in their place. It would give the central city a fresh start—the dying of the old and a beginning of the new.

Replacing several square blocks or even several square miles of slums with new projects where the same people move from the old to the new, somehow leaves the slum atmosphere hanging in the air. The vibrations of the old frustrations seem to penetrate the new shelters within a matter of months.

The imaginative real estate salesman of tomorrow will disperse the low income people into new areas, away from the slum smell, and assemble the ghetto land for decongested housing and new commercial development.

Blended with new beautifully landscaped factories, public buildings and parks, there could be a balanced mix of new low and moderate cost housing, but no more than ten families to an acre—preferably less.

The real estate men of tomorrow can make millions in assembling land in core areas and make it bloom with new centrally located business enterprises. For instance, why shouldn't the warehouses of department stores and food chains, which today are usually located on the outskirts of our cities, be located in the center of the city? Almost every business which deals on a metropolitan basis would be economically better off locating in the heart of the city and fanning out to all peripheral areas.

Businessmen might well ask: "What about the high cost of assembling land in the center of the city?"

The answer is that each city will have to subsidize the cost of this land. It will take a lot of money to move new business into old ghetto areas, but it will be worth it—in the short run and in the long run. In the short run, slum dwellers will be dispersed and the hearts of cities will be renewed, and in the long run their real estate tax bases will be increased to pay for the subsidization.

What is new about this concept is that it makes a clean sweep—out with old and in with the new. Sure, the cost will be astronomical, but not so high if we leave things as they are. What if we have to bend a few economic laws to straighten out past mistakes? It's a small price to pay for eliminating slums.

I realize it's easy to make sweeping generalizations. But sweeping theories created modern refrigerators. If we propound worthwhile goals, we increase our chances of reaping their specific benefits.

RE-ZONING THE SUBURBS
IS THE REAL ESTATE WAVE OF THE FUTURE

When economic laws are allowed to run their course in laissez-faire fashion, the confrontation between the haves and have-nots becomes inevitable. The last 30 years have seen the acceleration of this sociological and economic fact as our increased affluence built suburbia and left the central city to decay.

Conventional financing sought out the best loans and found them in the suburbs. In its early days even the FHA, in order to minimize its losses, eagerly insured loans in the newer areas and actually refused insuring them in the poorer parts of the city. Both the private and public financial attitudes thus contributed to divide the rich from the poor and accelerated their polarization. Each put economic feasibility ahead of people. It made short-range economic sense but long-range social chaos. We are now feeling its delayed sonic boom distress.

In the mid 1960's, open housing became a moral issue. It was voted locally and nationally, not out of conviction, but because it was the moral thing to do. But open housing did not budge the inexorable economic laws which continued to keep the low and moderate income groups from living alongside middle and upper class neighbors. Open housing did not bring the haves and have-nots together.

Now, something new is looming—re-zoning the suburbs. It's the real estate wave of the future. It is more practical than open housing because it gets closer to the economic guts of the problem. With the help of a more understanding FHA policy and enlightened private enterprise, many of the economically disadvantaged will be able to break through their economic prison walls and escape into the roomier countryside to join the suburbanites, but in an orderly, well-planned exodus. The controversial zoning practices of the suburbs are already beginning to feel the fresh air of change as they are being challenged in the courts by civil rights groups and legislators.

The 1970's can be a money-making decade for imaginative real estate men in two areas of development. One is the plowing up of slums and replacing them with industrial and commercial improvements. The other is to thin out the cities by dispersing millions of low and moderate income families into the outskirts and suburbs of America.

The handwriting is on the wall. The Department of Housing and Urban Development plans to give first priority in sewer, water and open space grants to towns that relax their zoning laws. If that fails, it favors cutting off aid to communities that keep out low and moderate apartment housing. A bipartisan bill mandating this harsher penalty has been filed in the Senate. At least four constitutional challenges to restricted zoning are in the Federal courts. The Massachusetts Legislature recently enacted a law creating a state committee empowered to overrule local zoning upon appeal by nonprofit or limited profit developers.

What does this mean for builders with a social conscience? New projects galore, more work for people, more profits and new housing more humanely mixed and better planned. It means building miniprojects to give more room and hope to the disadvantaged, but without disturbing the character of a suburb by overloading it with too many low income people.

Wholesale disregard for zoning laws would create more havoc than good. But judicious improvisation on present zoning laws, where there would be a proportionate and balanced mix of low, medium and higher cost housing is much to be desired. I can visualize at least 250 miniprojects of 20 to 30 families each in our Milwaukee metropolitan area. It would fulfill two desirable goals. It would begin the thinning out of our old areas to prepare them for razing and new commercial and industrial development, and the orderly exodus of the economically stockaded people into the outskirts and the suburbs.

Exclusivity, where the wealthy only talk to the wealthy, pauperizes the mind and shrinks the vision. Living in congested areas where the poor only talk to the poor is even worse. It builds uncontrollable frustration. Each would gain from living not far from the other. The haves would learn what goes on in the hearts and minds of the have-nots, and the have-nots, having an opportunity of seeing the haves in action, might try to emulate them. For instance, they might by example be prodded to maintain their properties and emulate some of their neighbors' more acceptable life patterns.

Re-zoning the suburbs, changing the face and functions of central cities, and dispersing the low and moderate income people in manageable proportions, are great money-making opportunities for the '70's. They are ideas ripe for action. Their time has come.

HERE ARE THE MONEY MAKING SPECIFICS FOR DISPERSING THE LOW INCOME FAMILIES

Our urbanologists, government officials and private entrepreneurs, mesmerized by the economies of mass production, have saddled us with people-problems which are crying out for answers. If, as has been shown over and over again, herding people in too small an area aberrates them, then one of the obvious solutions is to decongest them. It's simple, it's logical, we can do it and it will work.

We need to disperse the low-income families so they are absorbed in our population's mainstream. This will require two new convictions. One is that it pays to spend more money for more room and land per unit of housing at the outset, if we want to reap future social benfits. And two, we should reconcile ourselves to a sprinkling of neighbors with life styles different from our own, and say to ourselves that it is a small price to pay for a more orderly and stable society.

Here are the five necessary steps to implement the dispersal plan. It involves the federal government, the suburbs, private enterprise, nonprofit social agencies, and neighbors.

Step No. 1—The Federal Government

The federal government has already done its homework. It is more aware of the housing needs of the low income people than those on the state and local levels. Its various plans for rent subsidy and low interest rates make it possible for large families with low incomes and elderly with little income and no earning power, to live in homes and apartments for about half the cost of those who can afford to pay more.

Is it fair to subsidize the lower income groups of our country at the expense of others? One way to answer this question is to ask another. Is it fair to subsidize the farm industry five billion dollars a year?

I believe that if we give these questions some thought we must come to the conclusion that when basic needs like shelter and food are involved, the haves simply must help the have nots. There is no alternative.

European countries have been subsidizing housing in one form or another for the past several decades. They recognized it as a social stabilizer long before we did. Our 1968 Housing Act which initiated low interest and rent subsidies for the low income people is a long-belated step in creating housing for the needy. The federal government has made a start. It has given us the tools. It's step No. 1.

Step No. 2—The Suburbs

The counties and suburbs will have to do their part to implement the enlightened federal legislation. Local government often complains that the federal government interferes too much in their affairs (and often it does). But when the federal government does come up with an idea which is good for the country, it behooves local governments to cooperate.

The key to getting this cooperation from the suburbs, in my opinion, is to scatter miniprojects of 20 to 30 low income families throughout a metropolitan area, with no one site, however desirable, to carry a neighborhood changing brunt of a huge 200 or 300 family project. The ideal scattering ratio could be three new families to a stable and established family square block, and no more than 30 low income families to an apartment project.

This, of course, is not as economical as building huge housing projects, but what we are considering here is something much more important than building mass shelter through mass econom- ics. We want the disadvantaged to learn more orderly living habits by living alongside their more advantaged neighbors. By lifting them up socially as well as economically, we are hastening the day when the low income families can become more produc- tive, and eventually lessen the tax burdens of those who may be the first to complain in implementing this more humane popula- tion mix.

Enlightened real estate entrepreneurs should logically be at the fore-front of this orderly decongesting of people. They can make as much money unsnarling our housing mess as those who made it while getting us into it.

Step No. 3—Private Enterprise

The businessmen and industrialists, prodded by enlightened real estate men, can be the starters of change in our population mix. If business doesn't take this responsibility, and relegate it to govern- ment, it will have to reconcile itself to not having it done as well.

Here is how business and industry can become involved in remedying the housing mistakes of the past. Let each enlightened businessman interested in the social health of his community sponsor ten houses under Title 235, or a mini-rental project of 10 to 20 units under Title 236, in some part of the county or suburb. Since the government provides 100% financing for Title 235, and practically 100% for Title 236, there is no risk involved except a few thousand dollars of seed money which the sponsor gets back when the homes or apartments are completed.

The impact that several hundred businessmen would have on their community if they sponsored such housing would go far beyond providing shelter. It would show the have nots that the haves really care. And what makes this idea so exciting is that businessmen can do so much good, with so little effort, without risk and at no cost. All they have to do is lend the prestige of their names to a project and the real estate men and builders will do the rest.

County and suburban officials would be more likely to re-zone exclusive areas if business gets behind these rent and interest subsidy projects. The impact of caring businessmen and industrialists becoming directly involved in housing disadvantaged people can build trust and blunt confrontations.

If businessmen want a more stable environment in which to carry on commerce, they should not leave the dispersion of population to the government. If government bungles it, they will only have the satisfaction of saying, "They bungled it again." But they will not have domestic peace.

Step No. 4—Nonprofit Social Agencies

Dispersing the poor is going to be a many-faceted operation. We will need not only the subsidy programs of the federal government, the cooperation of the suburbs and the help of the businessmen, but the expertise of the social, nonprofit agencies as well. They work close to the disadvantaged—they can help find the most needy families and assist them with information on how to qualify for new homes and how to cope with their new environment.

The responsibility of the social agencies should not stop with finding deserving families. Since they know the habit patterns of the needy, the social workers are in the best position to help them adjust to their new neighbors. This is the key to the dispersal plan—getting the disadvantaged to adjust to the advantaged and vice versa. And this is more easily done if two or three low income families are dispersed among 20 or 30 established neighbors, than a 200 or 300 apartment project forced upon a stabilized community.

In a neighborhood where the old residents outnumber the newcomers 20 to 1, a social worker might be able to enlist the help of good intentioned neighbors to diplomatically guide a low income family to raise the quality of its behavior. This is almost impossible for the social worker to do when she visits her "case" in a milieu of squalor and frustration for blocks and blocks around.

In an orderly dispersal plan, the neighbors become the educators simply because they are there. Their more stable habits of maintenance and housekeeping have a far more educative impact than when a social worker lectures a poor family, surrounded by other poor families, who bring it down to their level as soon as the social worker leaves.

Step No. 5—Neighbors

This brings us to the final, and in many ways, the most important step of the dispersal plan—the neighbors—you and me. Remember, in the wild West movies, a town was cleansed of evil elements only when the whole town got up in arms—and cleaned it up. It became everybody's business.

The dispersal plan will not work unless the neighbors make it their business—unless they see the wisdom of diplomatically and voluntarily caring for isolated low income families. This cannot happen when they are forcefully swamped by too many. That's when it becomes a confrontation instead of cooperation.

The most advantaged instinctively like to help those who are less advantaged providing the problem is not insurmountable. With the help of understanding social workers a small, controllable number of low income families could easily integrate into a larger stable group. The few would try to emulate the many, and the many, with their innate desire to help, would do so, if it's on a manageable and personal basis.

Is it not a lot wiser to have thousands of small communities, each absorbing a small percentage of low income families, than loading up a few with too many? This is what will make the dispersal plan work. It makes practical sense. And it can be done if the federal government, business, the suburbs, the social agencies and neighbors join hands and become involved in what I believe to be a most idealistic and practical plan of meaningfully improving and stabilizing the social and economic structure of American society.

The real estate salesmen of tomorrow should be at the forefront of this dispersal idea, plugging it, implementing it and participating in its profits.

BUILD A "WILDWOOD" VILLAGE

You may not be able to build a city like Carthage, Rome or Constantinople, but you can build a village which could last for centuries. An interesting thought? Practical too, because you can make a lot of money doing it.

Today's superhighways are what the railroads were yesteryear, but more so. They interconnect almost everywhere. Along its highly trafficked lanes, within several blocks or miles, you can build a village which can be as picturesque and isolated as you like it, yet within minutes of the superhighway which could take you anywhere.

Now, to get started. When you're out for a drive anywhere within fifty miles of your city, let your eyes roam over the countryside, and when they chance upon a 200 acre sweep of land, preferably wooded, mark it down in your mind. When you get home, call a farm broker familiar with this area and find out if it is for sale. The chances are that it is.

You will probably have to pay from $300 to $500 an acre. Pay it and start building your village. It will be a fascinating project—one that may take five to ten years to finish—five to ten years of joy, if you adopt an artist's attitude toward your work. Don't hurry—savor the planning and execution of all the details—make it a work of love—exhilarate in it. Why not? The artistic geniuses have no monopoly on creative spirit.

Name your real estate project "Wildwood Village," or any name, perhaps your own, and begin planning it as you would a novel, a painting or a piece of sculpture. The fact that you may not get famous doing it should not distract you from your creative joy. Remember, some of the happiest people labor in anonymity, and some of the unhappiest ones are in the limelight of publicity.

Now what makes a village? People! And people must have jobs and a place to live. That's where you come in with your financial techniques, real estate knowledge and money making know-how.

Step No. 1, the most important, is to persuade some big city manufacturer or wholesale distributor to locate his plant or part of his plant on your acreage. In your sales presentation, point out to your prospective industrialist that you have immediate plans for the construction of homes and apartments, so that his workers will have adequate living quarters within walking distance of their work.

If you start with as few as 20 jobs and 20 living units, you've got a good beginning. It's a big enough nucleus to become a magnet to attract more industrialists, more workers and more homes. Now is a good time to begin planning your village as to its ultimate size, its character, its roads, its shopping area—yes, even its schools, churches and police protection.

Do you want your "Wildwood Village" to have 500 people? A thousand? More? Now is the time to decide. Delineate the skeleton plan in your mind, and take a decade to flesh it out.

Let's say you decide on a population of 1,000. Plan for about 150 industrial jobs, and about 50 commercial jobs to process the retail sales and services of the 150 workers. The commercial jobs such as gas station operators, a druggist or two, several grocery men, a few cocktail lounge owners, a dentist, a doctor and a dozen other sundry service jobs will round out a small community shopping development.

Besides planning the financial feasibility of the village, let's not forget or miss out on the fun of planning the physical aesthetics and the population mix.

First, with the help of an architect, designer, or perhaps your wife, if she has a flair for it, you should begin planning for a unique village character. The main architectural motif can be Western, New England or Southern, and if you like the old world flavor—French, Greek or Italian. Careful attention to detail design can make your dream for the unusual come true if you put your heart and mind into the planning.

The population mix of a new village presents an interesting challenge. Here is where you have a chance to express your sociological and philosophical values. If your political leanings are toward united world federalism, then you should try to attract a blendable proportion of different cultures and religions. to make your village a veritable pilot project of integration—a sort of blending of ethnic groups. And by mixing a few low income families in the potpourri with middle and upper class citizens, you'd have a one-world in microcosm. It would be an interesting place to live. Of course, you should live there too.

Whatever the architectural motif and population mix, a new village, in my opinion, ought to have these amenities: Country lanes, as rustic and authentic as you can make them, tennis courts, a baseball diamond, a par 3 golf course and an overnight camping site for children. For the adults, I suggest a public building where they can revive town hall politics, hear lectures and put on amateur plays. Attached to it there ought to be a wing for a bath house with a relaxing reading room nearby.

The quality of life in such a village would be superior to the sardine-packed living areas in the cities. It would even be of a higher quality than the $100,000 luxury condominium environment, or the $500 to $1,000 a month skyscraper apartments, where vision is limited to a birdseye view, not to the more natural human view close to the ground where man was meant to live.

Life in such a village would be secure and leisurely, contrasted to living in the city where, after dark, many of its tense citizens become prisoners in their own homes and apartments.

The village you build will become more livable and valuable as it grows and matures. The vacant land you have set aside for growth will increase in value, and the garden apartments and commercial real estate you will build will continue to show a greater return.

Although I do not suggest that you should be primarily motivated by monument building, nevertheless, founding a village that could live on for centuries should give you a feel of historical continuity.

If your creative juices run more abundantly by just reading about it, think what they could do for you if you actually went ahead and did it!

Index